Bluetooth End to

The Key Problem

How do I put Bluetooth technology to work for me?

Key Considerations

Bluetooth technology enables you to connect a variety of devices — for example, your cellular telephone, a personal digital assistant (PDA), and a computer — using a wireless signal, provided the devices are Bluetooth-enabled and are within a 10-meter range of each other. By eliminating the need to connect these devices with a cable, Bluetooth provides you with a convenient and easy way to synchronize your data and files.

For More Information

See the Chapter listed for each topic for more information:

- Bluetooth specifications — see Chapters 1 and 3
- Bluetooth operations — see Chapters 5, 6, 7, and 8
- Bluetooth-enabled devices – see Chapter 13

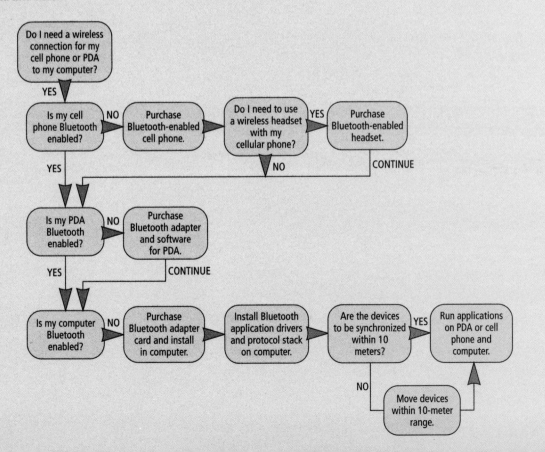

Bluetooth End to End

The Key Problem

What steps should my organization take to develop a Bluetooth-enabled product?

Key Considerations

A well-defined procedure exists for companies that want to develop a Bluetooth-enabled product. The Bluetooth specification details the usage models, profiles, and scenarios under which new Bluetooth products can be developed. With the amount of detail available in the specification, and with the product testing and approval process so well-defined, you have some very clear choices to make.

For More Information

- Bluetooth specifications — see Chapters 1 and 3

- Bluetooth operations — see Chapters 5, 6, 7, and 8

- Bluetooth components and interfaces — Chapters 9, 10, 11, and 12

- Bluetooth-enabled devices — see Chapter 13

- Bluetooth profiles, usage models, and applications — Chapters 2 and 13

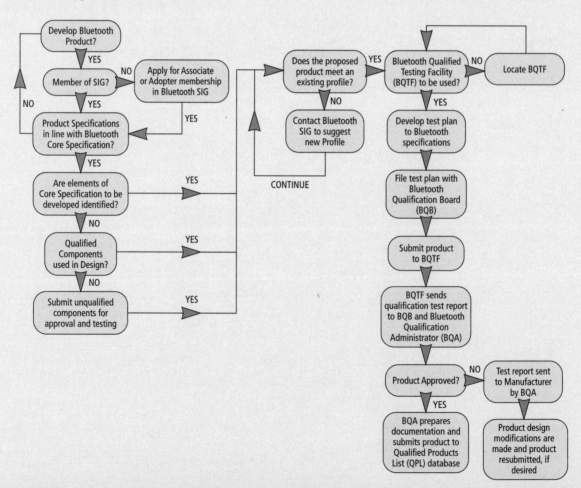

Bluetooth™
End to End™

Bluetooth™
End to End™

D.M. Bakker and Diane McMichael Gilster

Ron Gilster, Series Editor

M&T Books
An imprint of Hungry Minds, Inc.

**Best-Selling Books • Digital Downloads • e-Books • Answer Networks
e-Newsletters • Branded Web Sites • e-Learning**

New York, NY • Cleveland, OH • Indianapolis, IN

Bluetooth™ End to End™

Published by
Hungry Minds, Inc.
909 Third Avenue
New York, NY 10022
www.hungryminds.com

Library of Congress Control Number: 2001099735

ISBN: 0-7645-4887-5

Printed in the United States of America

10 9 8 7 6 5 4 3 2 1

1B/RZ/QS/QS/IN

Distributed in the United States by Hungry Minds, Inc.

Distributed by CDG Books Canada Inc. for Canada; by Transworld Publishers Limited in the United Kingdom; by IDG Norge Books for Norway; by IDG Sweden Books for Sweden; by IDG Books Australia Publishing Corporation Pty. Ltd. for Australia and New Zealand; by TransQuest Publishers Pte Ltd. for Singapore, Malaysia, Thailand, Indonesia, and Hong Kong; by Gotop Information Inc. for Taiwan; by ICG Muse, Inc. for Japan; by Intersoft for South Africa; by Eyrolles for France; by International Thomson Publishing for Germany, Austria, and Switzerland; by Distribuidora Cuspide for Argentina; by LR International for Brazil; by Galileo Libros for Chile; by Ediciones ZETA S.C.R. Ltda. for Peru; by WS Computer Publishing Corporation, Inc., for the Philippines; by Contemporanea de Ediciones for Venezuela; by Express Computer Distributors for the Caribbean and West Indies; by Micronesia Media Distributor, Inc. for Micronesia; by Chips Computadoras S.A. de C.V. for Mexico; by Editorial Norma de Panama S.A. for Panama; by American Bookshops for Finland.

For general information on Hungry Minds' products and services please contact our Customer Care department within the U.S. at 800-762-2974, outside the U.S. at 317-572-3993 or fax 317-572-4002.

For sales inquiries and reseller information, including discounts, premium and bulk quantity sales, and foreign-language translations, please contact our Customer Care department at 800-434-3422, fax 317-572-4002 or write to Hungry Minds, Inc., Attn: Customer Care Department, 10475 Crosspoint Boulevard, Indianapolis, IN 46256.

For information on licensing foreign or domestic rights, please contact our Sub-Rights Customer Care department at 212-884-5000.

For information on using Hungry Minds' products and services in the classroom or for ordering examination copies, please contact our Educational Sales department at 800-434-2086 or fax 317-572-4005.

For press review copies, author interviews, or other publicity information, please contact our Public Relations department at 317-572-3168 or fax 317-572-4168.

For authorization to photocopy items for corporate, personal, or educational use, please contact Copyright Clearance Center, 222 Rosewood Drive, Danvers, MA 01923, or fax 978-750-4470.

 is a trademark of Hungry Minds, Inc.

 is a trademark of Hungry Minds, Inc.

About the Authors

D.M. Bakker is a technical writer with over ten years of experience in the publications industry. For the past six years, she has focused on writing for the computer industry, where she has contracted with such companies as Intuit, QualComm, and Intel. Her experiences also include writing feature stories for a Midwestern newspaper, editing and writing for a bird-watching magazine, and editing books for various publishing companies. She currently resides in Southern California. She is a wine-enthusiast and loves to travel.

Diane McMichael Gilster (MCSE 2000, MCSE NT, Network+, i-Net+) has been active in computing for over 20 years and networking for more than 10 years. Diane's experience includes stints as a Network Manager, Network Consultant, and PC and Network Technician in both large and small networking environments, including wireless networking applications. Diane presently is active as an IT certification trainer, consultant, and author, with a currently popular book on home networking.

Ron Gilster, *End to End* Series Editor, is a best-selling author on the subjects of networking, PC hardware, and career certification. He has over 35 years of experience in computing, networking, and data communications, serving as a technician, consultant, trainer, and executive — most recently as the general manager of the Internet and backbone operations of a large regional wireless communications company.

Credits

ACQUISITIONS EDITOR
Katie Feltman

PROJECT EDITOR
John W. Pont

TECHNICAL EDITOR
Gayle Ehrenman

EDITORIAL MANAGERS
Ami Frank Sullivan, Kyle Looper

SENIOR VICE PRESIDENT, TECHNICAL PUBLISHING
Richard Swadley

VICE PRESIDENT AND PUBLISHER
Mary Bednarek

PROJECT COORDINATOR
Nancee Reeves

GRAPHICS AND PRODUCTION SPECIALISTS
Melissa Auciello-Brogan
Jackie Nicholas
Jacque Schneider

QUALITY CONTROL TECHNICIAN
John Bitter

PROOFREADING AND INDEXING
TECHBOOKS Production Services

From D.M. Bakker: To David, for helping me keep my priorities straight.
From Diane McMichael Gilster: To my precious girls, Kirstin and Jessica, who are the
loves of my life and have waited so patiently to play video games with their Mother.
This book is done, girls; let's go fly kites, play video games, and enjoy life together.
I also thank God for his help with this book and everything in our lives.

Preface

In today's mobile society, the need to connect communications and networking devices together with a physical cable is becoming more and more of a nuisance. With the emergence of the digital cellular telephone and handheld (and highly portable) computing devices, users are looking for a way to connect to their local network, the Internet, or even their own desktop computer from wherever they might be. Several emerging technologies can create a wireless world that supports this kind of freedom — freedom from wires; freedom from land-based telephone systems; and the freedom to access data truly "anytime, anywhere."

The Bluetooth technology, which was born from the cellular industry, is only one of the new cable-replacement technologies. Bluetooth, funny name and all, is being developed to provide mobile users with the levels of freedom they desire. Bluetooth technology is certainly a key part of creating what is being called "The Mobile Society." In a Bluetooth world, you can connect your handheld device — be it a cell phone, a notebook computer, or a personal digital assistant (PDA) — to your network or even to other Bluetooth-enabled devices to create ad hoc, peer-to-peer networks, using wireless technology. If you and a friend want to share data from one Palm Pilot to another, you don't need to hook up with a link cable. Bluetooth technology enables you and your friend to connect up over a wireless link that is automatically configured.

In this book, we offer many other examples of how Bluetooth can be put to use. We provide you with both a general overview of the Bluetooth technology and its applications as well as a more technical, but not too technical, look at the components and how Bluetooth operates to support its applications.

Acknowledgments

D.M. Bakker offers thanks to everyone who offered encouragement and support throughout this project. Special thanks to William Rachel, who took time away from his busy schedule to offer technical advice and assistance whenever needed.

Diane McMichael Gilster would like to thank her editor, Ron Gilster, for all his support and guidance with this book.

Contents at a Glance

Contents

Part II	The Technology of Bluetooth

Part I

Bluetooth Basics

IN THIS PART

There is some mystery surrounding just what the wireless technology with the funny-sounding name is. In this part of the book, we provide you with an overview of the basics of the Bluetooth technology and its governing body. We explain the history of Bluetooth's name and we take a brief look at the Bluetooth standard, its terminology, and its application concepts. We also explain the structure and the operations of the Bluetooth SIG (Special Interest Group) — the governing body for the Bluetooth standard.

Chapter 1

Introducing Bluetooth

In This Chapter

From the beginning, Bluetooth technology was intended to hasten the convergence of voice and data to handheld devices, such as cellular telephones and portable computers. Through the efforts of its developers and the members of the Bluetooth Special Interest Group (SIG), it is now emerging with features and applications that not only remain true to its original intent, but also provide for broader uses of its technology.

In this chapter, and throughout this book, we provide you with a look at the Bluetooth technology, its basic design, structure, and applications, as well as the processes involved to develop and launch new Bluetooth products. We keep the very technical jargon to a minimum and give you a detailed, thorough, yet understandable look at Bluetooth and its world. In this chapter, we address the following objectives, to help you get started on the road to implementing Bluetooth technology:

✓ Going back to Bluetooth's beginnings

✓ Getting a handle on Bluetooth terminology

✓ Examining Bluetooth concepts

In the Beginning

Bluetooth is an open standard specification for a radio frequency (RF)-based, short-range connectivity technology that promises to change the face of computing and wireless communication. It is designed to be an inexpensive, wireless networking system for all classes of portable devices, such as laptops, PDAs (personal digital assistants), and mobile phones. It also will enable wireless connections for desktop computers, making connections between monitors, printers, keyboards, and the CPU cable-free.

The idea of a cable-free, or wireless, technology was initially conceived by Ericsson in 1994, when the company began a study to investigate the feasibility of a low-power, low-cost radio interface between mobile phones and their accessories. The company's goal was to eliminate the need for cables.

The original idea was to create a small, inexpensive radio chip that could be used in mobile computers, printers, mobile phones, and so on, to transmit data between these devices. The radio chip, of course, would replace cables. The projected cost of the chip was around $5, and it was to require low power so that it could be used in devices that rely on battery life.

About the Name

For those who know little about the technology, and even for those who are more than a little acquainted with it, the name *Bluetooth* may seem odd. You may wonder, in fact, how it relates to wireless technology, or speculate that perhaps it's derived somehow from the founding members of the SIG. Neither of these ideas is correct. The name is a romantic gesture that in some sense indicates the excitement the technology generates as well as the belief in its value as a revolutionary concept. To combine these qualities in a name required ingenuity and delving into the past.

The name *Bluetooth* comes from Danish history. Harald Blatand, who was called Bluetooth, was the son of King Gorm the Old, who ruled Jutland, the main peninsula of Denmark. By the time Harald became king, he was a skilled Viking warrior. So, when his sister asked for help to secure control in Norway after her husband died, Harald quickly seized the opportunity to unite the countries and expand his kingdom. By 960 A.D., according to the story, Harald was at the height of his powers, and ruled both Denmark and Norway. He was later credited with bringing Christianity to his Viking realm.

Although it's popularly believed that King Harald had a blue tooth, and various stories explain how this came about, it's more likely that the Bluetooth name is the English derivative of the original Viking word, *Blâtand*. The Bluetooth name was chosen for the wireless technology because its developers and promoters hope it will unite the mobile world, just as King Harald united his world.

As the idea grew, a special interest group (SIG) was formed to create a standard for this technology. The original SIG, formed in 1998, consisted of five companies:

✓ Ericsson

✓ IBM

✓ Intel

✓ Nokia

✓ Toshiba

Four other major companies (Microsoft, 3Com, Lucent, and Motorola) later joined this founding group to form the Bluetooth Promoter Group. Many more companies have since become part of the Bluetooth revolution, expanding on the original vision, and helping drive the development of this new technology.

Bluetooth Components

A complete Bluetooth system will require these elements:

✓ An RF portion for receiving and transmitting data

✓ A module with a baseband microprocessor

✓ Memory

✓ An interface to the host device (such as a mobile phone)

We explain these terms and concepts in the section "Bluetooth Terminology," later in this chapter.

This basic system will vary, however, depending on whether the Bluetooth module is independent of the host or embedded. First, consider the module scenario.

The RF portion can be implemented as a module or as a single chip. Ericsson has a module available that includes a short-range radio transceiver, an external antenna, and a clock reference (required for synchronization). It can be used independently or with a baseband module, which Ericsson also offers. Other transceivers also are available for Bluetooth applications, and those transceivers also can be used with another company's baseband solution or with a packaged baseband processor.

In this type of arrangement, the lower-layer Bluetooth protocols are supported in the baseband module, and the host processor must support the upper-layer protocols (for example, file transfer). In other words, the RF/baseband solution provides the means to communicate with the host, but you need to implement a connection interface, as well as any upper-layer protocols, to use applications supported by the final product.

The upper layers of the technology support what are known as the *Bluetooth profiles* — in other words, a set of protocols. A set of protocols is optimized for a class of applications — for example, dial-up networking or file transfer. This feature is issue is important, because it enables interoperability among devices. Requiring a specific profile for devices that provide comparable applications ensures interoperability across a spectrum of devices.

Another option for manufacturers is to embed a fully integrated RF/baseband Bluetooth chip. In this scenario, the upper-layer protocols reside within the single chip, freeing the host processor from the protocol processing. The cost of the chip necessarily will be higher, but the fully integrated final design can be less complex, use less power, and reduce production cost. In this scenario, the Bluetooth unit can connect to the host device through a serial interface such as a universal serial bus (USB).

Yet another possibility for implementing Bluetooth is to integrate the Bluetooth baseband module with the host system. This option would involve owning and customizing the silicon chip for the device. In this case, the device manufacturer would have complete control of interfaces and features for the device, but development costs and investment risk could be high.

Bluetooth Terminology

The Bluetooth specification, while innovative, does not define a totally new technology. In fact, Bluetooth draws heavily on existing radio communications and networking technologies, which enables it to be operationally compatible with the existing devices that also use these technologies. Many of the various terms and concepts used in Bluetooth are borrowed from other areas and included in the specification of Bluetooth's elements, such as baseband, RF communications, and many of the upper- and lower-layer protocols (a few of which have been mentioned already in this chapter). What makes Bluetooth unique is how it applies its proprietary components and the existing technologies to define its central core operations and its application profiles. Regardless of their source, the terms that are integral to Bluetooth are worth examining a little more closely.

Bluetooth stack

As already noted, the baseband, or radio module, is the hardware that enables wireless communication between devices. The building block of this technology is the *Bluetooth stack*, which includes the hardware and software portions of the system. Figure 1-1 shows a graphic representation of the stack. Essentially, the stack contains a physical-level protocol (baseband) and a link-level protocol (Link Manager Protocol, or LMP) with an adaptation layer (Logical Link Control and Adaptation Layer Protocol, or L2CAP), enabling upper-layer protocols to interact with the lower layer.

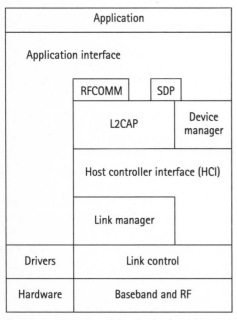

Figure 1-1: Overview of the Bluetooth stack

The Bluetooth stack has the following components:

- ✓ RF portion for reception and transmission
- ✓ Baseband portion with microcontroller
- ✓ Link control unit
- ✓ Link manager to support lower-layer protocols
- ✓ Interface to the host device
- ✓ Host processor to support upper-layer protocols
- ✓ L2CAP to support upper-layer protocols

The *radio frequency* (RF) portion provides the digital signal processing component of the system, and the baseband processes these signals. The *link controller* handles all the baseband functions and supports the link manager. It sends and receives data, identifies the sending device, performs authentication, and determines the type of frame to use for sending transmissions. The link controller also directs how devices listen for transmissions from other devices and can move devices into power-saving modes.

The *link manager*, located on top of the link controller, controls setup, authentication, link configuration, and other low-level protocols. Together, the baseband and the link manager establish connections for the network.

The *host controller interface* (HCI) communicates the lower-layer protocols to the host device (mobile computer or mobile phone, for example). The host contains a processor, the *L2CAP*, which supports the upper-layer protocols and communicates between upper and lower layers. The upper-layer protocols consist of service-specific applications that must be integrated into the host application.

Another element in the Bluetooth stack that relates to radio communications is the *RFCOMM protocol*, which allows for the emulation of serial ports over the L2CAP.

The *Service Discovery Protocol* (SDP) provides the means for Bluetooth applications to discover the services and the characteristics of the available services that are unique to Bluetooth.

The Bluetooth *device manager* provides for device inquiry and connection management services.

Chapters 3, 4, 5, and 6 provide a more detailed look at the Bluetooth protocol stack.

Links and channels

Links and channels are used to transmit data between Bluetooth units. First, the links are established. Bluetooth technology supports two link types: synchronous connection-oriented (SCO) and asynchronous connectionless (ACL) links. The SCO links are used primarily for voice communications. The ACL links are used for packet data. Bluetooth devices can use either link type and can change link types during transmissions, although an ACL link must be established before an SCO link can be used.

After the link has been established, Bluetooth uses five logical channels to transfer different types of information between devices:

✓ Link control (LC) manages the flow of packets over the link interface.

✓ Link manager (LM) transports link management information between participating stations.

✓ User asynchronous (UA) carries user data.

✓ User isochronous (UI) carries user data.

✓ User synchronous (US) carries synchronous (SCO) data.

Protocols

Bluetooth protocols are sets of conventions that govern the transmittal of data in upper and lower layers of the system. The lower-layer protocols pertain to establishing connections, and the upper layers correspond to specific types of applications.

LINK CONTROL PROTOCOL

The link control protocol is responsible for delivery of the basic data elements. All packet information is transmitted in a specific time-slot format (a single time slot in the Bluetooth system lasts 625 μs), and specific links are designed to transport a range of data types.

The symbol μ is the Greek letter *mu,* and it is used to represent microseconds in microprocessor technologies.

The Bluetooth link control protocol can be used to manage the associations and delivery of information between the various units within a Bluetooth network. This format is used for both synchronous (voice) and asynchronous (data) modes of operation, with specific formats specified for voice transport.

LINK MANAGER PROTOCOL

The link manager protocol (LMP) is a command-response system for transmitting data. It transports packets through the Bluetooth baseband link protocol, which is a time-slot-oriented mechanism. LMP packets are limited in size to ensure that they fit into a single time slot.

The format of the protocol data unit (PDU) is simple. Two fields are used:

✓ The OpCode identifies the type and sequence of the packet.

✓ The content field contains application-specific information.

The LMP also specifies a collection of mandatory and optional PDUs. Transmission and reception of mandatory PDUs must be supported. Optional PDUs don't need to be implemented, but can be used as necessary.

The protocol sequences are similar to client-server architectures, with the exchange of information following a similar request-response pattern. In general, a single response PDU is sent upon receipt of the original request. Because Bluetooth is an RF broadcast technology, a set of request messages can be broadcast to all participants on a network. In this case, one request can elicit several responses.

L2CAP

Logical link and adaptation protocol (L2CAP) enables transmission of data between upper and lower layers of the stack. It also enables support for many third-party upper-layer protocols such as TCP/IP. In addition, L2CAP provides group management by mapping upper-layer protocol groups to Bluetooth networks. It also is a factor in ensuring interoperability among Bluetooth units by providing application-specific protocols.

Other protocols interfacing to the L2CAP include service discovery protocol (SDP), radio frequency communication (RFCOMM), telephony control protocol specification (TCS), and IrDA Object Exchange Protocol (IrOBEX):

✓ **SDP** provides service discovery specific to Bluetooth. That is, one device can determine the services available in another connected device by implementing the SDP.

✓ **RFCOMM** is a transport protocol that provides serial data transfer. In other words, it enables legacy software applications to operate on a Bluetooth device.

✓ **TCS** is for voice and data call control. It provides group management capabilities and allows for signaling unrelated to an ongoing call.

✓ **OBEX** is a session protocol, and for Bluetooth devices, only connection-oriented OBEX is supported. Three application profiles have been developed using OBEX: synchronization (for phonebooks, calendars, messaging, and so on), file transfer between connected devices, and object push for business card support.

Bluetooth Networking

The Bluetooth technology provides both a point-to-point connection and a point-to-multipoint connection. In point-to-multipoint connections, the channel is shared among several Bluetooth units. In point-to-point connections, only two units share the connection.

Bluetooth protocols assume that a small number of units will participate in communications at any given time. These small groups are called *piconets*, and they consist of one master unit and up to seven active slave units. The master is the unit that initiates transmissions, and the slaves are the responding units. This type of Bluetooth network can have only one master unit.

If several piconets overlap a physical area, and members of the various piconets communicate with each other, this new, larger network is known as a *scatternet*. Any unit in one piconet can communicate in a second piconet as long as it serves as master for only one piconet at a time.

Figure 1-2 shows the intercommunication between units in different piconets.

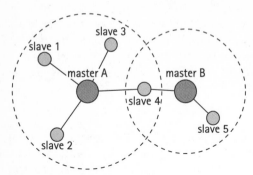

Figure 1-2: Piconets and scatternets

Bluetooth Concepts

Bluetooth is an emerging standard for wireless connectivity. It specifies a system — not just a radio — that encompasses the hardware, software framework, and interoperability requirements. And, the radio system is optimized for mobility. In other words, Bluetooth primarily specifies a cable-replacement technology that targets mobile users in the global marketplace.

Bluetooth connections

The major difference between Bluetooth wireless connectivity and the cellular radio architecture is that Bluetooth enables ad hoc networking. Rather than depending on a broadband system, which relies on terminals and base stations for maintaining connections to the network via radio links, Bluetooth implements peer-to-peer connectivity — no base stations or terminals are involved.

Using peer-to-peer connectivity, Bluetooth technology simplifies personal area wireless connections, enabling all digital devices to communicate spontaneously. Early applications are expected to include cable replacement for laptops, PDAs, mobile phones, and digital cameras. Because Bluetooth supports voice transmissions, headsets also are in line to become wireless. The Bluetooth technology offers the following advantages:

✓ Voice/data access points will allow, for example, mobile phone/Internet connections.

✓ Cable is replaced by a Bluetooth chip that transmits information at a special radio frequency to a receiver Bluetooth chip.

✓ Ad hoc networking enables personal devices to automatically exchange information and synchronize with each other. For example, appointments made on a PDA calendar automatically appear on a desktop calendar as well.

Figure 1-3 shows the three concepts that distinguish Bluetooth technology from other wireless connections.

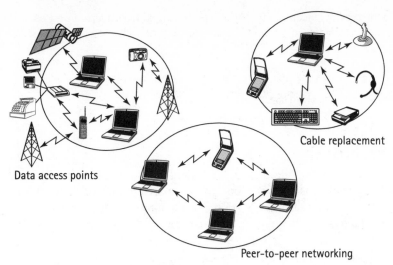

Data access points

Cable replacement

Peer-to-peer networking

Figure 1-3: Connecting with Bluetooth

Reliable and secure transmissions

Bluetooth technology also provides fast, secure voice and data transmissions. The range for connectivity is up to 10 meters, and line of sight is not required. The Bluetooth radio unit

✓ Functions even in noisy radio environments, ensuring audible voice transmissions in severe conditions.

✓ Protects data by using error-correction methods.

✓ Provides a high transmission rate.

✓ Encrypts and authenticates for privacy.

As with any wireless interface, Bluetooth must address issues involving reliable delivery of information. Noise and interference from other ISM (Industrial, Scientific, and Medical) band transmissions, for example, are factors that come into play. To help deliver accurate information, Bluetooth provides two error-correction mechanisms: forward error correction (FEC) and automatic repeat request (ARQ). Typically, FEC is applied to voice traffic for which the timeliness of the delivery takes precedence over the accuracy — late voice traffic being unacceptable. ARQ mechanisms are used for data applications.

Because Bluetooth operates in the unlicensed ISM frequency band, it competes with signals from other devices, such as garage door openers and microwave ovens. In order for Bluetooth devices to operate reliably, each Bluetooth network is synchronized to a specific frequency pattern. The Bluetooth unit moves through 1,600 different frequencies per second, and the pattern is unique to each network.

Bluetooth also implements various security measures, including authentication and encryption. Authentication is used to verify the identity of the device sending information, and encryption is used to ensure the integrity of the data.

Chapter 17 provides more information on Bluetooth security.

Low-power architecture

Because Bluetooth is intended for mobile devices, it implements a low-power architecture in which units move into lower-power modes when not actively participating on the network. Bluetooth units also consume less power during operation. For example, the Bluetooth radio consumes less than 3 percent of the power that a mobile phone consumes.

Global compatibility

Bluetooth architecture is compliant with global emissions rules, operating on a globally available frequency band (2.4 GHz ISM band), the unlicensed portion of the radio frequency spectrum. This ensures that Bluetooth devices will interact in the same way in any part of the world.

Bluetooth architecture also complies with airline regulations and is safe for use on airlines. Developers of the technology work with the FAA, JAA, FCC, airplane manufacturers, and airlines to ensure compliance.

Interoperability, standards, and specifications

Another key concept in the Bluetooth environment is the idea of interoperability among Bluetooth units regardless of manufacturer. Because Bluetooth is an open specification for short-range wireless communication, all Bluetooth products must conform to a standard. This ensures that wireless connections will be globally available, and Bluetooth units made anywhere in the world will be able to connect with and communicate information and services to other Bluetooth devices.

To this end, the Bluetooth SIG has developed detailed specifications for the hardware and software elements of Bluetooth units. The specifications consist of Core and Profiles documentation. The Core document discusses elements such as the radio, baseband, link manager, and interoperability with different communication protocols. The Profiles document delineates the protocols and procedures to be used for specific classes of applications. The specifications are intended to prevent discrepancies in end products due to different interpretations of the Bluetooth standard.

The SIG also has implemented a qualification process. This process defines criteria for Bluetooth product qualification, ensuring the Bluetooth standards are met in any product that sports the Bluetooth name.

Chapter 2 provides an overview of the prescribed processes used to qualify a Bluetooth product.

Summary

It can be said that the name *Bluetooth* refers not only to a technology, but also to a standard and a specification. And few standards have taken off as Bluetooth has, capturing the attention and development money of major corporations throughout the world. If it can live up to its expectations and meet the needs of a global marketplace in an easy-to-use, straightforward manner, it promises to become (like its eponymous King Harald) a uniting force in the wireless communications world. This chapter helps you get started with Bluetooth technology by covering the basics:

✓ The origin of the Bluetooth name

✓ An overview of the Bluetooth components

✓ An introduction to the terminology of Bluetooth

✓ A quick look at Bluetooth networking concepts

In the next chapter, we provide a look at the Bluetooth SIG (special interest group) and its organization, including the different levels of membership available to companies that want to produce Bluetooth-related products and the processes they must follow to have a product approved.

Chapter 2

The Bluetooth World

In This Chapter

The Bluetooth technology standards and specifications are developed, managed, and overseen by a group of companies — mostly hardware manufacturers and software developers — called the Bluetooth SIG (Special Interest Group). The SIG's activities are at the heart of the development, advancement, production, and promotion of the Bluetooth technology.

Special interest groups are very common to many emerging technologies. SIGs exist to define common standards of operation, manufacturing, and most important, interoperability among devices provided by different manufacturers or developers. SIGs exist for many of the technologies used in computing, communications, and networking. For example, the Peripheral Components Interface (PCI) SIG, the Interactive Audio (IA) SIG, and the I20 (Intelligent Input/Output) SIG each has the focus and purpose for its respective technologies, just as the Bluetooth SIG does.

To understand Bluetooth technology, including its origins, development, and future, you must understand the functions and purpose of the Bluetooth SIG. This chapter introduces you to the Bluetooth SIG, providing details about the following topics:

✓ Tracing the origin and development of the Bluetooth concepts

✓ Understanding the purpose and functions of the Bluetooth SIG

✓ Examining the activities of the Bluetooth Promoter Group

✓ Assessing the future of the Bluetooth SIG

✓ Exploring the Bluetooth Qualification Process

How It All Began

As society continues to become more mobile, facilitated by advances in emerging technologies that enable users to carry in their hands more computing power than the mainframes of the 1970s had, consumers are demanding still more computing power, applications, and connectivity. The cellular phone has been perhaps the greatest catalyst for the expansion of portable processing capabilities. The cell phone acquainted consumers to the power of wireless communications and technology.

The vision

Recognizing the growing demand for mobile computing capabilities, in 1994, the Swedish telecommunications manufacturer Telefonaktiebolaget LM Ericsson (known universally as Ericsson) began researching the possibilities of a low-cost, low-power, wireless means of communications between mobile phones and other portable devices, such as portable computers, using wireless technology and radio waves. Ericsson's researchers theorized that the hard-wire communications cables required at that time to connect networked devices could be replaced with electronic components that could communicate via radio signals. A driving concept of Ericsson's early development of this technology was to enable computer users to place cell-phone calls from their computers.

By applying the proposed concept, wireless users could set up impromptu connections between their wireless telephone, computer, personal digital assistant (PDA), and perhaps an earphone and speaker headset, enabling them to move about their home or office and remain connected to their system. Ericsson envisioned a wide range of cable-less household and personal devices with the ability to communicate with one another over a short distance.

Ericsson saw vast potential in applying wireless communications to personal devices. This new application of radio frequency (RF) communications held the promise of providing a host of benefits to consumers, including the following:

- ✓ Eliminating cables
- ✓ Providing a low-cost wireless personal network solution
- ✓ Providing instantaneous and transparent connections
- ✓ Facilitating ad hoc networking to both voice and data networks

ELIMINATING CABLES

The object of any wireless technology is to replace cables with radiofrequency connections. Home and office computer systems often result in a jumble of the device cables required to connect peripheral devices to the computer. Cables also define the scope of a personal work area. The length of its cable limits the distance a device can be from a computer. Wireless technologies, such as Bluetooth, expand the possibilities for spatial arrangements in a user's workspace, which means the user can arrange the devices to suit the furniture and the room, instead of the other way around.

Another benefit of the Bluetooth technology is the ability to move and use peripheral devices without the wear and tear of connecting cables. Although other technologies, such as infrared (IR) and radio frequency (RF), provide some capability in this area, devices that rely on these technologies must be positioned in a certain way relative to one another to create a connection, something Bluetooth would eliminate.

Chapter 12 provides a more detailed look at the IR and RF technologies and how they compare to Bluetooth.

REDUCING THE COST OF THE NETWORK SOLUTION

The defining principles of the Bluetooth technology call for smaller, less expensive, and easy-to-manufacture components, which should translate into lower-cost devices for the consumer. Ericsson and the other companies involved with developing the Bluetooth technology believe that these goals are essential if Bluetooth is to gain widespread acceptance in the industry and among consumers.

CREATING INSTANTANEOUS NETWORKS

Another key element of the Bluetooth technology concept is its ability to provide a single communications platform for myriad devices, enabling them to work together using a single, common "language." Bluetooth is envisioned as an always-on, short-range radio technology that can interconnect mobile devices. Implicit in the Bluetooth vision is the concept of transparent connections, or connections that are extremely easy to set up and use. Bluetooth must provide a means for instantaneous connections that are transparent to the user.

CONNECTING ON THE FLY

Ad hoc networking means that device users can connect to Bluetooth networks when needed, virtually without regard to where a user is currently located. In concept, mobile device users could have access to voice and data networks wherever they might be.

Making the dream a reality

Ericsson immediately began development on the first prototype components based on its proposed new wireless technology, which it later named Bluetooth. To prove the feasibility of the Bluetooth technology, Ericsson's engineers developed the integrated circuits (chips) and software modules that would form the basis for commercial product development. In early 2000, the first commercial Bluetooth product was developed: a network interface card.

Building the team

From its years in the cell-phone industry, Ericsson knew that without cooperation and collaboration from other wireless manufacturers, it probably would not succeed with the Bluetooth technology. The cell-phone industry has several strong manufacturers, all of which must adhere to a strict set of communications standards and guidelines to remain viable in the marketplace. Despite the competitiveness of the wireless industry, Ericsson recognized that it could not proceed alone if Bluetooth technology was to succeed.

So, in 1997, Ericsson invited other leading wireless, computing, and portable device manufacturers to join with it to develop and promote the Bluetooth technology: IBM, Intel, Nokia, and Toshiba. In addition to being the technology leaders in their markets, these companies also were very active in research and development of wireless technologies and products. In 1998, all four of the invited companies joined with Ericsson to form the Bluetooth Special Interest Group, which is more commonly known as the SIG.

The SIG

In today's environment of rapidly emerging and evolving technologies, a proprietary technology doesn't have much chance of being widely accepted by consumers. Proprietary technologies run the risk of becoming obsolete or unsupported as the market gives its support to more widely available technologies. The Betamax VCR is a case in point. Although many experts believed it was superior technology, the Betamax passed into oblivion in the consumer market because the VHS technology was more widely supported by manufacturers. Ericsson was trying to avoid this type of eventuality when it invited other computing and communications leaders to join it in creating the Bluetooth SIG.

The Bluetooth SIG is not a company, corporation, or any type of physical entity. It also is not like the Elks, Eastern Star, or Theta Chi. It does not have a secret handshake and its members do not wear ceremonial robes, hats, or rings. The Bluetooth SIG is an independent organization that meets periodically to review technology, products, and standards in the interest of defining and advancing the Bluetooth technology. The Bluetooth SIG now boasts nearly 2,500 promoter and adopter/associate members, all working together to define a standard technology specification for the benefit of all those who adopt, apply, or use the Bluetooth technology.

Moving forward together

Forming the Bluetooth SIG enabled Ericsson to pool its research and development resources with the other founding companies to define a technology that would be more widely accepted and adopted by manufacturing companies and consumers alike. The primary goal of the five founding members of the Bluetooth SIG was to create a technology specification that developers could use to design products capable of wireless communications, regardless of the device's manufacturer.

The SIG reasoned that developing an *open standard* (one available to anyone wanting to develop a product) was key to the acceptance of the Bluetooth technology in the marketplace. In addition, the contributions of independent manufacturers would enable the evolving Bluetooth specifications to provide interoperability between the devices designed and manufactured by different companies. Through cooperation, Bluetooth would be the next VHS and not another Betamax.

The Bluetooth Organization

The SIG includes three membership levels: Promoter, Associate, and Adopter (also called Early Adopter). Depending on its membership level, a company can participate on various boards, groups, and committees that deal with the issues of the evolving Bluetooth standards.

The current number of SIG members by membership type are as follows:

- ✓ Promoter members: 9
- ✓ Associate members: 199
- ✓ Early adopter members: 1,332 for Version 1.0 and 1,349 for Version 1.2

Many of the early adopter members have adopted both versions of the Bluetooth specification. The 1,349 early adopter members for Version 1.2 probably include the 1,332 that had adopted Version 1.0. For a list of the current member companies and organizations, visit www.opengroup.org/bluetooth/membership/.

Promoter members

The promoter members of the Bluetooth SIG comprise the original five companies, plus four companies that were later invited to join the SIG: 3Com Corporation, Lucent Technologies, Inc. (which recently changed the name of the division that works with Bluetooth to Agere Systems), Microsoft Corporation, and Nokia. The promoter members serve as a combination steering committee, board of directors, and advisory committee. The promoter members provide oversight for all activities of the SIG, including marketing, administration, regulatory issues, and standards development for the Bluetooth technology.

Figure 2-1 shows the organization structure of the Bluetooth SIG, indicating the lowest level of membership that can participate in a group, committee, or board. As Figure 2-1 indicates, promoter members participate at all levels and functions of the organization, including the primary decision-making, marketing, legal, and policy setting functions.

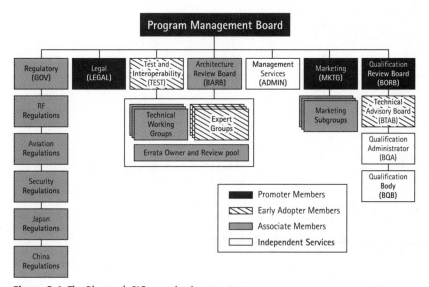

Figure 2-1: The Bluetooth SIG organization structure

Associate members

To become an associate member of the Bluetooth SIG, a company, organization, or individual must sign the Early Adopter contract and the Associate Member Amendment and pay an annual membership fee. Associate members can participate on several key boards, groups, and committees in the technical, architecture, and marketing areas (see Figure 2-1). Associate members also can participate on the Technical Working Groups (see "Working groups," later in this chapter).

For a complete list of the working groups on which associate members participate, go to www.bluetooth.com/sig/sig/sig.asp.

The Bluetooth SIG originally invited a group of 50 companies to join the SIG for a new level of participation. These companies were chosen because of their technical expertise in a particular field or technology and the resources they could provide in the research and development and promotion of the Bluetooth technology.

Early adopter members

Most members of the Bluetooth SIG are early adopters (also called adopter members), which means they have signed the Early Adopter contract. As an early adopter, a company or organization holds a royalty-free license to the Bluetooth intellectual property patent rights and can use the Bluetooth trademark and brand, provided the company has signed the Bluetooth Trademark Agreement. As illustrated in Figure 2-1, early adopter members can serve on many key groups and boards of the Bluetooth SIG.

Boards and subboards

As shown in Figure 2-1, the Bluetooth SIG is organized into a structure of boards, each of which has the responsibility for a specific segment of standards development, regulatory liaison, or promotion of the Bluetooth technology. These seven boards make up the first organizational layer of the SIG:

- ✓ **Regulatory:** Known as the GOV (or government relations) board, this board has five subordinate boards, each with a narrow scope and focus. The Regulatory board has five subboards:

    - ■ **Radio Frequency (RF) Regulations:** This body focuses on the adherence and proposal of new radio frequency regulations that impact Bluetooth technology applications.

    - ■ **Aviation Regulations:** This body focuses on the regulations that govern the use of wireless devices in and on aircraft.

    - ■ **Security Regulations:** This body is concerned with the security mechanisms incorporated into the Bluetooth technology and how they conform to local, regional, national, and international security regulations.

    - ■ **Japan Regulations:** This body is focused on the particular regulations that govern the use and development of wireless devices in Japan.

    - ■ **China Regulations:** This body is focused on the regulations governing the use and development of wireless devices in China.

- ✓ **Legal:** This board provides legal guidance to the Bluetooth SIG for all legal matters, such as contracts, agreements, and product development protections.

- ✓ **Test and Interoperability:** Arguably the most important board in the SIG, this body, known as TEST, is charged with defining the test and interoperability standards for new Bluetooth devices. It oversees, in conjunction with the BARB, the activities of the working groups and expert groups (see "Working groups" and "Expert groups," later in this chapter).

✓ **Architecture Review Board:** Known as the BARB, this group is the primary standards body of the SIG. The BARB oversees the activities of the working groups and expert groups (along with the TEST board) on the standards that specify the Bluetooth architecture.

✓ **Management Services:** All organizations, including the SIG, have some management and organization issues that must be administered. In the SIG, the Management Services board has the responsibility for these issues and activities.

✓ **Marketing:** This board, which is designated as the MKTG board, is to some people perhaps more important at this point of the Bluetooth technology development. Working with the marketing subgroups, the MKTG board is responsible for promoting and educating manufacturers, developers, and the public on Bluetooth standards, applications, and products.

✓ **Qualification Review Board:** Commonly referred to as the BQRB, this body has the responsibility for reviewing how well new products or applications meet the Bluetooth standards and determining which are added to the Qualified Products List (QPL). The BQRB oversees the product qualification program and works with three subgroups:

  ▪ **Technical Advisory Board (BTAB):** This group, made up of representatives from promoter member companies, provides guidance to the product qualification process.

  ▪ **Bluetooth Qualification Administrator (BQA):** This individual administers the qualification process for the BQRB and licenses facilities as Bluetooth Qualification Test Facilities (BQTFs).

  ▪ **Bluetooth Qualification Body (BQB):** This person has the responsibility of checking the documentation of products submitted to the qualification process, reviewing product test reports, and adding qualified products to the QPL.

Working groups

The working groups (technically, the Technology Working Groups) are teams made up primarily of promoter and associate members and have the responsibility for defining a specific Bluetooth function, interface, interoperability, or product area and generating the technical specifications for its implementation. The working groups, which work in conjunction with the expert groups and the Errata Owner and Review Pool, report directly to the BARB and the TEST boards.

Working groups vary in size, depending on the number of participants required for each group's assigned area of responsibility. The Bluetooth SIG guidelines recommend that a single member company or organization be limited to two individual representatives. However, in specific cases, a member can have three representatives. Although they may participate on the working groups, associate members do not have a vote unless one of their representatives is the chairperson of a group. Each member company has only one vote on each working group, regardless of how many representatives it may have on the group.

A great deal of interaction and overlap exist between the various working groups. For example, the Car Profile working group must work in conjunction with the Local Positioning, Personal Area Network (PAN), Audio/Video, Human Interface Device (HID), and Automotive expert groups to develop a standard that does not overlook the specifications and requirements established by overlapping product or service areas.

The following sections give an overview of the responsibilities of each of the current working groups.

AUDIO/VIDEO WORKING GROUP

The Audio/Video Working Group (AV) is responsible for defining the standards for wireless audio/video products that apply the Bluetooth technology — mostly consumer electronics, like the Ericsson mobile phone and headset shown in Figure 2-2 — and ensuring they meet the Bluetooth objectives as low-cost, low-power, interoperable devices. Representatives from Sony and Philips currently co-chair the AV Working Group.

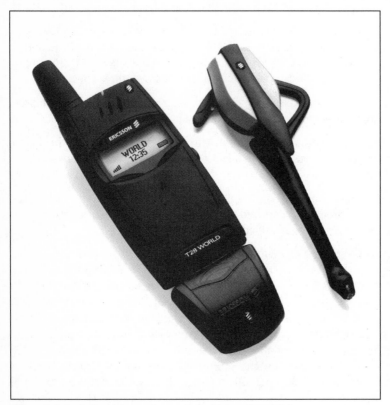

Figure 2-2: Audio headphones that apply the Bluetooth technology must use the standards developed by the AV Working Group.

The types of products that fall under the auspices of the AV Working Group include the following:

✓ CD-quality audio headphones, loudspeakers, and microphones

✓ Wireless short-range video displays

✓ Voice-quality dictation devices

✓ Wireless video cameras

✓ Videoconferencing devices

✓ Wideband voice-quality devices

CAR PROFILE WORKING GROUP

The Car Profile Working Group (CAR) is responsible for defining the standards for devices that operate inside cars and other motor vehicles. The standards and recommendations developed by the CAR Working Group, which is currently co-chaired by representatives from Nokia and Motorola, cover such products and functions as:

✓ The operation of a phone through an in-car device

✓ Portable devices that export the user interface to the car itself

✓ The personalization of a car and its Bluetooth devices

✓ Remote car-access and entry devices

✓ Call-handling between car-embedded and portable phones

✓ Devices that provide remote access to a car's location

✓ Devices that enable a car to communicate with the environment

✓ The diagnostics and programming used by car-compatible devices

COEXISTENCE AT 2.4 GHZ WORKING GROUP

The Coexistence Working Group (Coexist) addresses the issues arising from Bluetooth sharing the unlicensed 2.4-gigahertz (GHz) radio band with a wide range of wireless devices that also operate on this spectrum. The Coexistence Working Group is focused on ensuring that Bluetooth developers understand not only the effect other products have on Bluetooth devices, but also the effect Bluetooth devices have on products operating on other technologies. The 2.4-GHz band is an unlicensed radio frequency spectrum used throughout the world by wireless devices, including portable telephones, wireless Internet access, and even some baby monitors.

The Coexistence Working Group, which is currently chaired by a representative from Lucent, works closely with the Radio 2.0 Working Group to provide information and "Best Practices" white papers on the level of performance that Bluetooth developers can realistically expect in their products. The Coexistence Working Group has the following responsibilities:

✓ Identifying and quantifying the detrimental effects Bluetooth and other wireless products may have on each other

✓ Developing best-practice papers that describe the methods used to improve Bluetooth operation in the shared radio band

✓ Working with the Radio 2.0 Working Group on the coexistence issues of proposed radio specifications

EXTENDED SERVICE DISCOVERY PROFILES WORKING GROUP

The Extended Service Discovery Profiles Working Group (ESDP) develops Bluetooth specifications that enable Bluetooth devices (and perhaps non-Bluetooth devices) to discover each other and establish transparent personal networks. The ESDP Working Group, which is co-chaired by representatives from Microsoft and 3Com, is also responsible for defining and modifying the Bluetooth Service Discovery Protocol (BSDP).

The products of the ESDP Working Group, which are called *profiles*, map the service discovery protocols in use in the wireless industry. The first of the ESDP profiles is a mapping of Bluetooth discovery protocols with the Universal Plug and Play (UpnP) architecture, which has been developed by the Universal Plug and Play Forum (www.upnp.org) to provide the wireless industry with an easy and robust connectivity standard for standalone devices and PCs from many different vendors.

The usage models covered by the ESDP group include the following:

✓ Proximity, spontaneous, and personal networking

✓ Device and service discovery mechanisms

HUMAN INTERFACE DEVICE WORKING GROUP

The Human Interface Device Working Group (HID) develops profiles that provide specifications for the application of the Bluetooth technology to keyboards, pointing devices (mice, joysticks, trackballs, and so on), gaming devices, and human physiological monitoring devices. The HID Working Group, which is co-chaired by two representatives from Microsoft, is responsible for ensuring that HID devices are compatible, easy to use, and affordable.

The devices that fall under the responsibility of the HID Working Group include the following:

✓ Entertainment systems

✓ Smart home appliances

✓ Computer controls, including front panel knobs, buttons, slides, switches, and keypads

✓ Gaming devices, including throttles, steering wheels, and pedals

✓ Two-way interactive and force feedback devices, including game controllers and keypads that incorporate a display screen

✓ Bar-code readers

✓ Thermometers

✓ Digital voltage meters

IMAGING WORKING GROUP

The Imaging Working Group (Imaging) is responsible for developing profiles that define the exchange of digital images and related data between Bluetooth devices for the purpose of displaying, storing, transmitting, or printing the images. The Imaging Working Group, which is chaired by a representative of Nokia, works closely with the Personal Area Networking (PAN), AV, Printing, and Radio 2.0 Working Groups.

LOCAL POSITIONING WORKING GROUP

The Local Positioning Working Group (LP) has the responsibility for defining the methods used by devices to accurately determine their position, whether inside a building or outside. The LP Working Group is looking to supplement the use of Global Positioning Systems (GPSs) and cellular applications to improve their performance where their capabilities are reduced, such as inside a building. The LP Working Group, which is chaired by representatives from Nokia and Microsoft, is working to develop a location descriptor that will provide information to other 2.4-GHz positioning systems, working closely with the CAR and ESDP Working Groups.

The usage models of the LP group include the following:

✓ Enabling the user's device to accurately determine its position indoors and in other enclosed environments.

✓ Augmenting GPS and cellular positioning indoors, where their performance is reduced.

PERSONAL AREA NETWORKING WORKING GROUP

The Personal Area Networking Working Group (PAN) is concerned with the issues surrounding the creation of ad hoc, mobile IP (Internet Protocol)-based personal area networks (PANs), including the security of these networks. The PAN Working Group, which is co-chaired by representatives from Microsoft and Intel, is defining the use of the Bluetooth technology in establishing multi-user links that are operating system, programming language, and device-independent under the IEEE (Institute of Electrical and Electronics Engineers) 802.15 standards.

The PAN Working Group has the following objectives:

✓ Ensuring that the ad hoc network does not require the existence of any special-purpose products or infrastructure, although it should offer interoperability with such devices if they exist, in order to facilitate the ad hoc network or provide LAN access to a separate wired (or wireless) network

✓ Ensuring that all networking usage models fully support the TCP/IP protocol suite

✓ Ensuring that networking solutions will be backward-compatible with the Bluetooth specifications for L2CAP and the baseband

See Chapter 12 for more information on Bluetooth and personal area networks and Chapter 13 for a more detailed look at the profiles produced by the Bluetooth working groups.

PRINTING WORKING GROUP

The Printing Working Group (Printing) is charged with developing specifications that define how Bluetooth-capable printers connect to source devices and the print capabilities of Bluetooth printers. The Printing Working Group, co-chaired by representatives from Hewlett-Packard and Ericsson, also is working to define how printing operations work with mobile phones, personal digital assistants (PDAs), or personal computers, even if the printer is physically attached to another device or network.

RADIO 2.0 WORKING GROUP

The Radio 2.0 Working Group (Radio2) has the responsibility to recommend improvements to the original Bluetooth radio specification (Radio 1.0) in the development of a new and expanded radio standard, Radio 2.0. The original Bluetooth radio specification, which was announced in July 1999, included a common set of specifications for wireless voice and data transmission at up to 10 meters (about 33 feet). Radio 2.0 will not replace the Radio 1.0 specification but will add a set of optional extensions to the older specifications.

The Radio2 Working Group, chaired by representatives from Ericsson and Nokia, is developing improvements to the original Radio 1.0 specification that address issues in baseband communications and the Link Manager Protocol (LMP).

See Chapter 7 for more information on the Link Manager Protocol (LMP).

The responsibilities of the Radio 2.0 Working Group include the following:

✓ Improvements to the Radio 1.0 specification:

- Legacy compliance (backward-compatible with Radio 1.0)

- Improvements to radio, baseband, and LMP specifications

- Support for modulation schemes with a gross rate of 2 Mbps or more on packet payloads

- Support for profile features

✓ High-rate mode:

- Legacy compliance (backward-compatible with Radio 1.0)

- Compliance with Radio 1.0 improvements

- Worldwide use according to Radio 1.0

- Support for data rates of at least 10 Mbps

- Range of 10m at maximum data rate 10 Mbps, with link margin equal to or better than the 0dBm Radio 1.0

- Resistant to interference

- Coexistence with Radio 1.0 piconets and WLANs

- Concurrent support for low-rate and high-rate slaves in point-to-multipoint configurations

- Low-cost target ($10)

The usage models covered by the Radio2 group include the following:

✓ Data rate alignment with 2.5G and 3G cellular systems

✓ Access points to other networks (PSTN, or data networks of all types)

✓ Personal area networking

UNRESTRICTED DIGITAL INFORMATION WORKING GROUP

The Unrestricted Digital Information Working Group (UDI) concentrates on developing a standard that enables the UDI transfer services of the 3G (3rd Generation) cellular phone technology. The 3G technology is designed to support advanced global roaming and high-speed multimedia data and voice traffic on digital cell phones. The UDI Working Group has the task of developing a profile specification that is specifically aimed at the Japanese market, where UDI transfer is a requirement.

The usage models of the UDI group include the following:

✓ A circuit-switched and synchronous communication methodology to be independent of application

✓ UDI profiles to seamlessly extend UDI communication service of a 3G handset to external devices

Expert groups

Expert groups, which can have participants from promoter, early adopter, and associate members, operate independently but in support of the working groups to provide expertise on potential applications of the Bluetooth technology in specific industrial markets, such as security, automotive, and aviation.

Marketing board

The members of the Bluetooth SIG Marketing Board are the promoter member companies. They have the responsibility for the marketing and promotional activities for the Bluetooth technology. The marketing board operates through *marketing subgroups* — teams of promoter and associate members that are formed when needed to coordinate specific marketing and promotion tasks for the SIG.

Qualifying a New Product

One of the primary activities of the boards and groups of the Bluetooth SIG is the qualification of new products and services that adopt the Bluetooth technology. For this purpose, a formal process, officially called the Bluetooth Qualification Process, exists to ensure that new product applications of Bluetooth meet the specifications, performance goals, and objectives set forth by the Bluetooth SIG.

To qualify a new product, a company must go through the following steps:

1. If the manufacturer is not already a Bluetooth adopter member, it must become one by signing the Adopter Agreement.

2. As shown in Figure 2-3, the manufacturer must submit compliance documentation to the BQB, demonstrating that the product design complies with the Bluetooth specification. The manufacturer also must submit its Declaration of Compliance documents and all necessary documentation, such as technical product descriptions and a user's manual, which the Bluetooth Qualification Administrator (BQA) reviews. The BQA also oversees the qualification process and ensures that all required documentation is completed.

3. The manufacturer chooses a Bluetooth Qualification Test Facility (BQTF) from a list of approved facilities and submits the product for compliance and performance testing. In some cases, the BQTF could be an in-house facility, such as would be the case with a promoter member.

4. The BQTF produces a test report for review by the BQB, which then reviews the submitted documents and, if the product qualifies, prepares a qualified product notice that is used to update the Qualified Product List (QPL).

5. After all requirements are met, the BQB notifies the manufacturer that the product is qualified and listed in the QPL.

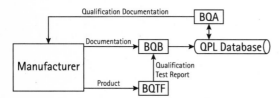

Figure 2-3: The Bluetooth qualification process

Every product that incorporates the Bluetooth wireless technology must be licensed. The Bluetooth name and logos are registered to Ericsson, but the Bluetooth SIG extends the licenses as Ericsson's agent. To be licensed, a product must successfully complete the qualification process.

The qualification process is not the same for every product. Products that are designed to be marketed as development or demonstration kits are exempt from the testing requirements. These products are qualified from their declaration of compliance documents. Products that incorporate a previously approved component only need to qualify those components not already qualified. All other products must be qualified through the qualification process.

Summary

Ericsson discovered early in the development of the Bluetooth specification that it needed to enlist the help of other manufacturers in order to gain wide acceptance and interoperability with their devices:

✓ Ericsson formed the Bluetooth SIG in order to help ensure the interoperability, compatibility, and universal acceptance of the Bluetooth technology.

✓ The Bluetooth SIG is made up of three levels of members: promoters, associates, and early adopters.

✓ The SIG's activities include specification and protocol development, marketing, product qualification, and standards development.

✓ The activities of the SIG are carried out through several boards and groups, each of which is assigned the responsibility for specific technological, market, industry, product, or interface issues that impact the application and extension of the Bluetooth technology.

In Chapter 3, we take a look at the components of Bluetooth and give an overview of their interactions and operations.

Part II

The Technology of Bluetooth

IN THIS PART

Bluetooth technology, as innovative as it may be, does not define much in the way of new technology. Most of the protocols and services that Bluetooth applies are borrowed from existing telephone and radio-frequency technologies. This part of the book looks at the components of the Bluetooth technology, including radio frequency, baseband communications, Bluetooth operating states, the Bluetooth Link Manager, the protocol stack, and software, as well as how those elements are combined into the operations of Bluetooth devices.

Chapter 3

Elementary Bluetooth

In This Chapter

The Bluetooth specifications describe and define how the Bluetooth hardware and software are to function in any device, regardless of manufacturer. This combination of hardware and software is known as the *Bluetooth stack*. The Bluetooth stack, according to the specifications, comprises upper and lower layers. The upper layer supports services for building application profiles, while the lower layer provides a combination of hardware and software to establish connections between devices. Any Bluetooth system has four basic components, as shown in Figure 3-1. These components are as follows:

✓ Radio that receives and transmits data and voice signals

✓ Baseband, or link control unit, that processes the data transmissions

✓ Link management software that manages data transmissions

✓ Supporting application software that enables the host device to do its job

Figure 3-1: Bluetooth components

The following sections describe these four basic elements of the Bluetooth system and indicate how they function together to establish wireless communication among Bluetooth devices. This chapter has the following objectives:

✓ Reviewing the basic components of the Bluetooth system

✓ Understanding radio frequencies

✓ Exploring the baseband

✓ Examining link management

✓ Taking a look at supporting software

Radio Frequencies

You can connect devices without wires in various ways, but because of its ease of use and flexibility, the Bluetooth SIG chose to use radio frequency (RF) communications as the Bluetooth standard. Radio frequencies in an unlicensed band provide a low-cost means of wireless communication. Also, the fact that radio requires low power is an advantage for mobile devices, because battery life is an important consideration for these devices.

The Bluetooth radio is a short-distance, low-power unit that operates in the unlicensed Industrial, Scientific, and Medical (ISM) spectrum of 2.4 GHz. The radio is both a receiver and a transmitter. Radio waves are generated when a transmitter oscillates at a specific frequency — the faster the oscillation, the higher the frequency.

An antenna is required to broadcast the radio waves. The Bluetooth antenna power used is 0 dBm, giving a range of 10 meters (about 33 feet). So, for devices to communicate, they must be within a 10-meter range. (The Bluetooth specifications indicate that a range of 100 meters can be achieved if a 20-dBm powered antenna is used.) To receive the broadcast signals, the Bluetooth receiver is tuned to the 2.4 GHz frequency.

The Bluetooth radio transmits data at a maximum gross rate of up to 1 Mbps; however, protocol overhead limits the data rate to a little over 721 Kbps. Other limitations include interference or being out of range, both of which can increase the bit error rate (BER), necessitating the retransmission of data packets, which further decreases the achievable transmission rate.

The ISM band is free for anyone to use, and currently it is used by many other devices, including the following:

✓ Microwave ovens

✓ 2.4 GHz cordless phones

✓ 802.11 wireless networks

✓ Garage door openers

✓ Many emergency radios

✓ Government communications in Spain, France, and Japan

✓ Home RF networks

Avoiding interference from other RF transmissions

Because so many other devices use the 2.4 GHz frequency, interference with Bluetooth transmissions is likely. To address this issue, Bluetooth technology uses a pseudo-random hopping sequence of 79 (or a reduced 23) hop frequencies that are spaced 1 MHz apart. The width of the frequency available is 83.5 MHz, so the frequency band is 2.4 GHz to 2.4835 GHz. The hop rate is 1,600 hops per second.

The specification attempts to reduce transmission interference by hopping along the frequencies. If a problem with transmission is encountered at a frequency, the master (sending) device waits until the hop to the next channel and then resends the data on the new channel. This process continues until the transmission is successful or times out.

The 79-hop frequency is the full frequency band implementation. In some countries, a reduced bandwidth is available due to national limitations. For example, in France, the smaller bandwidth available has 23 RF channels that are 1 MHz apart. The frequency range in France is 2.4465 to 2.4835 GHz. An upper and a lower band edge — the *guard band* — are defined in order to meet regulations in each country. Table 3-1 lists the differences in full and reduced frequencies. The full band specification gives the master, or transmitting, device more channels to send data to its slaves (recipients), while only 23 channels are available in the reduced band specification.

Table 3-1 Bandwidth

Band	Frequency Band	RF Channels
Full	2.4 GHZ to 2.4835 GHz	79
Reduced	2.4465 to 2.4835 GHz	23

Products developed for a reduced band market cannot be used with products developed for the standard full band version.

Channel arrangement and piconets

A specific channel is represented by a pseudo-random hop sequence, hopping through the 79 or 23 RF channels. The channel is divided into time slots (625 μ>s in length) in which each slot corresponds to an RF hop frequency, and consecutive hops correspond to different RF hop frequencies.

Two or more Bluetooth devices that use the same channel form what is known in Bluetooth terminology as a *piconet*. A piconet has one master (transmitting) device and one or more slave (receiving) devices. The hop sequence is unique for each piconet. This sequence is determined by the master unit's Bluetooth device address, and the hopping sequence phase is determined by the master unit's clock.

When a connection is made between the piconet devices, the master establishes a frequency-hopping scheme that is communicated to the slave devices. Frequency-hopping enables the communications to avoid frequencies that may have high levels of line noise or other problems. Also, as shown in Figure 3-2, some frequencies enable the master to send more slot packets per time slot.

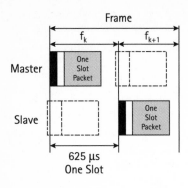

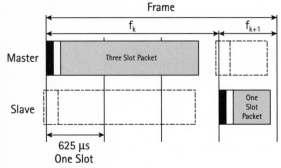

Figure 3-2: By applying frequency-hopping, a Bluetooth master device can take advantage of the frequency's characteristics.

A Time Division Duplex (TDD) scheme is used for transmissions, enabling the master and the slave to transmit alternately. As shown in Figure 3-3, the master unit starts the transmission in even-numbered slots, and the slave unit starts transmissions in the odd-numbered time slots.

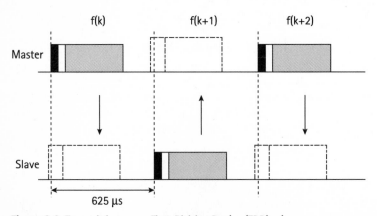

Figure 3-3: Transmitting over a Time Division Duplex (TDD) scheme

Baseband

In the Bluetooth environment, the *baseband* is the hardware that converts the received radio signals into a digital format that a host application can process. Conversely, the baseband also converts digital or voice data into a format that a radio signal can transmit.

When the master unit sends data to a slave unit, it must transfer the digital data into a radio signal. The baseband compresses the data, puts the data into packets, and adds the administrative information about the packet. In addition to the actual data that's being transmitted, each packet to be transmitted contains information about its origin, its frequency, and its destination. Packets also contain information about how the data was compressed for transmission, the order in which the packets were transmitted, and the effectiveness of the transmission.

The process is reversed for the slave, or receiving, unit. When the slave unit receives the signals, it needs to convert them into digital format so the host application can process the information. Also, when the data packet is received, it's checked for accuracy, extracted from the packet, reassembled, decompressed, and possibly filtered.

Link controller

The *link controller* is a supervisory function that handles all the Bluetooth baseband functions and supports the link manager. The link controller

- ✓ Sends and receives data.
- ✓ Identifies the device sending data.
- ✓ Performs authentication and ciphering functions.
- ✓ Determines the type of frame to use on a slot-by-slot basis.
- ✓ Determines how devices listen for transmissions or moves devices into various power-saving modes.

Links

A Bluetooth *link* is the actual data transmission method to be used among devices. The Bluetooth specification supports two types of links: synchronous connection-oriented (SCO) for voice communications, and asynchronous connectionless (ACL) for data. Each of these links supports up to 15 different packet types. The packet types actually used are dependent on the application. In the Bluetooth environment, devices can use either link type and can change link types during a transmission as necessary.

For more information about the various packet types that SCO and ACL links support, see Chapter 5.

Bluetooth supports one asynchronous data channel and three synchronous voice channels at 64 Kbps. Or, it can support simultaneous asynchronous data and voice. The asynchronous channel can support a link of 723.2 kilobits per second (Kbps) in either direction and a 57.6 Kbps link in the return direction.

Functional blocks

The components of the lower layer of the Bluetooth stack work together to enable connections between devices. The radio, or RF, portion of the system is the hardware that sends and receives the radio signals. The baseband processes the signals from the RF block and provides the digital signalprocessing component. The link manager resides on top of the baseband and controls link setup and configuration, accessing the underlying link controller for actually sending and receiving information. As shown in Figure 3-4, these functional blocks work together to establish the connections in a Bluetooth system.

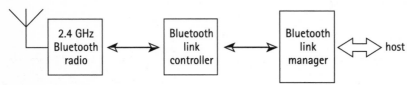

Figure 3-4: Bluetooth functional blocks

Link Management Software

The link management software runs on a microprocessor to handle connections between Bluetooth devices. Each Bluetooth device has a link manager (LM) that discovers other remote link managers and communicates with them. To perform its services, the LM relies on the functions provided by the hardware component, the link controller. The link controller functions include sending and receiving data, authenticating links, and setting up link types (SCO or ACL).

Communication between link managers occurs through messages, or protocol data units (PDUs), exchanged using the Bluetooth Link Manager Protocol (LMP). These messages perform the link setup, including invoking security features such as authentication and encryption if necessary. The PDUs also control and negotiate the baseband packet sizes, control the power modes and duty cycles of Bluetooth devices, and control the connection states of units in a piconet.

PDUs have a higher priority than user data, which means that a message sent by the LM will not be delayed by traffic sent in the higher layers. It is possible, however, that retransmissions of individual baseband packets will delay the PDUs. The messages are filtered out and interpreted by the LM in the receiving unit and are not propagated to the higher layers of the Bluetooth stack.

According to the Bluetooth specification, an explicit message acknowledgment is not needed because the link controller provides a reliable link. However, the time that elapses between receiving an LMP PDU and sending a valid response cannot exceed the response timeout threshold of 30 seconds.

The Bluetooth specification defines 55 different types of PDUs, and each PDU carries out a unique function. A 7-bit operations (op) code is assigned to each PDU and serves as a unique type identifier. The source and destination of each PDU are determined by the active member address contained in the packet header. Each PDU is either mandatory or optional, depending on the Bluetooth specification. If a PDU is optional, the LM doesn't need to transmit it, although it must be able to recognize all optional PDUs received and send a valid response if necessary. The PDU types include general response messages, authentication messages, and paging messages.

Figure 3-5 shows how the components of the lower layers of the stack function together to establish connections and transmit data.

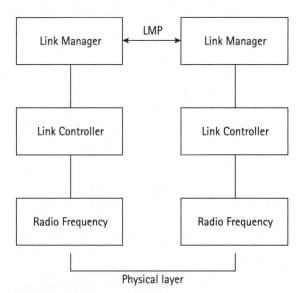

Figure 3-5: Link management

Supporting Application Software

The application software, which is embedded in the host device, operates an application over the Bluetooth protocol stack. Typically, in an embedded Bluetooth solution, the upper-layer protocols reside on a single chip in the host device. The Bluetooth unit can then connect to the host through a serial interface such as a universal serial bus (USB). Figure 3-6 indicates how the upper layers work over the baseband.

The application software enables the host device — a mobile phone, PDA, notebook computer, and so on — to do its job. To ensure interoperability, all Bluetooth devices must have compatible sections in their Bluetooth stack. The Bluetooth specifications, which define hardware and software components of the Bluetooth system, are the standard by which interoperability is ensured. Any product bearing the Bluetooth logo must be built according to the specifications and be certified by the SIG.

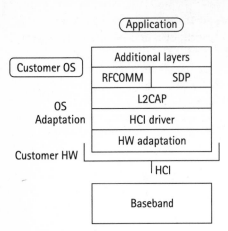

Figure 3-6: Upper layers

The Bluetooth specifications identify various usage models and scenarios that could use Bluetooth technology. Each usage model is tied to a Bluetooth profile, and each profile defines numerous protocols and features supporting the specific usage model. A *profile*, then, is a set of protocols that are used to implement an application (for example, dial-up networking or file transfer), and they are implemented in the upper layers of the Bluetooth stack. Each profile uses only a slice of the stack as necessary to support the application being implemented. To ensure interoperability among devices that host compatible applications, specific profiles are implemented; this serves to establish a standard profile for a given application.

The profiles for usage models that are defined in the Bluetooth specifications include the following:

✓ **Intercom profile:** Supports the usage scenarios that require a direct voice link between Bluetooth devices (for example, cell phones).

✓ **Cordless telephony profile:** Defines the procedures for making calls via a base station as well as making direct intercom calls between two terminals.

✓ **Headset profile:** Defines procedures for the usage model known as the *Ultimate Headset*, which can be implemented by devices such as cell phones and personal computers.

✓ **Dial-up networking profile:** Defines procedures for the usage model known as the *Internet Bridge* and used by devices such as modems and cell phones. (Enables a device to act as a wireless modem in order to connect a computer to a dial-up Internet access server.)

✓ **Fax profile:** Defines procedures for devices implementing the fax usage model. For example, a cell phone that is Bluetooth-enabled may be used by a computer as a wireless fax-modem to send or receive faxes.

✓ **LAN access profile:** Defines procedures for using Bluetooth wireless technology to access the services of a local area network (LAN). In this usage model, multiple data terminals use a LAN access point as a wireless connection to a LAN, thus enabling access to all services provided by the LAN.

The profiles listed in this chapter support specific usage models, as defined by the Bluetooth specifications. Their purpose is to define the specific messages and procedures used to implement various application features — some of which are mandatory, some optional, and some conditional. When a feature is implemented, it must be according to the protocols defined in the appropriate profile in order to ensure interoperability.

In an embedded Bluetooth solution, in which the upper-layer protocols that implement the host applications reside on a single chip, the host processor is freed from intensive protocol processing — the Bluetooth chip takes care of it.

Summary

Any hardware or software approved through the Bluetooth qualification program must meet the specification for basic and core components:

✓ All Bluetooth devices must have four basic components:

  ▪ A radio that receives and transmits data and voice signals

  ▪ Baseband operations or a link control unit to process data transmissions

  ▪ Link management software that manages data transmissions

  ▪ Supporting application software that enables the host device to do its job

✓ Each basic component must be developed in accordance with the Bluetooth specifications.

✓ The Bluetooth certification procedures are rigid and designed to ensure global interoperability among Bluetooth and other devices using the protocols in the Bluetooth stack.

✓ Bluetooth hardware and software components are intended to interact seamlessly and provide a reliable, convenient, and low-cost means of wireless connectivity.

Chapter 4 takes a look at wireless communications and provides an overview of radio frequency communications.

Chapter 4

RF and Bluetooth

In This Chapter

Although we typically think of radio as a way to listen to news, weather, music, and sports in our car, office, or home, radio frequency communications also serve as the basis for most wireless communications. Most wireless communications technologies in use today, including cellular telephones, point-to-multipoint broadband wireless services (such as LMDS, or local multipoint distribution service, and MMDS, or multichannel multipoint distribution service), Home RF (radio frequency), and even Bluetooth, use radio frequency communications technologies to carry voice and data signals.

In this chapter, we provide a look at a few of the wireless technologies that compete with Bluetooth in the market and the technology space. We also look at radio frequency communications and the role it plays in the Bluetooth technology. Radio frequency communications can be a very technical and detailed topic to cover, but we narrow down the focus to the parts of RF technology that are included in Bluetooth and compatible technologies. This chapter has the following objectives:

- ✓ Examining the most common wireless communication methods
- ✓ Understanding radio waves
- ✓ Explaining the radio frequency spectrum
- ✓ Defining spread-spectrum frequency-hopping
- ✓ Understanding baseband signaling

Wireless Communication Methods

Bluetooth technology did not invent wireless communications for local area networks (LANs), but Bluetooth is adapting wireless communications technology to create new networking applications, including what is called a Wireless Personal Area Network (WPAN). A LAN, or any network for that matter, exists to share resources between devices that are connected by some form of communications media. A WPAN, on the other hand, is not a network in the true sense of this definition, but it does interconnect wireless devices to create a personal workspace. Through other applications of wireless communications technology, Bluetooth developers are looking for ways to extend its range and capabilities to include transparent and instantaneous connections to specialized LANs, CANs (Campus Area Networks), and even WANs (Wide Area Networks).

At the heart of these capabilities are wireless communications technologies. Wireless communications date back to the early days of radio and television, and the basic technology is not new. More recently, infrared signals, like those used in your television remote control and other similar devices, wireless cellular communications, like that used in your cell phone, and adaptations of radio frequency (RF) communications are being adapted to carry voice, data, and multimedia between mobile devices.

Although this chapter focuses on providing you with background on RF communications, a quick look at other wireless communications technologies will help you to understand the competitive environment of RF communications and the Bluetooth technology.

Infrared communications

As the use of infrared signals began to emerge as a means for transmitting data between devices, the Infrared Data Association (IrDA) was formed in 1993. IrDA, which is an industry association much like the Bluetooth SIG, focuses on the development of infrared communications technology and the standards that define its use with computer devices, as well as several other applications.

INFRARED TECHNOLOGY

In an infrared (IR) communications application, data is sent between two devices using a light beam from the infrared spectrum, which falls just beyond the light visible to the human eye. The sending device emits a light beam, using various wavelengths to represent the data being transmitted. The receiving device "sees" the wavelengths and interprets them into binary data, which it passes on to the host device, usually a PC.

The receiving device must "see" the incoming light wavelengths, which makes IR technology a *line-of-sight* technology. In other words, the sending and receiving devices must be placed so the IR transceiver on the sending device has a clear, unobstructed path to the receiving IR transceiver. If the two devices are not directly lined up, or if anything — a body, a book, a wall, or any other obstruction — blocks the line-of-sight, the light beam carrying the data is interrupted and the devices cannot communicate.

Another problem in IR communications is distance. IR has a relatively short *attenuation point* (the point at which the signal loses the integrity of its data), which means that IR devices also must be in close proximity to one another.

Because of these limitations, IR is not appropriate for all situations. Specifically, walls, doors, equipment, and so on must not separate communicating devices, nor must the devices become easily misaligned through jarring, bumping, or moving.

IR DEVICES

IR technology is currently used for a wide range of PC peripheral devices. Many PC systems, especially high-end systems, now come with an IR port (transceiver) as a standard feature. The range of devices that support IR communications includes the following:

✓ Notebook computers

✓ Mice

✓ Keyboards

✓ Handheld devices (palmtop computers)

    ✓ Pocket PCs

    ✓ Scanners

    ✓ Digital cameras

    ✓ Printers

    ✓ Cell phones

    ✓ Pagers

One of the main benefits of wireless technologies is that they free users from fixed-point operations. With a technology like IR, you can locate devices anywhere you want in relation to the other devices to which they must communicate, as long as the devices share a line-of-sight pathway and are in close enough proximity. For many users, mobility and flexibility are the chief benefits of wireless technologies, regardless of their inherent limitations.

Not wireless, but mobile

Another technology that supports mobile communications is called *cable synchronization*. Technically, cable synchronization is not wireless because it requires some form of a physical cable to connect the devices. However, devices that support cable synchronization are completely mobile with respect to one another, except, of course, when they are communicating with one another. You may not think these devices strictly qualify as mobile devices, but many of the wireless technologies, including Bluetooth and IR, specifically target this group of devices.

Common cable synchronization devices include personal digital assistants (PDAs), such as a Handspring Visor Edge (shown in Figure 4-1) or a Palm Pilot, flash card readers (like those used in digital cameras), and other forms of data- or image-capture devices. These devices are connected to a computer through a cradle or with a proprietary cable. Some also connect via Universal Signal Bus (USB) or IEEE 1394 (FireWire) cables and ports.

Bluetooth breaks the bonds

Like the wireless cellular technologies, Bluetooth has solved the line-of-sight and temporary-cabling connection problems by using RF technology to transmit data. Radio frequency, or radio wave, technology (see "Radio waves," later in this chapter) is a more robust technology than infrared technology or cable synchronization because the equipment does not require line-of-sight or physical connectivity at any point during the communication.

If the equipment is moved or rearranged, within the maximum signal distance zone, the move will not cause the device to lose its connection within the network. Radio waves can travel "through" and around walls or large objects so they do not reduce the devices' signal. RF technology needs no cables, at any time. Bluetooth technology and the 802.11 (wireless LAN) technologies differ in terms of how they operate and in their signal range and use.

We examine these differences and the IEEE (Institute of Electrical and Electronics Engineers) 802.11 wireless LAN standards more thoroughly in Chapters 7, 11, and 18.

Figure 4-1: Many personal digital assistant (PDA) devices require cable synchronization to communicate. Photo courtesy of Handspring, Inc.

Mobile Wireless Devices: Breaking Free of the Cable

With the advancement of wireless technologies, many cable synchronization devices are now available with wireless modules that eliminate the need to attach the mobile device to a fixed base for communications.

For example, the Handspring Visor, shown in Figure 4-1, has an optional snap-on module that can be added to the device to support wireless voice and data communications. Most of the competing products to the Visor, like the Palm Pilot series, have similar modules that can be added to provide wireless features, such as caller ID, call waiting, three-way calling, speed dial, call history, voicemail, SMS (short messaging service) text messaging, and with the addition of software on the handheld device, wireless modem services to provide Internet, e-mail, and remote synchronization access. These capabilities are not limited to PDAs. In fact, many palmtop and handheld computers also offer similar built-in or add-on wireless communications options.

The wireless technology used on these devices is generically cellular wireless communications, such as is used by cell phones. However, several types and variations of wireless cellular communications currently in development will be applied to the full range of handheld devices. Perhaps, a short overview of the evolution of wireless communications, defined by its generations, is in order. First, however, we need to define a few important terms.

Narrow-, wide-, broad-, and basebands

You cannot discuss wireless (or wired) communications without discussing the different transmission bands used by the various technologies. Bluetooth uses baseband transmissions, which we describe briefly later in this chapter (see "Baseband Communications"). Other wireless technologies use narrowband, wideband, and broadband transmission modes. Here are brief definitions of these transmission modes:

- ✓ **Narrowband** supports transmission rates between 50 bps (bits per second) and 64 Kbps (kilobits per second).

- ✓ **Wideband** supports transmission rates between 64 Kbps and 2 Mbps (megabits per second).

- ✓ **Broadband** is a high-speed transmission mode that typically refers to the bandwidth provided by T-1 (1.544 Mbps) lines or above, but broadband services are available from DSL (Digital Subscriber Lines), cable modems, and other dedicated Internet access services with speeds as low as 250 Kbps. Broadband services can carry analog (voice), digital (data), or video transmissions. In effect, broadband transmissions are the opposite of baseband transmissions, which carry only digital transmissions.

- ✓ **Baseband** is a digital transmission mode that is used in virtually all networking environments. Bluetooth is a baseband technology, and we explain baseband in more detail later in this chapter (see "Baseband Communications") as well as in Chapter 5.

Wireless cellular generations

Wireless cellular communications have evolved through three generations to date. Each generation has advanced the capabilities and utility of the cellular device users with an incredible range of functions and features.

1G

The first generation (1G) of wireless cellular communications supported analog voice transmissions, using such technologies as the Advanced Mobile Phone Service (AMPS), Nordic Mobile Telephone (NMT), and Total Access Communication System (TACS). Here is a brief overview of these 1G technologies:

- ✓ **AMPS:** This analog wireless cellular technology is used in North and South America and more than 30 other countries around the world. The AMPS technology, which has been in use in the United States since 1983, is an 800-MHz (megahertz) system.

- ✓ **NMT:** This analog wireless cellular system is used throughout Europe. As its name implies, it was first used in Scandinavia (in 1979). NMT, which supports both 450-MHz and 900-MHz transmissions, was the first analog wireless technology implemented.

✓ **TACS:** This is another analog wireless cellular system used mostly in European countries. TACS is based on the AMPS model and has several variations in use, including ETACS (Extended TACS), ITACS (International TACS), IETACS (International ETACS), and NTACS (Narrowband TACS).

The 1G technologies are Frequency Division Multiple Access (FDMA) services. FDMA divides radio frequency channels into a range of subfrequencies, and only one user can use a channel at one time. The channel cannot be used for other calls until a user's call is terminated or passed on to another channel by the system.

2G

In the 1990s, the second generation (2G) of wireless cellular communications emerged and offered digital transmissions. The technologies of 2G — Code Division Multiple Access (CDMA), Global System for Mobile Communications (GSM), and Time Division Multiple Access (TDMA) — are primarily voice transmission technologies. However, GSM does include SMS support.

Advancements that provide improved data speeds for enhanced e-mail and Internet access have been and are still being developed for the 2G technologies. These advancements are included in what is called 2.5G or 2G+.

Here is a brief description of these wireless cellular communications technologies:

✓ **CDMA:** This wireless cellular system assigns a unique identifier to each system user and combines multiple transmissions on a single wideband channel. The identifier, which is called a *pseudo-random code sequence*, is used to distinguish conversations between the mobile device and the base station. CDMA uses a frequency-hopping technique called *spread spectrum.*

✓ **GSM:** GSM is the reigning 2G wireless cellular technology in Europe, but it is also used regionally in the U.S. GSM differs from CDMA and TDMA in that it defines an entire communications system and is not limited to just the wireless transmission interfaces. Nearly one-half of all cellular phones in use in the world are on the GSM system.

✓ **TDMA:** This type of wireless cellular system divides radio channels into time slots, which allows the channel to support a greater number of calls. GSM and Personal Digital Cellular (PDC) systems are based on TDMA services. Like FDMA, a TDMA channel (time slot) is limited to one call at a time.

3G

The third generation of wireless cellular communications is designed to transmit high-speed voice, data, and multimedia to handheld devices, primarily cell phones. When fully implemented, which is projected to be in the 2003 to 2005 timeframe, 3G technology is expected to provide high-quality audio and video transmissions as well as advanced global roaming for cell-phone users. Its objective is to enable a wireless cell-phone user to be handed off automatically to the best available service, such as an in-house phone system, the cellular system, a satellite communications system, or whatever compatible system is available.

Wireless Communications and the Movie Star

Technology often has its origins in the strangest places. For example, the underlying principles for CDMA were first conceived back in 1940 when the movie star Hedy Lamarr was talking with composer George Antheil at a cocktail party. While discussing their disdain for Nazi Germany and its control of Europe, they came up with the idea for a new wireless communications technique that would prevent the Germans from disrupting Allied communications. The next day, Hedy and George met to discuss their idea and they later patented a frequency-hopping scheme that was subsequently developed by QualComm.

The original idea used player piano rolls to synchronize the frequency-hopping patterns. Modern systems perform this process digitally. Neither Ms. Lamarr nor Mr. Antheil ever made any money from their patent. Their ideas were not put to use until 1962, three years after their patent had expired.

The 3G technology standards are being developed under the guidance of the 3rd Generation Partnership Project (3GPP), which consists of an alliance of several standards organizations from around the world. 3GPP is divided into two specialty areas focusing on the development of the Wideband CDMA (W-CDMA) and cdma2000 technologies.

The 3G technologies, some of which are operating regionally in Europe, Japan, and the U.S., are

- ✓ **cdma2000:** This 3G wireless technology increases the data transmission rates of CDMA (now referred to as cdmaOne) to 144 Kbps, with hopes to raise the rate to 4 Mbps in its second phase.

- ✓ **NTT-DoCoMo:** This technology, which is under development by the Japanese company with the same name, is another 3G system based on W-CDMA. DoCoMo means *anywhere* in Japanese.

- ✓ **Universal Mobile Telecommunications System (UMTS):** UMTS is the 3G system implemented in Europe and is based on the W-CDMA technology.

- ✓ **Wideband CDMA (W-CDMA):** This 3G technology replaces TDMA with CDMA in the GSM system.

Radio Frequency Communications

For most of your life, you have probably been using RF communications in one form or another. You probably have a radio in your home or car, and you may own a cell phone. If your TV remote control works from another room or out of sight of the TV or your satellite dish tuner, you are also using radio waves to control that device.

Understanding the Bluetooth technology requires an understanding of radio frequency technology and how radio waves and radio spectrums are used to carry data, voice, and video between devices.

Radio waves

Radio-wave transmissions are electromagnetic waves transmitted from a radio antenna. There are two basic types of radio-wave transmissions:

✓ **Square wave:** This type of radio wave, illustrated in Figure 4-2, is an electrical current that changes from an off power to on power (current flow). For example, repeatedly switching the voltage on a wire from 0v (no power) to 2v creates a square wave that oscillates between 0 and 2 volts. The on and off signals will match the switching of the voltage, but in most cases the rise and fall of the signal wave typically are equal in length and duration.

✓ **Sine wave:** A sine wave, which is the basic form of radio wave, is a continuously varying electrical current. The image of a sine wave, shown in Figure 4-3, is a simple, smoothly transitioning wave that is consistent in its form of alternating peaks and valleys. However, a sine wave can vary in the time or distance, length, and strength of its states.

Figure 4-2: The pattern produced by a square-wave radio signal

Figure 4-3: The pattern produced by a sine-wave radio signal

A square radio wave is representative of binary data being transmitted over a cable or wire. The sine wave is the basis for radio communications and is explained in more detail in the next section.

Sine waves

Only a few basic electrical components are required to produce a sine wave: a capacitor, an inductor, and a few transistors. The capacitor stores the electrical charges, the inductor is an electromagnet that keeps the electrical current flowing at a steady pace, and the transistor amplifies the current that is flowing (the wave) into a signal. Sending a sine wave through a wire creates a simple radio transmitter. The result is the creation of a simple radio station. However, this radio station's radio wave doesn't include any data at this point. All that has been created is a carrier wave.

For the radio wave to contain information, it must be modulated. In other words, the radio wave must be varied or changed. Sine waves are modulated using three different methods: pulse modulation, amplitude modulation, and frequency modulation.

PULSE MODULATION

Pulse modulation is similar to a square wave in that the wave is turned on and off. However, in a pulse modulation sine wave, the signal fluctuates from one signal state to another for specified periods of time. This pattern, shown in Figure 4-4, continues at a pulse-like rate. An early example of a pulse-modulated signal is Morse code.

Figure 4-4: An example of a pulse modulation sine wave

AMPLITUDE MODULATION

In amplitude modulation (AM), a carrier wave is added to the data signal to create a sine wave that matches the rise and fall of the carrier wave. The modulation of the data wave is adjusted to fit the peak-to-peak voltage of the carrier wave. In other words, the intensity, which is called *amplitude*, of the resulting wave varies with the modulating signal. Figure 4-5 illustrates the effect of amplitude modulation.

Figure 4-5: An example of the effect of amplitude modulation on a radio wave

FREQUENCY MODULATION

Frequency modulation is also known as FM, as in FM radio transmissions or signals. Applying *frequency* — that is, the speed or distance of the fluctuations of the signal — alters the resulting sine wave's frequency to match that of the data wave. Figure 4-6 illustrates the effect of frequency modulation. Notice that it is the reverse of amplitude modulation.

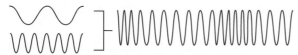

Figure 4-6: An example of the effect of frequency modulation on a radio wave

MODULATING OVER THE PUBLIC AIRWAVES

When you listen to your favorite FM radio station, you frequently hear the announcer identify the station's FM frequency and call letters. The call letters of the station, such as KDMG, identify the station to an assigned frequency in the radio band (*spectrum* — see "Radio Spectrum," later in this chapter) — for example, 102.7. In terms of radio waves, this means the station is broadcasting an FM signal using a radio wave that modulates at 102.7 MHz, or million times per second.

The frequency of the radio wave differentiates it from the signals of other radio stations, all of which use a different frequency to modulate their signals. This is the radio stations' *broadcast spectrum*, which we explain in the next section of this chapter.

An AM (amplitude modulation) radio station modulates its *amplitude*, or signal strength, in line with its assigned spectrum. For example, WHMI, which is at 930 on your AM dial, broadcasts its signal with a modulation of 930 KHz (thousands of cycles per second). Again, this differentiates it from other AM radio stations, which use different modulation frequencies.

Radio Spectrum

Radio receivers can be tuned to receive signals from an individual radio frequency. The capability of a radio receiver determines the range of frequencies it can receive. A particular type of radio receiver can be tuned to receive signals only within a specific range of radio frequencies. Not every radio frequency is available for any purpose. In fact, the frequencies used by radio transmitters and receivers to communicate over the public airwaves are tightly controlled and, in many cases, licensed by government agencies.

Radio frequency assignments

In the United States, the Federal Communications Commission (FCC) determines which frequencies are available for specific purposes and issues licenses to radio, television, fixed wireless, cellular, and other broadcasters for the particular frequencies over which they operate. Table 4-1 lists the common frequency bands assigned to various broadcasters and radio services.

Table 4-1 Common Radio Frequency Allocations

Frequency Band Range	Usage
535 KHz to 1.7 MHz	AM radio
5.9 MHz to 26.1 MHz	Short wave radio
26.96 MHz to 27.41 MHz	Citizens band (CB) radio
40 MHz to 50 MHz	Cordless phones
54 MHz to 88 MHz	TV channels 2 through 6
88 MHz to 108 MHz	FM radio
174 MHz to 220 MHz	TV channels 7 through 13
824 MHz to 849 MHz	Cell phones
900 MHz	Cordless phones
2.45 GHz	ISM communications

Literally thousands of other radio frequency allocations have been made, including frequencies set aside for baby monitors, garage door openers, deep space communications, and more.

The 2.4 GHz spectrum

As indicated in Table 4-1, the 2.45-gigahertz (GHz — billions of modulations per second) range has been set aside under an international agreement for use by industrial, scientific, and medical devices (ISM). The Bluetooth technology uses the ISM frequency range along with numerous common devices, including high-frequency cordless phones, baby monitors, wireless Internet services, and some remote control electronic toys.

A major concern during the development of the Bluetooth specification has been the potential interference caused by these and other devices that share the ISM frequency range. The developers of Bluetooth technology have solved this problem by applying spread-spectrum frequency-hopping.

Spread-Spectrum Frequency-Hopping

Bluetooth devices send signals at a very weak level to avoid interfering with other systems. These signals are sent out at 1 milliwatt (one-thousandth of a watt), compared to 3 watts, which is the strength of the signal transmitted by the more powerful cellular telephones. Because of their weaker signal strength, Bluetooth devices are limited in their receiving range to around 10 meters (approximately 33 feet).

However, Bluetooth's 10-meter transmitting and receiving range is oblivious to walls, doors, or other solid objects, because radio waves are not subject to the problems of line of sight, temperature, or light. The transmissions of a Bluetooth device are very much like the radio signals you receive from your local radio stations. However, Bluetooth signals are transmitted on a different frequency and amplitude.

To further avoid interference from other devices sharing the same frequency range, as well as other Bluetooth devices within the same transmitting and receiving range, Bluetooth uses a technique called spread-spectrum frequency-hopping.

A spread-spectrum frequency-hopping device randomly chooses from among 79 different channels within the frequency range assigned to it in the United States and Europe. In other countries, only 23 channels are available for use. Under the spread-spectrum frequency-hopping technology, the Bluetooth device switches the frequency on which it is sending at regular intervals.

A channel is a specific frequency within a wireless medium, such as RF signals.

Bluetooth devices apply the spread-spectrum frequency-hopping technology on an advanced level, changing frequencies at the rate of 1,600 frequency changes per second. This feature increases the availability of any one frequency and the number of devices that can use the designated frequency spectrum. Other benefits of spread-spectrum frequency-hopping are that it creates more resistance to interference and a better base for security.

Using spread-spectrum frequency-hopping greatly reduces the chance of two Bluetooth devices using the same frequency at the exact instance. The same holds true for other non-Bluetooth devices operating on the same 2.4 GHz frequency range. Spread-spectrum frequency-hopping virtually eliminates the risk of these devices interfering with Bluetooth transmissions. If a non-Bluetooth device signal happens to interfere with a Bluetooth transmission, the interruption would last only a fraction of a second.

Serial Versus Parallel Transmissions

Two communications methods are used to transmit and receive data over a network: serial transmissions and parallel transmissions. Bluetooth technology sends data using a serial transmission. Here is a closer look at the advantage of using serial transmissions over parallel transmissions:

✓ **Serial transmissions** send data in a sequential fashion, meaning that each bit is followed by another bit of data through the communication link to the remote device. Using this mode of transmission requires only one communication link per connection, allowing several more devices to communicate with each other using the same bandwidth. Figure 4-7 compares a serial transmission to a parallel transmission.

✓ **Parallel transmissions** send the data bits of a single character or byte (8 bits) at the same time using separate channels. In other words, parallel transmissions send 8 bits at a time, with each bit transmitted over a separate wire or channel. As a result, parallel transmissions are eight times faster than serial transmissions. However, parallel systems can be more expensive than serial systems, primarily because of the additional wires, connectors, and pins required. In addition, extra channels or wires are used to transmit a clock signal and possibly acknowledgment and control signals. Parallel transmissions require the use of several channel frequencies at the same time, which diminishes the amount of bandwidth available for other Bluetooth devices.

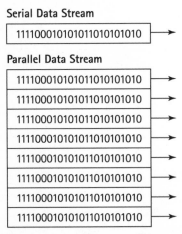

Serial Data Stream

| 111100010101011010101010 |

Parallel Data Stream

| 111100010101011010101010 |
| 111100010101011010101010 |
| 111100010101011010101010 |
| 111100010101011010101010 |
| 111100010101011010101010 |
| 111100010101011010101010 |
| 111100010101011010101010 |
| 111100010101011010101010 |

Figure 4-7: Serial versus parallel transmission modes

Synchronous versus Asynchronous Communications

Network communications can be either synchronous or asynchronous in their transmission timing. Synchronous communications are communications in which the transmissions from both communicating stations are synchronized to a common timing device. A synchronous link is established by a series of synchronizing signals, and then data is transmitted as a continuous stream.

In asynchronous communications, the time interval between message units is not always the same. For example, the interval between packets 1 and 2 is not necessarily the same as the interval between packets 2 and 3. Asynchronous events are not coordinated (synchronized) by a time standard, such as a system clock, and can begin a new event prior to the completion of the current event. Asynchronous transmissions send each character or message unit as a self-contained element that has its own start and stop bits. Async (as it is commonly known) transmission is the method commonly used between a computer and a modem. However, a modem often uses synchronous transmissions when communicating with another modem.

To create a contrast for you between synchronous and asynchronous transmissions, a synchronous transmission looks something like this example:

```
a b c d e f 1 2 3 4 5 6 g h i j k 1 7 8 9
```

An asynchronous transmission may look like this:

```
abc d ef 1234 5 6 gh ijk 1 78 0
```

Bluetooth technology is designed to work with a multitude of products in a multitude of circumstances, each requiring its own method of communication; therefore, Bluetooth works with both synchronous and asynchronous communicating devices. A speakerphone is an example of a device that requires asynchronous communication links. The cordless phone in a typical household uses a synchronous, or two-way, communication link. Transmission of multimedia data is another example in which a synchronous communication link must be used. As you can see, for Bluetooth technology to work with a variety of devices, it had to be designed to work in both synchronous and asynchronous fashion.

Whether the signal is to be sent synchronously or asynchronously, it will require a network layer to manage the transmissions being sent and received. The managing Bluetooth network layer is called the *baseband layer*. The baseband layer is made up of the hardware, which physically processes the data, and the software, which manages and organizes the transmission of the data.

Baseband Communications

Another aspect of the way that Bluetooth devices communicate over radio frequencies is that they are baseband devices. Baseband communications transmit signals without changing their modulation. The drawback to baseband, which is also the communications technique used on most LANs, is that it is limited in range. However, it also does not require the use of complex communication control mechanisms such as those required for broadband communications.

Baseband communications (discussed again in Chapter 5) use the full bandwidth of the channel over which they are transmitted. The ability to transmit multiple simultaneous sets of data is achieved through the use of Time Division Multiplexing, or TDM. TDM slices the available bandwidth into frames. Each frame contains a set number of time slots, and each time slot can carry a set number of bits. The number of frames and time slots the bandwidth is divided into depends on the physical characteristics of the medium. The combination of frames and time slots enables what seems like simultaneous data transmissions over a baseband network. Figure 4-8 illustrates the effect of applying TDM to baseband communications.

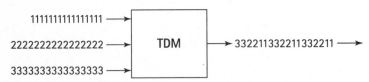

Figure 4-8: Time Division Multiplexing (TDM) interleaves data from multiple transmissions.

When TDM is used with Bluetooth communications, the effect is that a baseband signal is able to support multiple devices sharing the available channels, which maximizes the utilization of the available bandwidth.

Summary

The underlying technology of Bluetooth is radio frequency communications, which is true for most of the competing wireless technologies as well:

- ✓ Bluetooth technology competes with infrared (IR), Home RF, and other wireless cable replacement technologies.

- ✓ Bluetooth is a baseband technology.

- ✓ Bluetooth uses spread-spectrum frequency hopping in the ISM (Industrial, Scientific, and Medical) frequency band at 2.45 GHz.

- ✓ Bluetooth supports both synchronous and asynchronous transmissions.

Chapter 5 looks deeper into baseband communications and the ways Bluetooth uses this transmission mode to send data.

Chapter 5

Baseband Communications

In This Chapter

The baseband is the physical layer of the Bluetooth protocol stack. It is the hardware that converts received radio signals into a digital format so the host application can the process them. The baseband also converts digital and voice data into formats that can be transmitted using a radio signal.

Built on top of the radio in the Bluetooth stack, the baseband essentially acts as a link controller. It works with the link manager to carry out link-level routines for connection and power control.

The baseband manages asynchronous and synchronous links and their respective data packets. It implements paging and inquiry in order to access other Bluetooth-enabled devices. The baseband takes care of converting data, compressing it, putting it into packets, taking it out of packets, and assigning identifiers. Then, it reverses the process for data received. The baseband also handles error correction, designates hop selection, and implements security in the lower layers.

To help you understand the baseband's role in a Bluetooth environment, this chapter covers the following topics:

✓ Reviewing the basics of baseband communications

✓ Understanding Bluetooth baseband operations

✓ Establishing a Bluetooth connection

Contrasting Broadband and Baseband Communications

In the wireless communications world, services are available with either broadband or baseband transmission modes. Bluetooth is a baseband service, but to help you understand the differences between these two types of services, this section offers an overview of broadband services.

Broadband, which comprises a wide band of frequencies, is a communications network in which a frequency range is divided into multiple independent channels for simultaneous transmission of voice, data, or video signals. Most systems that support mobile communications are based on cellular radio architecture, which is a broadband service. In the near future, broadband services will be available over a wide variety of media, including cable television, upgraded telephone services, satellite communications, and terrestrial broadband radio, which is another name for fixed point-to-point radio communications. Because of its capacity, broadband radio meets the needs of a wide range of applications and services, especially Internet services and applications.

The broadband architecture has the following elements:

✓ A mobile network established on a wired infrastructure that uses one or more base stations at strategic locations to provide local cell coverage

✓ Terminals that maintain connections to the network via radio links to base stations

✓ Strict separation between base stations and terminals

✓ Base station control of channel access, allocation, traffic, and interference

✓ Connections that are established or released according to control channel protocols

Unlike this type of system, Bluetooth enables ad hoc communications among Bluetooth units, and a Bluetooth system has no distinctive (fixed or otherwise) base stations and terminals. Bluetooth communications are peer-based, so a Bluetooth network differs from the broadband world in the following ways:

✓ No wired infrastructure

✓ No central controller

✓ No support for coordinating communications among devices

✓ No intervention of operators

Bluetooth instead allows a large number of ad hoc connections to exist in the same area without mutual coordination. It does this by means of the baseband protocol, which is the focus of this chapter. Baseband is the Bluetooth physical layer, which enables peer-to-peer communication among Bluetooth devices.

Bluetooth Baseband

The Bluetooth stack has several layers, as shown in Figure 5-1. These layers include a data-link layer (Link Manager), an adaptation layer (L2CAP), and a physical layer — the baseband. The components of this layer consist of physical characteristics such as channels and link types, data packets, channel control, error control, and flow control as determined by SIG specifications.

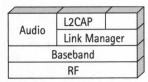

Figure 5-1: The protocol layers of the Bluetooth stack

Baseband interacts with the link manager for link-level routines such as connection and power control. Baseband also manages asynchronous and synchronous links, transmits packets, and performs paging and inquiry routines to establish a connection with or discover other Bluetooth units.

Physical characteristics

The Bluetooth technology provides for a point-to-point connection between two units and a point-to-multipoint connection that multiple units share. Two or more units sharing a connection channel form what is known as a *piconet*.

A piconet has a single master unit and one or more slave units. Source and destination transmissions characterize the relationship among units. That is, the unit sending data (initiating connection) is known as the *source*, or *master*, unit. The unit receiving the transmission is known as the *destination*, or *slave*, unit.

Although each slave can have only one master in any given piconet, units can participate in other piconets simultaneously, and a slave in one piconet can be a master in another. Multiple piconets overlapping in their coverage area are known as a *scatternet*.

In order to establish a piconet or a scatternet, a physical channel must be set up to enable communication among Bluetooth units.

PHYSICAL CHANNEL

A channel enables units to exchange communication packets in either a point-to-point link or a point-to-multipoint link. The channel consists of a pseudo-random hopping sequence that is unique for each piconet. This hopping sequence is determined by the master unit's internal clock.

Bluetooth devices exchange information in packets, as we explain in the section "Packets," later in this chapter.

The channel is divided into time slots, and each slot corresponds to an RF hop frequency. All Bluetooth units participating in a piconet are time- and hop-synchronized to this channel.

Time slots are the means by which Bluetooth units transmit information packets in a piconet. A single time slot in the Bluetooth system lasts 625(s. (Think of a time slot as the time needed to transmit one packet between Bluetooth units.) The slots are numbered according to the master unit's clock.

Bluetooth technology uses a time-division duplex (TDD) scheme in which master and slave alternately transmit, with the master using the even-numbered slots and the slave using the odd-numbered slots. The hop frequency, based on the master unit's clock, remains the same for the duration of the packet transmission.

PHYSICAL LINKS

Sending transmissions between units in a piconet requires establishing a link between them. Bluetooth uses two types of links for this purpose:

✓ Synchronous Connection-Oriented (SCO)

✓ Asynchronous Connection-Less (ACL)

The SCO link is a point-to-point link between a master and a single slave. The ACL link is a point-to-multipoint link between the master unit and all slave units in a piconet.

SCO LINK   This point-to-point link between a master and a single slave typically supports time-bound information such as voice data. It's a synchronous, or circuit-switched, connection. The master supports up to three SCO links to the same slave or to different slaves, while a slave can support up to three links from the same master or two if from different masters. SCO links are never retransmitted. This type of link is used primarily to send SCO packets.

For more information about SCO and other Bluetooth packets, see the section "Packets," later in this chapter.

Using the link manager (LM) protocol, the master establishes a link by sending an SCO setup message to the slave. The master sends SCO packets at regular intervals in the reserved master-to-slave time slots. Each packet contains information that enables the slave to initialize its clock to the master clock. The slave responds with an SCO packet in the slave-to-master slot. Even if a slave doesn't read its address in the packet header, it can still return an SCO packet in the reserved slot.

ACL LINK   An ACL link is a point-to-multipoint, asynchronous, packet-switched link between the master and slave device connected on a Bluetooth piconet, but only a single ACL link can exist between a master and a slave. ACL packets are sent over any link not reserved as an SCO link. One difference between SCO and ACL links is that most ACL packets are retransmitted to ensure data integrity. An ACL link supports both asynchronous and isochronous services.

A slave can return a packet in a slave-to-master slot only if it has been addressed in the preceding master-to-slave slot. If the slave doesn't decode its address in the packet header, it's not allowed to send a packet. Also, packets not addressed to specific slaves are read by every slave as broadcast packets. Transmission doesn't take place on an ACL link if there's neither data to transmit nor polling required.

LOGICAL CHANNELS

Bluetooth uses five logical channels on which to transmit different types of information:

✓ **Link Control (LC):** This channel carries low-level link control information, such as ARQ (automatic repeat request), flow control, and payload information. Link control is carried in the header of every packet except ID, which has no header. All other channel links are identified in the packet payload.

✓ **Link Manager (LM):** This channel carries control information that is exchanged between the link managers of masters and slaves. It's typically used for protected DM packet types and can be carried on either an SCO or ACL link.

✓ **User Channel (UA):** This channel carries L2CAP transparent asynchronous user data. Typically, it's carried in the ACL link.

✓ **User Channel (UI):** This channel carries L2CAP transparent isochronous user data. Typically, it's carried in the ACL link. It's supported by timing start packets at higher levels.

✓ **User Channel (US):** This channel carries transparent synchronous user data. It's carried in the SCO link only.

See Chapter 9 for more information on the networking concepts we describe throughout this chapter. You also can find many of these terms in this book's "Bluetooth Terminology" appendix.

Packets

Data on piconet channels is sent in packets. Each packet can contain the following:

✓ Access code

✓ Header

✓ Payload

Figure 5-2 shows the contents of the Bluetooth piconet packet.

Figure 5-2: The standard format of the Bluetooth piconet packet

The Bluetooth packet may come in one of three variations:

✓ Access code only

✓ Access code and header

✓ Access code, header, and payload

ACCESS CODE

Each packet starts with an access code, which is used for synchronization, clock offset compensation, and identification. The access code is 72 bits in length and is used for identifying the packet, for device paging, and for inquiries.

The access code portion of the Bluetooth packet has three fields:

- ✓ **Preamble:** This 4-bit field is a fixed binary (zeroes and ones) pattern that is used to facilitate *DC compensation*, which attempts to offset the voltage levels produced by a radio amplifier.

- ✓ **Sync word:** This 64-bit code is used for timing synchronization.

- ✓ **Trailer:** A 4-bit fixed binary bit pattern also may be used for DC compensation.

All packets sent in the same piconet are preceded by the same access code.

HEADER

The packet header, which is 54 bits in length, is divided into six fields:

- ✓ **Active member address (AM_ADDR):** The master unit assigns a temporary active address to each slave that joins the piconet. This temporary active address distinguishes the slave from others on the piconet. When a slave disconnects or parks, it gives up this temporary active address. When it rejoins the piconet, it's assigned another temporary active member address.

- ✓ **Type code (TYPE):** Bluetooth devices can transmit 16 different types of packets, as specified by a packet's TYPE code. This doesn't mean there are 16 different packet formats, only that the contents of the packet can create 16 different packet types. How the TYPE code is interpreted depends on the physical link on which the packet is sent. After it's determined to be either ACL or SCO, it can further be broken down to which type of ACL or SCO packet it is. TYPE also indicates how many slots the current packet occupies, so slaves that are not addressed can stop listening to the channel for the remaining slots.

- ✓ **Flow control (FLOW):** This field is used for flow control of packets on the ACL link. For example, when the buffer for the ACL in the slave is full, a STOP indication is returned to stop the flow of data. When the buffer is empty, a GO indication is returned, indicating that data can be transmitted.

- ✓ **Acknowledge indication (ARQN):** This field is used to inform the master unit about a transmission of payload data. It can be a positive acknowledgement (ACK) or a negative one (NAK). NAK is the default return. If no response is returned, NAK is assumed.

- ✓ **Sequence number (SEQN):** The sequence number helps filter out retransmissions at the destination by providing sequential numbering to order the data stream.

- ✓ **Header error check (HEC):** The header error check provides a means of checking the integrity of the header in a data packet.

See "Packet types," later in this chapter, for more information on Bluetooth packet types.

PAYLOADS

The payload portion of a Bluetooth packet carries the voice or data being transmitted. Depending on whether the packet is carrying voice or data, the format of the payload varies. The payload also varies in length, from 0 bits in an inquiry or error message to 2,745 bits in a data packet. The format of the payload changes with the type of link over which it is sent. Synchronous (SCO) packets do not include a payload header (with one exception), and asynchronous (ACL) packets do.

A voice (SCO) payload has the following characteristics:

✓ HV (High-quality Voice) packets range in size from 80 to 240 bits, depending on the type of FEC applied.

✓ DV (Data Voice) packets have a fixed length of 80 bits

✓ HV packets have no payload header; DV packets have an 8-bit header

See "Error Control," later in this chapter, for more information on FEC. See Table 5-3 for the formats of SCO packets.

A data (ACL) payload has the following characteristics:

✓ A 1- or 2-byte (8 or 16 bits) payload header, depending on whether the payload is in a Data Medium-rate (DM), Data High-rate (DH), or auxiliary (AUX) packet type.

✓ A data field that varies from 0 to 339 bytes, depending on the packet type. (For more information on packet types, see Tables 5-3 and 5-4, later in this chapter.)

✓ A cyclic redundancy check (CRC) code, except in the auxiliary (AUX) packet type.

Table 5-1 summarizes the data segments of the payload.

Table 5-1 Payload Data Segments

Data Segment	Size in Bits	Description
Header	8 (single slot)	Only contained in data fields
	16 (multi-slot)	Indicates logical channel
		Controls flow on channel
		Has payload length indicator
		(Continued)

Table 5-1 Payload Data Segments (Continued)

Data Segment	Size in Bits	Description
Body	0–2,745 (length indicated in header)	Includes user host information
		Determines effective user transmission
		Body length indicated in header
CRC	16	Used to verify delivery address
		Determines whether retransmission is necessary

PACKET TYPES

When a packet is transmitted on a piconet, its format is specific to the physical link on which it is transmitted. The two physical links pertinent to this discussion are the SCO link and the ACL link. There are 15 different packet types for each of these links. Table 5-2 describes the types common to both ACL and SCO links. Table 5-3 describes SCO packet types, and Table 5-4 describes ACL packets.

Table 5-2 Link Control Packets Common to ACL and SCO Links

Packet Type	Description
ID	Stands for *identity packet.*
	Consists of the device access code (DAC) or inquiry access code (IAC).
	Fixed length = 68 bits. Robust packet.
	Receiver uses a bit correlator to match the received packet to the known bit sequence of the ID packet.
	Used in paging, inquiry, and response routines.
POLL	Upon receipt, slave responds with a packet even if it has no information to send.

Packet Type	Description
	Return is acknowledgment of the POLL packet.
	Can be used by the master in a piconet to poll the slaves.
FHS	Control packet indicating the Bluetooth device address and clock of sender.
	Used for frequency-hop synchronization.
NULL	Has no payload; consists of channel access code and header.
	Used to return link information to master, indicating success of previous transmission (ARQN) or the status of buffer (FLOW).

SCO packets defined are typically used for speech transmission and are routed to the synchronous I/O (voice) port. Table 5-3 lists the SCO packet types.

Table 5-3 SCO Packet Types

Packet Type	Description
High-quality Voice 1 (HV1)	Used for transmission of voice and transparent synchronous data.
	Packet is never retransmitted.
HV2	Carries 2.5 ms of speech at a 64 Kbps rate.
	Has to be sent every four time slots.
HV3	Carries 3.75 ms of speech at a 64 Kbps rate.
	Has to be sent every six time slots.
Data-Voice (DV)	A combined data-voice packet.
	Voice and data fields are treated separately.
	Voice is normal SCO packet and never retransmitted.
	Data is checked for errors and retransmitted if necessary.

ACL packets can carry user data or control data. Table 5-4 details the formats of ACL packets.

Table 5-4 ACL Packet Formats

Packet Type	Description
DM1	Stands for *data-medium* rate.
	Carries information data only.
	2/3 FEC encoded.
	Carries 0 to 18 bytes of data information bytes and covers a single time slot.
	Supports control messages in any link type.
	Contains 16-bit cyclic redundancy check (CRC) code, so retransmitted if necessary.
DH1	Stands for *data-high* rate.
	Similar to DM1 except payload information not FEC encoded.
	Carries 0 to 28 bytes of data and covers a single time slot.
	Contains CRC code, so retransmitted if necessary.
DM3	Stands for *data-medium* rate.
	Carries information data only.
	2/3 FEC encoded.
	Carries 0 to 123 bytes of data and covers up to three time slots.
	Contains CRC code, so retransmitted if necessary.
DH3	Stands for *data-high* rate.
	Similar to DM3 except payload information not FEC encoded.
	Carries 0 to 185 bytes of data and covers up to three time slots.
	Contains CRC code, so retransmitted if necessary.
DM5	Stands for *data-medium* rate.
	Carries data information only.

Packet Type	Description
	Carries 0 to 226 bytes of data and covers up to five time slots.
	Contains CRC code, so retransmitted if necessary.
DH5	Stands for *data-high* rate.
	Similar to DM5 except payload information not FEC encoded.
	Carries 0 to 339 bytes of data and covers up to five time slots.
	Contains CRC code, so retransmitted if necessary.
AUX1	Carries data information only.
	Similar to a DH1 packet, but contains no CRC code.
	Carries 0 to 30 bytes of data.
	Not retransmitted.

Channel control

The master unit determines the characteristics of the channel on which members of a piconet communicate. In other words, the master unit's Bluetooth device address, system clock, and polling scheme provide the means for maintaining control as transmissions are sent and received by all units that make up the piconet.

The master unit's Bluetooth device address determines the frequency-hopping sequence and the channel access code (CAC) for the channel. The system clock determines the phase in the hopping sequence and sets the timing. And traffic is controlled on the channel by the use of a polling scheme.

Device addresses

Four types of addresses can be assigned to Bluetooth units:

✓ Bluetooth device address (BD_ADDR): Unique 48-bit address given to each Bluetooth transceiver.

✓ Active member address (AM_ADDR): Temporary address assigned to an active member on a channel.

✓ **Parked member address (PM_ADDR):** Distinguishes parked slaves. Valid only as long as a slave is parked.

✓ **Access request address (AR_ADDR):** Determines slave-to-master half-slot the slave should use to send access request messages. Because some procedures and applications produce two packets per baseband time slot, Bluetooth divides the time slot into two halves and uses the AR_ADDR to indicate which half-slot an access request is to use. The AR_ADDR is valid only as long as the slave is parked, and this address is not necessarily unique.

Park and *unpark* are concepts used in Bluetooth to indicate a device's status on a piconet. Park is very similar to sniff, although the rules for waking up are a bit different. A parked device gives up its device ID and sleeps. Periodically, the parked device wakes up and looks for unpark messages that re-establish the device on the piconet.

See Chapter 6 for more information on the Bluetooth operating states.

Bluetooth clocks

Every Bluetooth unit has an internal system clock (called the CLKN) that determines the timing and hopping of its transceiver. This clock ticks every 312.5μs, which yields a clock rate of 3.2 kHz. Slave devices on a Bluetooth piconet synchronize to the master device's clock by adding an offset to their own clocks. The clock is vital to a device's transceiver because it determines critical periods and triggers events in the Bluetooth receiver.

The Bluetooth clock has no relation to time of day; therefore, it can be initialized at any value.

As already noted, in a piconet, the master unit's internal clock determines timing and frequency-hopping. After a piconet is established, the master clock is communicated to the slaves, and the slaves add offsets to their native clocks to synchronize with the master, which gives an estimated clock value. These offsets are then updated on a regular basis via data packets.

The exact value of the offset is calculated from the difference between the master device's clock and the slave device's clock and represents the number of clock cycles needed to adjust the slave's clock to the master's — for example, 10μs, 20μs, and so on.

The clock has different appearances, depending on a unit's state or mode. These differences are denoted as follows:

✓ **CLKN:** The free-running native clock of the current Bluetooth device that is referenced by all other clocks.

✓ **CLKE:** The slave's estimate of the recipient's CLKN.

✓ **CLK:** The master clock that defines the timing and scheduling of activities on a piconet.

A Bluetooth device derives its CLKE and CLK from the CLKN by adding an offset. To remain synchronized with the master's CLK, a slave device must regularly update its offset. The offset for the master clock is zero, because CLK and CLKN are the same.

States and substates

To provide more channel control, Bluetooth also implements various states and substates for use with the units on a piconet. Bluetooth implements two main states — Standby and Connection — and seven substates: page, page scan, master response, slave response, inquiry, inquiry scan, and inquiry response.

The default state is standby. This state uses low power, and a unit in this state does not interact with any other device. In the connection state, as the name implies, a connection is established between units. In the connection state, master and slave can exchange packets. The substates provide further flexibility in maintaining a piconet.

Chapter 6 describes these states and substates in detail.

Error control

Bluetooth technology provides three means of error correction:

✓ ARQ (for data)

✓ 1/3 rate Forward Error Correction (FEC)

✓ 2/3 rate FEC

In the 1/3 rate, every bit is repeated three times for redundancy. For the 2/3 rate, a generator polynomial encodes 10- to 15-bit code, which is a shortened Hamming code. FEC reduces the number of retransmissions sent on a channel. However, it can create unnecessary overhead in an environment that is reasonably error-free, and thus reduce throughput. Therefore, Bluetooth does not require the use of FEC in the payload. The 1/3 FEC is always used in the packet header, because it contains link information and must be able to sustain more errors.

A Hamming code is an error-detecting and correcting binary code that can detect 1- and 2-bit errors and correct single-bit errors. Hamming codes insert check bits after a certain number of data bits, depending on the FEC rate in use. The receiving device uses the check bits to detect and correct 1-bit errors.

ARQ SCHEME

The Automatic Repeat Request (ARQ) scheme is for data only. It retransmits DM, DH, and the data field of DV packets (on SCO links) until acknowledgment is received or until the transmission times out. ARQN values are set to enable fast, unnumbered positive or negative acknowledgment of transmissions. If the transmission times out, the packet is flushed and the next packet is sent.

Table 5-5 details the two types of ARQ schemes.

Table 5-5 ARQ Schemes

Type	Description
ARQ	Transmits and retransmits packets until acknowledgment is received.
	This information is in the return packet header.
	CRC code added to packet. Determines whether payload is correct.
	Packet header and voice data not protected by ARC scheme.
Unnumbered ARQ	Provides fast packet acknowledgment.
	One of these acknowledgments is returned: ACK (ARQN=1) or NAK (ARQN=0).
	NAK returned if no access code detected, HEC or CRC fails.

The ARQ scheme is never used for broadcast packets, because these packets are never acknowledged. Broadcast packets are checked only for CRC.

RETRANSMISSIONS

A data payload is retransmitted until a positive ACK is received or timeout is exceeded. Retransmissions occur either because the packet or response transmission failed. To be successful, an incoming packet must pass the HEC and CRC check (if CRC is included).

FLUSHING PAYLOADS

Because of retransmission time, the ARQ scheme can cause delays. For certain links, however, only limited delay is allowed. When the limit is reached, the current packet is flushed (which could result in some data being lost), and the Bluetooth controller sends the next packet instead.

Broadcast packets

A broadcast packet is one that is transmitted by the master of the piconet to all slaves at the same time. These packets aren't acknowledged, so they are repeated for a set number of times. If a broadcast message is time-critical, it may override a retransmission. An example of this type of message is one sent to unpark a slave.

For more information about parking and unparking, see Chapter 6.

ERROR CHECK

The controller uses the channel access code, HEC, and CRC to check for errors. When a packet is received, the access code is checked first to determine whether the packet has been delivered to the correct address. HEC and CRC are further checks for correct delivery. CRC also checks for correct payload, and HEC checks for header errors.

FLOW CONTROL

To facilitate the flow of traffic on the ACL and SCO links, the Bluetooth technology implements transmission and reception routines specific to these links. The transmission routines are referred to as TX, and the receptions as RX.

TX routines are carried out separately for SCO and ACL links. Buffers are used for both links on which information is read and loaded. Each TX buffer consists of two first-in, first-out (FIFO) registers:

- ✓ **Current:** The register on which the link controller reads packets that are composed and sent.

- ✓ **Next:** The register on which the link manager loads new information.

All ACL packets use the ACL buffer, while all SCO packets use the SCO buffer, except for the DV packet. For the DV packet, voice is handled by SCO and data by ACL. A separate TX ACL buffer is used in the master for each slave, but one or more TX SCO buffers can exist for each SCO slave.

In ACL traffic, as long as the link manager loads new information, the link controller automatically transmits the payload, and retransmissions are sent if errors occur. For SCO traffic, if control information with high priority is sent between a master and a slave, SCO information is discarded, and the control information is used instead.

The default packet type on an ACL link is NULL for master and slave. Because the SCO packet type is negotiated at the LM level when the link is established, whatever is agreed upon at that time is the default for SCO links.

When receiving transmissions, an RX routine is implemented. The RX routine is carried out separately for ACL and SCO links. In an ACL link, all slaves share a single RX buffer. For SCO links, the manner in which the links are distinguished determines whether extra buffers are required.

The link manager fills the queues, and the link controller empties them automatically using a FIFO (first-in, first-out) process. When the queues are full, flow control prevents packets from being dropped, and a stop indication is transmitted to the sender to indicate that data cannot be received. When the stop indication is received, the FIFO queues are frozen. (In multi-slave configurations, only transmissions to the slave issuing the stop indicator are stopped.) When the receiver is ready, a go packet is sent, resuming the transmission flow.

Establishing a Bluetooth Baseband Connection

Before the connection state can occur, Bluetooth units need a means of finding other Bluetooth units. The Bluetooth technology provides an Inquiry procedure for this purpose. An Inquiry procedure enables one unit to discover other devices that are in range and available for connection. The Inquiry procedure also enables the inquiring unit to discover the Bluetooth addresses and clocks of the discovered devices. A Bluetooth address is needed to establish a connection. Knowledge of the clock accelerates the connection procedure.

After the inquiry procedure has discovered other devices, a Page procedure is implemented to establish the actual connection between units. The unit that initiates the connection and carries out the Page procedure automatically becomes master of the connection.

The connection state begins with a POLL packet sent by the master unit. This packet is used to verify that the slave has switched to the master's timing (CLK) and frequency-hopping. When the slave sends a response to this POLL packet (and it can be any kind of packet transmission), the connection is established and a piconet is formed.

Three things are necessary to transmit on a piconet:

✓ Channel-hopping sequence

✓ Phase of the sequence

✓ Channel Access Code (CAC) to place on packets

For the channel-hopping sequence, the Bluetooth device address of the master is used. The system clock of the master determines the phase in the hopping sequence, and the CAC is derived from the Bluetooth device address of the master.

A piconet can consist of one master unit and up to seven slaves. Each piconet has its own master, and each piconet hops independently with its own channel-hopping frequency and phase, which the master determines. Packets on the channel are also preceded by a CAC. If multiple piconets cover the same area, a Bluetooth unit can participate in two or more of the overlaying piconets. A unit can act as a slave in several piconets, but as a master in only one. A group of piconets in which connections overlap is known as a *scatternet*.

Summary

Bluetooth is a baseband system. In this chapter, we detail the various links, packet types, channels, and mechanisms applied to establish a Bluetooth piconet on a baseband link. Here are the key points from this chapter:

✓ Bluetooth uses baseband communications.

✓ Bluetooth establishes two types of links: SCO and ACL.

✓ Bluetooth uses five types of logical channels. Two link channels, link control (LC) and link manager (LM), and three user channels (UA, UI, and US).

✓ Generally, a Bluetooth packet has three basic elements: an access code, a header, and a payload.

✓ Bluetooth uses 15 packet type variations, depending on the link type, as well as whether the packet is carrying voice or data and whether it is sent using a medium data rate or a high data rate.

✓ FEC and ARQ are used for error detection and correction.

✓ A Bluetooth baseband connection requires three elements: a channel-hopping sequence, a sequence phase, and a channel access code.

Chapter 6 extends the discussion on Bluetooth communications with a look at the various Bluetooth operating states.

Chapter 6

Bluetooth Operating States

In This Chapter

A piconet has a single master unit and one or more slave units. The relationship among units is characterized by source and destination transmissions. That is, the unit sending data (initiating connection) is known as the source, or master, unit. The unit receiving the transmission is known as the destination, or slave, unit. The terms *master* and *slave* refer only to the protocol on a given channel; the Bluetooth units themselves are identical and can become masters or slaves in any piconet, depending on which unit initiates the transmission.

This chapter describes the two major states, seven substates, and four modes used in the Bluetooth link controller for the purpose of controlling the activity of units on a piconet channel. These states, substates, and modes have various functions, including entering low-power modes that enable Bluetooth units to conserve capacity for other tasks, enabling units to scan for incoming pages or inquiries, and enabling units to page for other units or discover Bluetooth units within range.

Manipulating Bluetooth units in a piconet by moving them in and out of the various states and substates provides flexibility and efficiency in the Bluetooth environment. It also provides a means of juggling the number of units in a piconet without putting too much strain on the system.

In this chapter, you explore the following topics regarding Bluetooth operating states:

- ✓ Reviewing the Bluetooth operational states, substates, and modes

- ✓ Understanding states and substates

- ✓ Defining communication requirements

- ✓ Finding and accessing other Bluetooth units

- ✓ Entering the connection state and connection modes

States and Substates

The Bluetooth link controller uses two major states, seven substates, and four modes. Bluetooth units move in and out of these states, substates, and modes through commands from the Bluetooth link manager or from internal signals in the link controller. Figure 6-1 depicts a piconet and its slave units in various states and substates, which we describe in the following sections.

Why a 3-bit Field Can Address Only Seven Devices

In binary numbers, which is the number system used inside electronic devices, each bit represents a power of 2. In fact, *bit* actually stands for binary digit. Reading right to left, each bit in a 3-digit binary number represents 2^0, 2^1, and 2^2, respectively, or the equivalent of 1, 2, and 4 in decimal values.

Regardless of the binary value of the bits, only eight combinations of ones and zeroes can be placed in three positions:

```
000
001
010
011
100
101
110
111
```

If the all-zero combination is set aside, as it is in the Bluetooth AM_ADDR field, then only seven available combinations can be assigned.

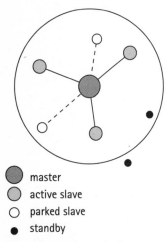

● master
◐ active slave
○ parked slave
● standby

Figure 6-1: A Bluetooth piconet

Major states

The major operating states of the Bluetooth specification control the status or state of the connection of a device to a piconet. The two major states are

✓ **Standby:** This is a Bluetooth unit's default state. The standby state requires low power and is used to free up capacity on a piconet, where only seven devices can be active at any one time. If more than seven devices are on the piconet, a device can be placed into standby state so it does not occupy one of the seven open slots. In the standby state, only the unit's native clock is running, and the unit has no interaction with other units. All units remain in standby until the link controller leaves this state to perform some new operation.

✓ **Connection:** In the connection state, two or more units have established an active connection and can pass data packets back and forth.

By default, unconnected Bluetooth devices are in standby mode, in which they listen for messages — a process called *scanning*. Scanning can be divided into two groups: page substates and inquiry substates. These substate groups are used to add or remove Bluetooth units from a piconet. Page substates enable devices to connect to another unit. Inquiry substates enable a unit to search for other Bluetooth units in range and available.

Paging substates

Bluetooth uses three paging substates to locate and build a connection between a master and a slave:

✓ **Page scan:** In this substate, slave devices scan for their DAC (Device Access Code) every 11.25 ms (the length of the scan window). Slaves scan using only one of the possible 32 frequency hops available. The master unit scans the piconet using a *page train*, which provides a means for the master to include all the 32 frequency hops and locate slave units, each of which is scanning on only one frequency hop.

✓ **Page:** In this substate, the master repeatedly transmits the DAC of the slave, trying to establish a connection between itself and the slave. This process is repeated for each frequency hop in a page train. When a response is received from a slave unit, the master moves to the master response substate.

✓ **Page response:** In this substate, which is really a general substate that includes the master response and the slave response substates, the master and the slave devices exchange the information needed to establish a connection.

In a page train, a different frequency hop is scanned every 1.28 seconds. Page trains are made up of two page train groups. The first page train (Page Train A) includes one-half of the possible frequency hops. If no slaves are identified during Page Train A, then Page Train B is used to continue the scan.

Inquiry substates

Bluetooth devices also may use three inquiry substates. Inquiry substates use essentially the same procedures as the paging substates. The difference is in the information that passes between the devices. The inquiry substates are

✓ **Inquiry scan:** In this substate, the master is looking for potential slaves but doesn't know the DACs needed to create connections.

✓ **Inquiry:** In this substate, the master obtains the DAC needed to establish a connection with a responding slave.

✓ **Inquiry response:** The slave responds with its DAC so the master can enter the page substates to begin establishing a connection.

Connection substates

When a Bluetooth device is in the connection state, it can be in any of the following modes:

✓ **Active:** In active mode, a Bluetooth device is connected and participating on the piconet, and its traffic is scheduled based on its needs. Active devices are assigned an Active Member Address (AM_ADDR). The AM_ADDR is a 3-bit field and can address only seven devices. (The zero address is reserved.)

✓ **Hold:** The hold mode is a reduced-power mode that enables a device to hang onto its AM_ADDR and support SCO packets (voice), but not ACL (data) packets. A device uses hold mode so it can process other tasks, like page and inquiry scans, and remain active on the piconet.

✓ **Sniff:** The sniff mode is another reduced-power mode that enables a device to support both ACL and SCO packets and keep its AM_ADDR. A device uses sniff mode to reduce its power usage or to share time between two piconets.

✓ **Park:** The park mode enables a device to remain synchronized to its channel and listen for broadcast messages, but not actively participate on the piconet. When a device enters park mode, it gives up its AM_ADDR and is assigned a Parked Member Address (PM_ADDR). Because it is an 8-bit address, the PM_ADDR can address up to 255 parked slaves.

How Units Communicate

Each Bluetooth unit has characteristics that make it unique and distinguishable from other units. When Bluetooth units search for other units in range or when they send and receive transmissions, this unique information comes into play. These unique characteristics include

✓ **Bluetooth address:** The Bluetooth address of the master unit determines the access code and hopping frequency of the piconet.

✓ **Internal native clock:** This is the master clock, which sets the phase of the hopping frequency in use on the piconet.

Depending on a unit's state or substate, it may or may not have this information about another device. In order to establish a connection, however, the unit must use inquiry and page procedures to obtain the information.

Bluetooth addresses

Each and every Bluetooth transceiver is assigned a unique 48-bit Bluetooth device address (BD_ADDR) that is divided into three fields:

✓ LAP field: Lower address part, consisting of 24 bits

✓ UAP field: Upper address part, consisting of 8 bits

✓ NAP field: Nonsignificant address part, consisting of 16 bits

The Bluetooth address is used when establishing a connection between units, and the access codes are based on this address.

Access codes

Access codes are used for timing synchronization, clock offset compensation, and paging and inquiry routines. These codes are derived from the LAP (lower address part) of the device address. The three access codes pertinent to this discussion are

✓ Device access code (DAC): Used in page, page scan, and page response substates.

✓ Channel access code (CAC): Used in channel setup as an ID packet and in random access procedures while a device is in park mode.

✓ Inquiry access code (IAC): Used in inquiry operations.

Clocks

The transmissions and signals used by the link controller to move units in and out of states and substates are tied to a unit's internal system clock, which determines timing and hopping of the transceiver. Each Bluetooth unit has such a clock, and it is derived from a native clock that is never adjusted and never turned off.

In a piconet, the master unit's Bluetooth clock determines timing and frequency hopping. After a piconet is established, the master clock is communicated to the slaves, and the slaves add offsets to their native clocks in order to synchronize with the master. These offsets are updated on a regular basis via data packets. However, all units do not have to be active or connected to receive updates and remain on the piconet channel.

Hopping sequences

To send page and inquiry transmissions, the master unit must determine a hop frequency on which to send them, as shown in Figure 6-2. It does this by means of its internal clock.

Bluetooth has ten defined hop frequencies: five for the 79-hop system and five for the 23-hop system. These systems differ only in frequency range and segment length. The main hopping sequence used in Bluetooth systems is the channel-hopping sequence. Other hopping sequences are specific to inquiry and page procedures.

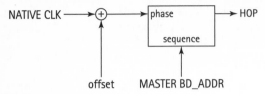

Figure 6-2: Hopping frequency

Table 6-1 shows the defined hop frequencies. (Numbers for the 23-hop system are in parentheses.)

Table 6-1 Hopping Frequencies

Sequence	Definition
Page	32 (16) unique wake-up frequencies distributed equally over 79 (23) MHz with a period length of 32 (16).
Page-response	32 (16) unique response frequencies in a one-to-one correspondence to the current page hopping sequence.
	Different rules for master and slave to obtain the same sequence.
Inquiry	32 (16) wakeup frequencies distributed equally over the 79 (23) MHz.
	Period length of 32 (16).
Inquiry-response	32 (16) unique response frequencies in a one-to-one correspondence with the current inquiry hopping sequence.
Channel-hopping	Has a long period length that doesn't show repetitive patterns over a short time interval.
	Distributes hop frequencies equally over the 79 (23) MHz during a short time interval.

Links

Bluetooth uses two types of links to send transmissions between units in a piconet:

- ✓ Synchronous Connection-Oriented (SCO)
- ✓ Asynchronous Connection-Less (ACL)

The SCO link is a point-to-point link between a master and a single slave. The ACL link is a point-to-multipoint link between the master unit and each slave unit in a piconet. Depending upon the type of packet that is to be transmitted, either an ACL or SCO link is used. ACL packets contain data, while SCO packets are primarily time-bound voice packets. To move units from one state to another, messages can be transmitted on either an ACL or an SCO link. An ACL link must be established before an SCO link can be created.

Accessing Other Units

To look for Bluetooth units in range and then establish connections between them, inquiry and page procedures are performed. The master and slave units are in their respective substates during these procedures, but until they are addressed, all devices remain in standby mode by default. When the master initiates a page procedure, it is in the page substate. When it initiates an inquiry procedure, it is in the inquiry substate.

Slave units move into the correlatives of page and inquiry — that is, page scan and inquiry scan substates — in order to respond to the master transmissions. The inquiry and page procedures exist to establish communication between units — in other words, to create a piconet.

When one unit knows nothing about other units, the following process is implemented to find units in range and establish a connection:

1. First, the inquiry procedure is implemented, enabling a unit to discover devices in range and obtain information about their addresses and clocks. (The range for Bluetooth devices is 10 meters.)

2. After inquiry locates other devices, page procedure actually establishes a connection.

3. Units enter the connection state when the master unit sends a POLL packet to verify that the slave has switched to the master's timing and channel-hopping frequency.

Inquiry procedures

The inquiry procedure is used for applications in which the source device doesn't know the destination device's address and clock. Such devices may include printers, fax machines, or LAN access points. The inquiry procedures serve to discover which other units are in range and, during this discovery period, to obtain the device addresses and clocks of all units that respond to the inquiry message. Then, at a later time, the discovering unit can connect to any of these devices using the page procedure.

INQUIRY

A unit moves into the inquiry substate when it wants to discover other Bluetooth devices in range and available. The inquiring unit continuously transmits a message of inquiry at different hop frequencies, as shown in Figure 6-3. Other units that are in the inquiry response substate can respond to the message.

During the inquiry, the discovering Bluetooth unit gets the device address and clock of each responding unit. The discovering unit can then connect to any of these units by using the page procedure. The inquiry substate continues until the link manager stops it or timeout is reached.

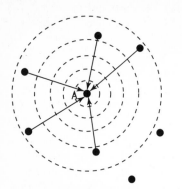

Figure 6-3: A Bluetooth inquiry action

A Bluetooth unit can enter the inquiry substate from either standby or connection state. In standby, a unit can use all its capacity for inquiry, while in connection state, a unit needs to reserve capacity for inquiry (by placing ACL connections in hold or park mode).

RESPONDING TO THE INQUIRY

In the inquiry procedure, no master response is required, only a slave response. The master unit listens between inquiry messages for a response, but even after receiving a response from the slave, the master unit can continue transmitting inquiries.

When the slave receives an inquiry message from the master, it responds by sending an FHS packet containing its address, native clock, and other information. The FHS packet is returned at semi-random times. The slave then returns to standby or connection state for the duration of these random time slots.

An inquiry scan substate is similar to the page scan substate. However, instead of scanning for a DAC, the unit scans for a general or dedicated inquiry access code (IAC). As in page scan, the unit wakes up periodically to scan for these codes. If an inquiry message is recognized, the unit can reenter the inquiry scan substate or the inquiry response substate, depending on what is needed.

A unit can enter inquiry scan substates from either connection or standby state. As with page and page scan, the dedicated capacity of standby enables the unit to easily carry out inquiry scan. In connection mode, capacity can be maximized by placing other units in park or hold mode.

In summary, the inquiry process works as follows:

1. The source unit enters inquiry state and sends out inquiry packets.

2. The destination unit(s) must be in the inquiry scan substate in order to receive the inquiry packets.

3. The destination unit then enters the inquiry response substate in order to send an inquiry reply back to the source unit.

4. When the previous steps are successful, the page procedure is implemented to set up the connection and enable units to enter the connection state.

Page procedures

The procedures used to establish connections between Bluetooth devices are known as *page procedures*. These procedures consist of paging, page scan, and page response (master and slave). The Bluetooth unit that initiates the page transmission automatically is the source, or master, of the connection.

PAGE

The master unit uses the page substate as a means of activating and connecting to a slave unit. To do this, the master unit sends out signals to another unit that wakes periodically and scans for messages. Because the master and slave clocks aren't synchronized at this point, the master doesn't know when the slave unit will wake up or what hop frequency it's on. So the master unit can only send out the slave's device access code (DAC) in an ID packet repeatedly until the slave unit wakes up and responds. (For common packet definitions, see Table 6-2, later in this chapter.)

Precisely how the master implements the page procedure involves several variables. The slave's DAC is known, and this is used to determine the page-hopping sequence, which is how the master will reach the slave. The phase in the sequence, however, is not yet known to the master, nor is the slave unit's native clock. The master unit may estimate the slave's clock based on a previous connection with the unit or from a previous inquiry procedure.

Using this estimate, the master predicts the hop channel on which the slave unit's page scan will start. This prediction, of course, can be incorrect. To compensate for inaccuracy, the master unit sends its page message during a short time interval on numerous wakeup frequencies. The page message is sent until the slave enters the page scan substate and responds, or until the page times out.

A Bluetooth unit can enter the page substate from standby or connection state. In the low-power standby state, no connection has been previously established, so the unit can use all its capacity to perform the page. When entering the page substate from the connection state, a Bluetooth unit needs to free as much of its capacity as possible for transmitting.

RESPONDING TO THE PAGE

When the slave receives a page message, master and slave begin a response procedure to exchange information necessary to continue connection setup. The units must use the same access code and channel-hopping sequence, and their clocks must be synchronized. This information is exchanged in the packets that are sent, and the information is derived from the master unit.

PAGE SCAN The correlative of the master unit's page substate is the slave unit's page scan substate. The master unit pages, while a slave unit uses page scan to listen for master signals. Thus, in the page scan substate, a unit listens for its own device access code during its scan window. The scan window lasts long enough to scan 16 page frequencies. When a unit enters the page scan substate, it selects the scan frequency based on its page-hopping sequence, which, as previously mentioned, the master determines from the slave's DAC. This is a 32-hop sequence in which each hop is unique. As already indicated, the phase in this sequence is determined by the unit's native clock — information the master does not yet have and can only predict.

When the slave unit receives a message that matches its DAC, it enters the slave response substate, which is preliminary to establishing a connection with the master unit.

A unit can enter the page scan substate from either standby or connection state. On standby, a unit can use all its capacity for page scans, whereas in connection state, a unit needs to reserve capacity for scanning (by placing ACL connections in hold or park mode).

SLAVE RESPONSE   When a unit receives its own DAC during page scan, the unit enters the slave response substate and sends a message back to the master unit in response. The slave unit's receiver is then activated and waits for an FHS packet (see Table 6-2, later in this chapter) to be sent by the master unit.

When the slave receives the FHS packet, it returns another response to acknowledge receipt of the FHS packet. The FHS packet includes the Bluetooth device address and clock of the sender. The slave then changes to the master unit's channel access code and clock. At this point, the slave unit enters the connection state.

The actual connection starts with a POLL packet sent by the master. However, if the slave doesn't receive the POLL packet, or the master does not receive the slave response, the units return to page scan and page substate, respectively.

MASTER RESPONSE   After the slave (destination) unit recognizes its DAC sent by the master unit, it enters slave response substate and sends a reply to the master unit. When this occurs, the master unit moves from the page substate to enter the master response substate. After master and slave enter their respective response substates, their clock input to page and page response hop selection is frozen.

After the clock input is frozen, the master sends an FHS packet containing the real-time clock, address, device class, and other information to the slave. When this packet is sent, the master unit waits for another response from the slave. If no response is received, the master retransmits the packet with an updated clock until a response is received or until the response interval times out. If the response interval times out, the master unit moves back into the page substate and can begin the process again.

If a second slave response is received, however, the master unit enters connection state and sends the slave unit a POLL packet. If the slave does not receive the POLL packet or if the slave fails to respond, the units reenter their page and page scan substates, respectively. If the slave unit sends a response to the master unit, a connection between the units is established.

In summary, the page process works as follows:

1. The source unit enters page state and pages another unit (destination unit).

2. The destination unit must be in page scan substate to receive the page.

3. The destination unit enters the slave response substate and sends a reply to the source.

4. The source unit enters the master response substate and sends an FHS packet to the destination.

5. The destination unit, still in slave response substate, sends a second reply to the source.

6. The destination unit remains in slave response substate, and the source unit remains in master response substate in order to switch to the source channel parameters necessary for establishing a connection.

Packet types

Packets that are sent on a piconet are related to the physical links in which they are used. For purposes of this discussion, two physical links have been defined: the SCO link and the ACL link. The SCO link is for transmissions a master unit sends to all slaves on the piconet. The ACL link is for transmissions sent to specific slaves. Table 6-2 identifies the packet types common to both the SCO and ACL links.

Table 6-2 Bluetooth Link Control Packets

Packet Type	Description
ID	Identity packet consists of the device access code (DAC) or inquiry access code (IAC).
	Fixed length = 68 bits.
	Robust packet.
	Receiver uses a bit correlator to match the received packet to the known bit sequence of the ID packet.
	Used in paging, inquiry, and response routines.
POLL	Upon receipt of a POLL packet, the slave responds with a packet even if it does not have information to send.
	Return is implicit acknowledgment of the POLL packet.
	POLL packet can be used by the master in a piconet to poll the slaves.
FHS	Special control packet indicating the Bluetooth device address and clock of the sender.
	Used for frequency-hop synchronization.

Of the packets defined in Table 6-2, the FHS packet is particularly critical to establishing a connection between units. This special control packet provides the Bluetooth device address and the clock of the sender. During connection setup, an FHS packet transmitted from the master to the slave establishes the timing and frequency synchronization between the units.

The FHS packet is transmitted during the master response and inquiry response procedures. While the unit is in the master response substate, the packet is retransmitted until the slave acknowledges its reception or a timeout occurs. The packet contains real-time clock information that is updated before each retransmission. The FHS packet also is used for hop synchronization before a piconet channel has been established or when an existing piconet changes to a new piconet.

Connection State

In the connection state, a connection has been established between Bluetooth devices, and data packets can be sent back and forth between the units. The connection state begins with a POLL packet (see Table 6-2) sent by the master unit to verify that the slave unit has switched to the master timing and channel frequency. When the slave responds, with any type of packet, the connection is established.

The master or the slave can close the connection between Bluetooth units at any time. A detach message is sent from one unit to the other informing the unit of the reason for closing the connection. After detachment, the address and clock information remain valid. Should a link get snapped for any other reason, it can be reestablished through a reset message.

Modes

While in the connection state, Bluetooth units can be in various operational modes, including active mode, sniff mode, hold mode, and park mode. The last three modes are low-power modes. In increasing order of power efficiency, sniff mode has the higher duty cycle; next is hold mode with a lower cycle; and finally, park mode has the lowest duty cycle.

ACTIVE MODE

Typically, a master unit schedules transmissions to and from different slave units and also supports regular transmissions to keep slaves synchronized to the channel. In active mode, a Bluetooth unit actively participates on a piconet channel by listening for packets. However, when not specifically addressed, the active slave can sleep until the next transmission.

SNIFF MODE

When a slave is on an ACL link, it listens in every ACL slot for master transmissions. In sniff mode, however, the number of time slots in which the master unit transmits to a slave is reduced. Thus, the duty cycle of the slave's listening activity can be reduced.

To enter sniff mode, a master or a slave sends a message through the LM protocol indicating a sniff interval and an offset. The offset determines the timing of the sniff mode.

HOLD MODE

If a slave doesn't need to receive ACL packet transmissions for a period of time during the connection state, the master can place the ACL link in hold mode. With a device in hold mode, additional capacity exists on the piconet for scanning, paging, inquiring, or attending another piconet. While in hold mode, a Bluetooth unit can also enter a low-power sleep mode.

Before entering hold mode, a master and slave determine a time length for the slave to remain in this mode. A timer is initialized with a value, and when the timer expires, the slave wakes up, synchronizes with traffic on its channel, and waits for further direction from the master unit.

PARK MODE

In park mode, a slave can remain synchronized to its channel but doesn't need to participate on it. A parked slave wakes at regular intervals to listen to the channel, checking for messages and resynchronizing with the master clock. This low-power mode requires very little activity in the slave unit. A master signal is sent at fixed intervals to support a unit in this mode.

As well as using park mode for low-power consumption, Bluetooth units also use it when more than seven slaves are to be connected to a single master. Although only seven slaves can be active at one time, parking slaves while others are active increases the number of slaves virtually connected to as many as 255. Also, an unlimited number of slaves can be parked in a piconet.

Three addresses come into play when a master unit parks a slave:

✓ Active member address

✓ Access request address

✓ Parked member address

When placed in park mode, a slave is given an access request address and a parked member address and gives up its active member address. Although the parked member address is unique, the access request address is not necessarily unique. When placed in park mode, the slave gives up its active member address.

To unpark the slave, the master sends a transmission using the slave's parked member address as well as a message that includes the active member address the slave will use when it rejoins the piconet. An unpark message can include more than one slave addresses in order to unpark multiple slaves at once.

RETURNING FROM HOLD, SNIFF, AND PARK

As previously indicated, a slave in park or sniff mode wakes up periodically to listen to transmissions from the master unit and resynchronize clock offsets. Unlike these two modes, a unit in hold mode does not send or receive information. Before being placed in hold mode, the master and slave agree to a hold duration during which time the slave doesn't send or receive messages. After the hold duration expires, the slave synchronizes to the traffic on the channel and waits for messages from the master.

Connection breakdown

In order to protect against an unexpected connection breakdown, Bluetooth technology provides a means of monitoring SCO and ACL links between units. A connection may break down, for example, when a device moves out of range, or a power failure may cause connection failure. Because either of these circumstances may happen without any warning, links on both the master and slave side must be monitored to avoid problems.

Both master and slave use timers to detect link loss due to devices moving out of range or similar types of connection failure. A timeout period is negotiated at the link manager (LM) level, and its value is chosen so that the supervision timeout will be longer than hold and sniff periods. In the case of a parked slave, the link can be managed by unparking and reparking the slave. The same timeout value is used for both SCO and ACL connections.

State Transitions

The Link Manager (LM), using link manager protocol (LMP), along with the link and adaptation level protocol (L2CAP), is the means by which Bluetooth moves units in and out of the various states and modes. Figure 6-4 shows where L2CAP and Link Manager reside in the Bluetooth stack.

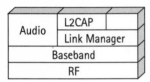

Figure 6-4: The Bluetooth stack

The LM establishes a physical link between units at the baseband level. The L2CAP establishes a channel after the physical link is created. An LM in one Bluetooth unit discovers and communicates with the LM in another Bluetooth device via the LMP, which consists of various protocol data units (PDUs) that are sent between LMs. Using predefined commands, the receiving LM filters out and interprets the PDUs.

Just as link managers communicate with each other using the link manager protocol, so other Bluetooth protocols are implemented in the L2CAP. The L2CAP transmits events and commands between the upper and lower layers of the Bluetooth stack. A connection is established in the lower layers when the LM establishes a physical link. L2CAP establishes the channel for the connections.

The following procedure demonstrates how the LM and L2CAP function as units to transition in and out of hold mode. The procedure is representative of how units move in and out of the various states and modes.

The master or slave in a piconet can force hold mode or request it. The master or slave can force hold mode if a previous request was accepted. The hold time in the PDU sent by the unit forcing hold mode cannot be longer than when the unit initially accepted the hold request.

The following steps are taken when a master unit forces a slave into hold mode:

1. The master LM finalizes the transmission of the current ACL packet with L2CAP information and stops L2CAP transmission.

2. It then selects the hold instant.

3. The master LM queues the LMP_hold to its link controller for transmission.

4. A timer is started.

5. When the timer expires, the connection enters hold mode.

6. When the unit exits hold mode, the L2CAP transmission is enabled.

A similar procedure is used when a master or slave *requests* hold mode. Similar procedures are invoked when moving units in and out of park and sniff modes as well. The master-slave switch is another example of state transitions involving both L2CAP and the LM protocol.

Summary

The Bluetooth specification defines the mechanisms used to establish communications between two Bluetooth devices:

✓ The Bluetooth specification defines three procedures for establishing communication among units: link, channel, and connection establishment.

✓ After a physical link is created, a logical channel is set up between the devices, and a connection is established.

✓ To maximize the efficiency of this communication process while minimizing power consumption, the Bluetooth system incorporates various states, substates, and modes into the operating environment.

✓ Moving units in and out of the various states and substates provides efficiency in the piconet environment, and moving units in and out of the various connection modes offers flexibility in the management of piconets.

Central to communications on Bluetooth devices is the link manager, which we examine in Chapter 7.

Chapter 7

The Bluetooth Link Manager (LM)

In This Chapter

The Bluetooth link manager (LM) is one of the key elements in the Bluetooth protocol stack. As shown in Figure 7-1, the link manager resides between the baseband and L2CAP layers. The link manager has several responsibilities: managing security, setting up and controlling links, communicating with the link managers of other Bluetooth devices to exchange control information and data (through the link controller), and acting as a go-between for upper-layer applications and protocols to negotiate transmission and operating characteristics (such as power consumption and security levels) with other link managers and protocols.

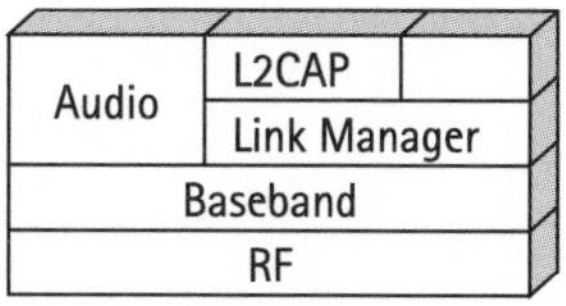

Figure 7-1: The Bluetooth protocol stack

The link manager also facilitates the master-slave switching and mode-switching procedures that force or request a device to change to a different connection mode as well as the parking and unparking of devices on a piconet.

The link manager is important enough that we devote an entire chapter to it. This chapter has the following objectives:

- ✓ Reviewing the operations of the Bluetooth link manager
- ✓ Detailing the functions of the link manager to establish a link with another device

Link Manager Operations

The tasks handled by LM include security management, link configuration, and establishing L2CAP links.

Authentication and encryption management

Authentication and encryption are features used in the Bluetooth technology to provide secure communication between Bluetooth devices. Authentication and encryption require connections to higher layers in the Bluetooth stack, so the L2CAP comes into play in these transmissions. Authentication is the process of verifying who is on the other end of a link, while encryption is intended to ensure security of data.

AUTHENTICATION

The process of authentication involves one unit (verifier) issuing a challenge to another device (claimant). The other device, in turn, responds by sending a PDU (protocol data unit) based on the challenge, the unit's BD_ADDR, and the link key shared between the devices. If the link key returned by the claimant matches the verifier's link key, authentication is successful.

See "Packet data units," later in this chapter, for more information on the PDU types mentioned in this section.

Authentication is application-specific. Some applications require only one-way authentication, while others need mutual authentication. In mutual authentication, each unit is the challenger, and two authentication procedures take place. For example, after unit one successfully authenticates unit two, unit two challenges unit one. The verifier is not necessarily the master of the connection; each application indicates who needs to be authenticated by whom.

If authentication fails, a certain time interval must pass before another attempt can be made. For each subsequent authentication failure, this interval increases exponentially, so that on the second attempt the required interval will be twice as long as the first. Conversely, this interval will decrease exponentially if no new failed attempts occur during a certain time period.

Figure 7-2 provides an overview of the authentication process.

ABOUT KEYS

For authentication to take place, link keys must be generated and given to Bluetooth units. Because they are for security purposes, the keys are secret. This means they can't be exchanged through an inquiry routine in the way that Bluetooth addresses are exchanged. In this case, keys must be exchanged during the initialization process, and this process must occur between two units that want to use authentication and security for their connection.

For more information about inquiries, see Chapter 6.

The process has the following elements:

✓ Generation of the initialization key

✓ Generation of the link key

✓ Link key exchange

✓ Authentication

✓ Generation of the encryption key (optional)

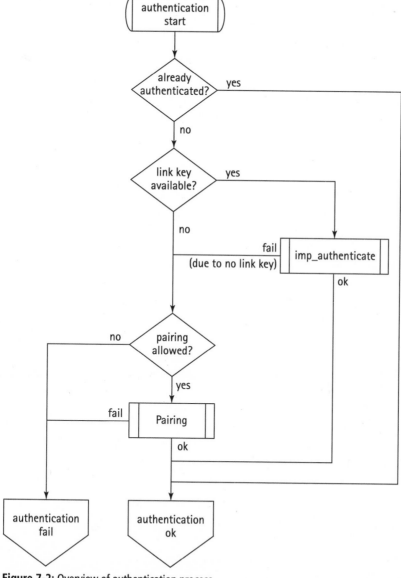

Figure 7-2: Overview of authentication process

After initialization takes place, the units can establish a connection or end the link.

If the units establish a connection after initialization, a link key is generated and then exchanged by the units. The link key can be either temporary or semipermanent, as indicated in Table 7-1.

Table 7-1 Link Key Types

Key Type	Description
Link key	Contains 128-bit random number.
	Shared by two or more units.
	Basis for all security between units.
	Used as parameter for determining encryption key.
	Can be either semipermanent or temporary.
Current link key	Key currently in use.
	Used for all authentication in an ongoing connection.
	Used for generation of encryption keys in ongoing connections.
Semipermanent link key	Stored in nonvolatile memory.
	May be used in subsequent sessions.
	Can be changed.

Four link keys are used in Bluetooth security: initialization key, unit key, master key, and combination key. Which one is used depends on what it is used for and is determined as follows:

- ✓ The initialization key serves as the link key in the initialization process.
- ✓ If one unit sends LMP_unit_key, and the other unit sends LMP_comb_key, the unit key will serve as the link key. (For more information about the PDUs mentioned in this section, see "Packet data units," later in this chapter.)
- ✓ If both units send LMP_unit_key, the master's unit key serves as the link key.
- ✓ If both units send LMP_comb_key, the two units generate random numbers that are combined to serve as the link key.

Table 7-2 describes link keys.

Table 7-2 Link Keys

Key Type	Description
Initialization key	Used during initialization process.
	Protects transfer of initialization parameters.
	Derived from a random number, a PIN code, and BD_ADDR of the claimant unit.
Unit key	Generated at the installation of a Bluetooth unit and rarely changed.
	Used by Bluetooth units with little memory in which to store keys.
Master key	Temporarily replaces original link key.
	Can be used only for current session.
	Used when master wants to transmit to several units at once.
Combination key	Derived from information in both units in a connection.
	Always dependent on these two units.
	Derived for each new combination of Bluetooth units.
	Used for applications requiring higher security.
	Requires more memory.

ENCRYPTION

Bluetooth ensures the security of data sent between units by encrypting the payloads of packets transmitted between the units. Bluetooth enables encryption with a stream cipher that is resynchronized for each payload. The stream cipher consists of the following:

- ✓ A payload key generator
- ✓ A key stream generator
- ✓ Encryption/decryption capability

The payload key generator combines input bits in an appropriate order and shifts them to the four Linear Feedback Shift Registers (LFSR) of the key stream generator. The LFSR width totals 128 bits, which enables effective encryption key length that is selectable between 8 and 128 bits.

Before encryption is activated, the master and slave must agree on whether to use it, they must decide what mode to use, and they must negotiate key size. An encryption mode request message is sent from one unit to the other to determine whether encryption will be used.

If the units agree to use encryption, the next step is for the units to determine encryption key size. The encryption key is derived from the link key and automatically changes every time a Bluetooth device enters encryption mode. Which encryption modes are available depends on whether a device uses a semipermanent link key or a master key. For example, if a unit key or a combination key is used, broadcast traffic over a piconet is not encrypted, while individually addressed messages can be either encrypted or not. If a master key is used, the following three encryption modes are possible:

✓ **Mode 1:** Nothing is encrypted.

✓ **Mode 2:** Broadcast traffic is not encrypted, but the individually addressed traffic is encrypted with the master key.

✓ **Mode 3:** All traffic is encrypted with the master key.

As previously indicated, the encryption key size can vary from 8 bits to 128 bits, so the size of the encryption key used between two devices needs to be negotiated. Each device has a parameter that defines the maximum key length allowed. When the master sends a message suggesting encryption key size to the slave, the slave can accept the suggestion, acknowledge it, or send another suggestion, based on its maximum allowed key length. Negotiation continues until the devices agree on a key length or until one of the units stops the negotiation. If the units cannot agree on an acceptable key size, they cannot use encryption.

After encryption has been activated, it can be stopped when desired. Messages are sent by the master to the slave requesting to stop it. When the slave accepts the master's request, encryption stops. If the encryption key or mode needs to be changed, the units first have to stop encryption and then restart with the new parameters.

LOGICAL LINK CREATION

While link managers communicate with each other using the link manager protocol, other Bluetooth protocols are implemented in the logical link control and adaptation protocol (L2CAP) layer. L2CAP provides the interface to the link controller and allows for interoperability between Bluetooth devices.

The L2CAP protocol transmits events and commands to or receives them from upper and lower layers of the Bluetooth stack. It provides management by mapping upper protocol groups to Bluetooth piconets, it provides segmentation and reassembly of packets between layers, and it negotiates and monitors quality of service (QoS) between devices.

To enable this functionality, the Bluetooth baseband provides an ACL link over which the L2CAP link layer can operate. Then, using LMP, the LM sets up a single ACL link that is always available between a master and an active slave. This provides a point-to-multipoint link, supporting both asynchronous and isochronous data transfer.

After a link-level connection has been created, an L2CAP channel can be established. L2CAP then provides services to upper-level protocols by transmitting data packets over the L2CAP channels. The three types of L2CAP channels are

✓ Bidirectional signaling channels that carry commands

✓ Connection-oriented channels for bidirectional, point-to-point connections

✓ Unidirectional, connectionless channels that support point-to-multipoint connections (enabling connection to a group of remote devices)

Data is transmitted in packets across the L2CAP channels. A connection-oriented channel uses packets with a header, payload, and a destination channel identifier (CID). The payload contains information that is received from or being sent to the upper-level protocol. Connectionless channel packets include a header, followed by a 16-bit protocol/service multiplexer (PSM). The PSM is used to indicate the upper-level protocol from which the packet originated and to enable packet reassembly on a remote device. The PSM field is not required for connection-oriented channels because they're bound to a specific protocol when a connection is established.

Similar to data packets, signaling packets include a header indicating payload length and the remote CID. Signaling packets contain commands that include requests and responses related to connecting, configuring, and disconnecting channels. In addition, a Command Reject command is used to respond to an invalid or unrecognized command.

The L2CAP enables segmentation and reassembly of packets between upper-level and lower-level protocols. This capability is necessary because packets from the upper-level protocols cannot exceed a maximum transmission unit (MTU) negotiated during configuration. These upper-level packets are segmented into protocol data units (PDUs) that are small enough for the lower-level protocol. All PDUs for a packet must be sent over the baseband before another packet can be sent to the same remote device.

The LMP also uses underlying baseband services to send packets. LMP packets, which are sent in the ACL payload, are distinguished from L2CAP packets by a bit in the ACL header. The LMP packets are single-slot and higher priority than L2CAP packets. This helps maintain link integrity during high traffic periods.

Connection management

The procedure for establishing a connection between two Bluetooth units involves the following steps:

1. First, one unit must find the remote device with which it wants to connect. This is done through Inquiry.

2. After a remote device is located, the initiating device moves into page mode and begins the page procedure.

3. The master unit then polls the slave with a maximum poll interval.

4. The LMP procedures for clock offset request, LMP version, supported features, name request, and detach can be performed.

5. A connection request can be transmitted, and either accepted or rejected by the slave. If accepted, a connection is established.

6. After the connection request is transmitted, the following actions can be taken:

- Procedures that involve connecting to layers above LM (such as pairing, authentication, or encryption) are performed.

- Master-slave switch can occur. After the switch is completed, the old slave replies with accepted or rejected to the connection request.

7. Finally, the setup complete message can be sent. When both devices have sent the setup complete message, the first data packet can be transmitted on a channel other than LMP.

Integration with hardware

The components of the Bluetooth technology consist of hardware and software elements. They stack up and work together as described in the following sections.

BASEBAND

The baseband is the hardware that turns radio signals into digital form so the host application can process them. The baseband also converts digital or voice data into a form that can be transmitted by radio signal to other Bluetooth units.

The baseband processor then transmits data packets over a channel. Each data packet contains information about the packet's origin, its frequency, and its destination. Data packets also can contain information about how the data was compressed, the order of packet transmission, and information verifying the effectiveness of the transmission. When data is received, the baseband checks it for accuracy, extracts it from the packet, reassembles it, decompresses it, and filters it if necessary. This baseband function is called the link controller.

ACL AND SCO LINKS

Bluetooth uses two standard links to transmit data. The SCO and ACL links each support 16 different packet types. Any two devices may use either link type and can change link types during a transmission, if desired.

LINK MANAGER

Link manager is the software that runs on a microprocessor and manages communication between devices. Each Bluetooth device has its own link manager, which handles various tasks, such as discovering other link managers, setting up links, negotiating features, authenticating QoS, and encrypting data on a link.

LINK CONTROLLER

The link controller is a supervisory function used to handle all baseband functions and support the link manager. Its tasks include sending and receiving data, identifying remote devices, performing authentication, and moving devices into power-saving modes.

L2CAP

This software is used for protocol multiplexing above the basic layers. It handles packet segmentation and reassembly and conveys QoS information. It too relies on the baseband to transmit packets on ACL or SCO links via logical channels.

Linking into the Network

An LM in one Bluetooth unit discovers and communicates with the LM in another Bluetooth device via the link manager protocol (LMP), as shown in Figure 7-3. The LMP consists of various protocol data units (PDUs) that are sent between LMs.

Figure 7-3: The Bluetooth link manager
protocol

Using predefined commands, the receiving LM filters out and interprets the PDUs. LMP enables LMs to set up, terminate, and manage baseband connections between units.

LMP functionality

Because LMP enables LMs to communicate, understanding LMP functionality is important. Using LMP, an LM handles the following tasks:

✓ **Piconet management**, enabling units to

■ Attach and detach slaves

■ Switch between master and slave status

■ Establish ACL and SCO links

■ Handle low-power mode

✓ **Link configuration**, enabling units to

■ Determine supported features

■ Implement Quality of Service (QoS), usable packet types

■ Enable power control

✓ **Security management**, enabling units to establish

■ Pairing

■ Authentication

■ Encryption

Packet data units

An LM transmits PDUs to other LMs by using the LMP. These PDUs are specific to the required task. A PDU is either mandatory (M) or optional (O). *Optional* indicates that the PDU relates to the services supported by a Bluetooth unit. The LM doesn't need to be able to transmit a PDU that is optional; however, it does need to recognize optional PDUs and be able to send valid responses, such as *this is an unsupported LMP feature*. If an optional PDU doesn't require a response, the recipient doesn't send one. If desired, a device can request to know which optional PDUs another device supports.

Table 7-3 lists the mandatory and optional PDUs of the LM.

Table 7-3 Mandatory and Optional LM PDUs

Use	Support	Type
General response	Mandatory	LMP_accepted
		LMP_not_accepted
Authentication	Mandatory	LMP_au_rand
		LMP_sres
Pairing	Mandatory	LMP_in_rand
		LMP_au_rand
		LMP_sres
		LMP_comb_key
		LMP_unit_key
Change link key	Mandatory	LMP_comb_key
Change current link key	Mandatory	LMP_temp_rand
		LMP_temp_key
		LMP_use_semi_permanent_key
Clock offset request	Mandatory	LMP_clkoffset_req
		LMP_clkoffset_res
Slot offset request	Optional	LMP_slot_offset
Timing accuracy information request	Optional	LMP_timing_accuracy_req
		LMP_timing_accuracy_res
LMP version	Mandatory	LMP_version_req
		LMP_version_res
Supported features	Mandatory	LMP_features_req
		LMP_features_res

Use	Support	Type
Name request	Mandatory	LMP_name_req
		LMP_name_res
Detach	Mandatory	LMP_detach
Master-slave switch	Optional	LMP_switch_req
		LMP_slot_offset
Hold mode	Optional	LMP_hold
		LMP_hold_req
Sniff mode	Optional	LMP_sniff_req
		LMP_unsniff_req
Park mode	Optional	LMP_park_req
		LMP_unpark_PM_ADDR_req
		LMP_unpark_BD_ADDR_req
		LMP_set_broadcast_scan window
		LMP_modify_beacon
Power control	Optional	LMP_incr_power_req
		LMP_decr_power_req
		LMP_max_power
		LMP_min_power
Channel quality-driven change (between DM and DH packets)	Optional	LMP_auto_rate
		LMP_preferred_rate
Quality of Service (QoS)	Mandatory	LMP_quality_of_service
		LMP_quality_of_service_req
SCO links	Optional	LMP_SCO_link_req
		LMP_remove_SCO_link_req
Control of multislot packets	Mandatory	LMP_max_slot
		LMP_max_slot_req

Continued

Table 7-3 Mandatory and Optional LM PDUs (Continued)

Use	Support	Type
Paging scheme	Optional	LMP_page_mode_req
		LMP_page_scan_mode_req
Link supervision	Mandatory	LMP_supervision_timeout
Connection establishment	Mandatory	LMP_host_connection_req
		LMP_setup_complete
Test mode	Mandatory	LMP_test_activate
		LMP_test_control
Error handling	Mandatory	LMP_not_accepted
Encryption	Optional	LMP_encryption_mode_req
		LMP_encryption_key_size_req
		LMP_start_encryption_req
		LMP_stop_encryption_req

The following sections describe the various types of PDUs transmitted by LMs.

GENERAL RESPONSE (M)

These mandatory PDUs are used to send general responses between units. They are used for various procedures and are identified by the operation code of the message to which a response is being made. If an LM sends a not-accepted message, it also sends a reason for not accepting the request.

AUTHENTICATION (M)

Before connecting to a remote device, the LM of the discovering device needs to verify the remote device's identity. It does this via the authentication process, for which support is mandatory. The verifying unit sends an LMP_au_rand message to the remote device. This PDU contains a random number, which serves as the authentication challenge to the other unit. The response, LMP_sres, contains the remote unit's BD_ADDR and a secret (link) key. When the response is returned, the discovering unit checks its accuracy.

For a successful authentication response, the two units must share a link key. If the response is incorrect, the discovering unit can end the connection by sending an LMP_detach PDU. This PDU provides a reason for the failure, and the reason code in this case would be *authentication failure*.

If the respondent does not have a link key, it sends the LMP_not_accepted response. The reason code given in this case is *key missing*.

PAIRING (M)

Authentication is accomplished either by using a stored link key or by creating an initialization key. When two devices communicate for the first time, a procedure known as *pairing* generates the link key. LM automatically starts this process if no link key is available. The initialization key is based on a PIN, a random number, and a Bluetooth device address.

The PIN code is a number that can be fixed or selected by a user. The user also can change it. A PIN can be entered into just one device — this is called a *fixed PIN* — but entering it in both devices offers greater security.

The following pairing scenarios may take place:

✓ Accepting pairing:

1. The initiating LM sends an LMP_in_rand PDU.

2. If the responding LM accepts, it sends an LMP_accepted PDU.

3. Both units calculate the initialization key and complete the procedure by creating the link key.

✓ Fixed/variable PIN:

1. The initiating LM has a variable PIN. It sends an LMP_in_rand PDU.

2. If the responding LM has a fixed PIN, it generates a new random number and returns that number to the initiator in the LMP_in_rand PDU.

3. Because the initiator has a variable PIN, it must accept the response and return LMP_accepted.

4. Both units then calculate the initialization key and create the link key.

✓ Fixed/fixed PIN:

1. If both units have a fixed PIN, the LMP_in_rand that the responding unit sends back is rejected by the initiating unit.

2. It sends back LMP_not_accepted.

3. The reason code indicates that pairing is not allowed, and the procedure is ended.

CHANGE LINK KEY (M)

Only a link key that is derived from combination keys can be changed, providing that the current link is the semipermanent link key. However, if the link key is a unit key, the linked units will need to repeat the pairing procedure to change the link key. The initiating unit sends the PDU LMP_comb_key, and the responding unit can either accept by sending LMP_comb_key or reject by sending LMP_not_accepted.

If successful, the old link key is discarded, the new link key stored in memory, and it will serve as the link for all subsequent connections between the units unless or until the key is changed again.

CHANGE CURRENT LINK KEY (M)

The current link key is either a semipermanent or a temporary link key. It can be changed temporarily, but the change is only valid for the current session. For example, units may change to a temporary link key because the piconet needs to support encrypted broadcasts. The semipermanent link key allows subsequent connections using the same key.

A temporary key change is valid only for the current connection. After issuing a random number, the master of the piconet sends LMP_temp_rand. Both sides calculate another random number, and then the master sends LMP_temp_key containing the new number to the slave. After the units change to the temporary key, authentication is made to confirm that the same key has been created in both units.

If desired, after the temporary link key has been created, it can be changed back so the semipermanent link key becomes current again. To accomplish this, the master sends the slave LMP_use_semi_permanent_key, and the slave responds with LMP_accepted.

CLOCK OFFSET REQUEST (M)

The clock offset request is used to calculate the difference between a master and a slave's clock. Each time a packet is received, it updates the clock offset. Anytime before, during, or after connection setup, the master will know the slave's page scan channel and therefore the channel on which to issue a wakeup after the slave leaves the piconet. This will speed up the page time on subsequent page attempts. The master sends LMP_clkoffset_req, and the slave responds with LMP_clkoffset_res.

SLOT OFFSET REQUEST (O)

The slot offset request supplies information about the difference between slot boundaries in different piconets, which can be useful in interpiconet communication. The PDU transmits the slot offset parameter and the BD_ADDR. The LMP_slot_offset PDU the master sends to the slave contains the slot offset information. This request also is used for master-slave switching. It must be transmitted from the device that will become master in the switch procedure.

TIMING ACCURACY INFORMATION REQUEST (O)

Timing accuracy information is used to extend or decrease the hold time of a slave returning from hold mode, the time when scanning for sniff mode slots, or time scanning for park mode beacon packets. The master sends the LMP_timing_accuracy_req PDU, and the slave responds with LMP_timing_accuracy_res.

A beacon packet is a broadcast packet sent at regular intervals that tells transmitting devices when to send data to receiving devices.

LMP VERSION (M)

The LMP version transaction provides information about the version of the LM protocol in use. Companies can create their own unique implementations of the LM and will then have unique identifiers. So, this PDU supports requests for the information. The initiating LM transmits LMP_version_req, and the responding LM returns LMP_version_res.

SUPPORTED FEATURES (M)

Not every Bluetooth-enabled device will support all available features; therefore, one unit can request to know which features another unit supports. In fact, only certain packet types can be sent until one device is aware of which features the other device supports. The initiating unit sends LMP_features_req, and the response is LMP_features_res. Support for this PDU is mandatory.

NAME REQUEST (M)

The Bluetooth system allows units to choose easily recognizable, user-friendly names. The name request PDU enables one unit to request the user-friendly name of another. The name can be as many as 248 bytes. The initiating unit sends LMP_name_req, and the responding device transmits LMP_name_res, which includes the name offset, name length, and name fragment. This information is fragmented and sent over one or more DM1 packets.

DETACH REQUEST (M)

The detach request PDU enables the master or the slave to close the connection between them at any time. The transmission includes a reason parameter indicating why the connection is being closed. The unit initiating the disconnection sends LMP_detach.

MASTER-SLAVE ROLE SWITCH REQUEST (O)

Bluetooth allows for the switch of master-slave roles when necessary. The master or the slave can initiate the request. When the slave initiates, it first sends the LMP_slot_offset, followed immediately by the LMP_switch_req. The master unit can accept or reject the request.

If the master initiates the request, it sends LMP_switch_req. If the slave accepts, it sends LMP_slot_offset in response, followed by an LMP_accepted. If the slave does not accept, it sends LMP_not_accepted.

HOLD MODE REQUEST (O)

When a slave does not need to send data for some time, it can enter the lower-power hold mode. During the hold period, the master does not transmit ACL packets to the slave.

The master or the slave can force hold mode by sending LMP_hold. This PDU sets the hold instant and transmits the instant to the other unit. The master or slave can also request hold mode. In this case, the initiating unit sends LMP_hold_req, and the response is LMP_accepted or LMP_rejected.

SNIFF MODE REQUEST (O)

Sniff mode is another optionally supported lower-power mode. To enter this mode, the slave and the master negotiate sniff intervals and offset. They do this via LMP_sniff_req, which contains information about timing, sniff attempts, and sniff timeouts. To move from sniff to active mode, the unit transmits an LMP_unsniff_req PDU.

PARK MODE REQUEST (O)

Park mode enables a unit to remain synchronized to a frequency without having to participate on the channel. Park is a lower-power mode. Master or slave can initiate the request for park mode by transmitting LMP_park_req, which is either accepted or rejected. Broadcast PDUs are the only type that can be sent to a slave in park mode.

A slave is assigned a unique park mode address (PM_ADDR) when placed in park mode, and the master uses that address to unpark the slave. The master can unpark one or multiple slaves by sending the broadcast PDU LMP_unpark_PM_ADDR_req. Slaves can respond with LMP_accepted or LMP_not_accepted.

POWER CONTROL (O)

If a unit wants to increase or decrease another unit's TX (transmit) power, it can request a change in the received signal strength indication (RSSI) value. This change may be necessary if the units differ too much in power.

The initiating unit can send LMP_incr_power_req to request an increase. If the other unit is already at maximum power, however, it returns an LMP_max_power response. If a device wants a decrease in power, it can send LMP_decr_power_req. Again, if the other unit already transmits at minimum power, it returns an LMP_min_power response.

CHANNEL QUALITY-DRIVEN CHANGE BETWEEN DM AND DH REQUEST (O)

How a unit transmits a given packet type depends on the RF channel quality. The quality measurements in the receiver of one device can determine the packet type to be transmitted from another device and set for optimal results. For example, the controlling device may prefer to use DM packets (data-medium rate) rather than DH (data-high rate) packets on a given channel. After receiving the LMP_auto_rate PDU, the controlling device sends back LMP_preferred_rate, with a parameter indicating the preferred coding and slot size.

The transmitting device is not required to change to the preferred packet type and is not allowed to do so if the packet is larger than the maximum allowed number of slots, even if the preferred size is greater than this value.

QUALITY OF SERVICE (M)

LM enables the master and slave to negotiate poll intervals and the number of times broadcast packets are retransmitted — thus determining what kind, or quality, of service will exist between the two units. The master can notify the slave of a change in quality of service (QoS) by sending LMP_quality_of_service. When it receives this transmission, the slave cannot reject it.

The master or slave can also request a change in service by sending the LMP_quality_of_service_req. The responding unit can accept or reject the request.

SCO LINKS (O)

The LM must establish an ACL link before it can create an SCO link. An SCO link is a synchronous (circuit-switched) connection for reserved bandwidth communications such as voice. To establish an SCO link, the master sends a request with parameters specifying timing, packet type, and coding to be used for the link. These parameters determine the time slots for the link. When the master initiates the SCO link, it sends LMP_SCO_link_req. The slave can accept or reject the request. If the slave rejects the request, it indicates why in the error reason field of the PDU. The master can then adjust and try again.

If the slave initiates the SCO link, it sends LMP_SCO_link_req, but the timing parameters will be invalid (because timing is determined by master clock). If the master cannot establish a link using this information, it rejects the request. If it can, it sends back LMP_SCO_link_req with the appropriate parameters.

The master and slave can also request a change of link parameters or request removal of the link. To remove the link, the initiating unit sends LMP_remove_SCO_link_req. This PDU will contain a reason for the requested link removal. The responding unit can accept or reject the request.

CONTROL OF MULTISLOT PACKET (M)
A maximum number of slots can be provided for a remote device to use by sending it the LMP_max_slot PDU. Or, a device can request the maximum number of slots for use by sending the LMP_max_slot_req PDU. The responding device can accept or reject the request.

PAGING SCHEME (O)
Bluetooth allows the use of optional paging schemes, and LMP provides the means for negotiating the use of an optional paging scheme. The paging device can initiate the request for an optional paging scheme by sending LMP_page_mode_req. The responding device can accept or reject the request. A request to switch back to the mandatory scheme can also be rejected.

A device receiving the page can also initiate a page scheme request. In this case, it would send LMP_page_scan_mode_req. The responding device can accept or reject an optional paging scheme but must accept a request for the mandatory paging scheme.

LINK SUPERVISION (M)
Link timers are used to detect link loss, and an LMP procedure is implemented to set the value of the supervision timeout. To establish the value, the master sends LMP_supervision_timeout to the slave.

CONNECTION ESTABLISHMENT (M)
To create a connection involving layers above LM, a paging device sends LMP_host_connection_req. When this request is received, the host is informed of the incoming connection. The responding device sends LMP_accepted or LMP_not_accepted.

If LMP_host_connection_req is accepted, LMP security procedures (pairing, authentication, and encryption) can be invoked. If no further security procedures are to be initiated, the device sends LMP_setup_complete. Both devices need to send LMP_setup_complete PDUs before the first packet on a logical channel other than LMP can be transmitted.

TEST MODES (M)
Different Bluetooth test modes are used for certification and compliance testing of the radio and baseband. LMP supports these test modes with LMP_test_activate and LMP_test_control PDUs.

ERROR HANDLING (M)
Error handling comes into play when a link manager receives a PDU with unrecognized code. The LM responds with LMP_not_accepted, indicating in the reason code *unknown LMP PDU*. Also, if the LM receives a PDU with invalid parameters, it responds with LMP_not_accepted, the reason

code indicating *invalid LMP parameters*. Further, if the maximum response time is exceeded or if a link loss is detected, the unit waiting for the response will determine that the procedure has terminated unsuccessfully.

Errors in LMP messages can be caused by errors on the channel or errors in transmission. To detect errors in transmission, the LM should monitor the number of erroneous messages and disconnect if the number exceeds a threshold.

ENCRYPTION (O)

Before encryption takes place, the master and slave must agree to use it. Before encryption can be implemented, authentication must take place between units. The units also must determine whether encryption will apply only to point-to-point packets or to broadcast packets as well.

If the master wants all slaves in a piconet to use the same encryption parameters, it must issue a temporary key and make it the current link key for all slaves in the piconet before starting encryption. This must happen if broadcast packets are to be encrypted.

To implement encryption, the initiating LM sends an LMP_encryption_mode_req. The request can be accepted or rejected. If encryption is accepted, the next step is to determine encryption key size. So, the master sends LMP_encryption_key_size_req, indicating a suggested key size. If the slave rejects the key size, it sends back the PDU suggesting another key size. This is negotiated until both devices agree, or until the devices recognize that they can't reach an agreement. If agreement can't be reached, the LMP_not_accepted PDU is returned with the reason code indicating *unsupported parameter value*. If this occurs, the units cannot use encryption in their communication.

The initiating unit can stop encryption by sending LMP_encryption_mode_req with the parameter for encryption mode equal to zero — no encryption.

Summary

The Link Manager specifications define a variety of protocol data units (PDUs) that enable the LM to communicate with other link managers and devices. From this chapter, you should have an appreciation for the complexity of the tasks managed and controlled by the Bluetooth link manager:

- ✓ Authentication and encryption
- ✓ Connection management
- ✓ Integration with hardware
- ✓ Piconet management
- ✓ Link configuration

While the LM enables devices to establish and manage links, the applications running on each device must interface to the Bluetooth API in order to access Bluetooth technology. Chapter 8 examines the Bluetooth API and explains how it is used to support applications.

Chapter 8

Interfacing to Bluetooth

In This Chapter

Although connecting your notebook computer to your cell phone using a Bluetooth interface is very exciting, the excitement will soon fade if you cannot do something with that connection. Using the Bluetooth API (application programming interface), your computer, cell phone, or any other Bluetooth-enabled device has the ability to send and receive data in a format it can use.

The Bluetooth API is an essential element in the Bluetooth technology and its ability to provide function on user devices. This chapter focuses on the what and how of the Bluetooth API, with particular emphasis on the following topics:

✓ Understanding the role of Bluetooth application programming interfaces (APIs)

✓ Interfacing an application to Bluetooth

✓ Assessing Bluetooth's compatibility with Windows, Linux, and UNIX systems

Understanding Bluetooth Application Programming Interfaces (APIs)

A Bluetooth application programming interface (API) is the means by which various applications interact with the Bluetooth technology. In other words, an API provides a programming interface for developing Bluetooth software, and it exposes objects and uses methods to perform the Bluetooth communication functions.

Several companies have created APIs intended for use with Bluetooth technology — such companies include Digianswer, Axis, Ericsson, and Nokia. With these APIs, which are typically part of the SDKs (software development kits) available for purchase, application developers can use Bluetooth technologies to connect Bluetooth devices without writing extensive low-level code or having to know the technical intricacies of the Bluetooth stack and the hardware on which it runs.

Bluetooth protocols can be written only in Microsoft C or C++ because only these languages support the relevant driver development tools. However, because you can implement a Bluetooth API as an out-of-process Common Object Model (COM) server, you can write Bluetooth applications and profiles in any language that supports the Microsoft Common Object Model, including Microsoft Visual Basic, Visual C++, C#, and Java.

Because Bluetooth is an evolving, dynamic technology, the APIs must be extensible so they can accommodate changes to existing profiles and protocols as well as support the addition of new ones. Figure 8-1 shows a modular structure for Bluetooth APIs, indicating modules that correspond to existing Bluetooth profiles and protocols. In this type of architecture, developers can easily add new modules, as necessary.

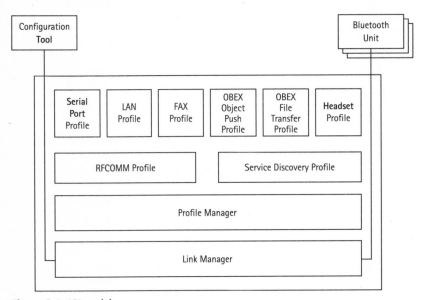

Figure 8-1: API modules

This architecture for Bluetooth APIs comprises the following modules:

✓ **Link Manager:** Handles establishing links, discovering devices, and determining link-level settings for security, encryption, and device name.

✓ **Profile Manager:** Manages profile implementations and ensures that all profile modules are ready to be run.

✓ **RFCOMM profile:** Provides serial port emulation for legacy applications using standard Windows COM ports.

✓ **Service discovery profile:** Provides service information for Bluetooth-aware applications.

✓ **Serial port profile:** Emulates a serial connection between Bluetooth devices.

✓ **LAN profile:** Enables local area network access using Point-to-Point Protocol.

✓ **FAX profile:** Supports FAX connections.

✓ **OBEX object push profile:** Sends and receives data.

✓ **OBEX file transfer profile:** Provides a set of functions that enable access to OBEX file transfer, including pushFile and pullFile.

✓ **Headset profile:** Supports audio input and output.

The Configuration Tool shown in Figure 8-1 represents approved software used to configure a Bluetooth device and the elements of the Bluetooth API that are applied to the device. The Bluetooth Unit in Figure 8-1 represents the hardware of the Bluetooth device.

Interfacing an Application to Bluetooth

In the Bluetooth environment, a *profile* is a set of protocols — or procedures — optimized for use with specific classes of applications. An API implemented for a specific profile necessarily will be application specific. A Bluetooth profile uses a slice of the protocol stack as needed to support an application. For example, the service discovery profile defines the features and procedures an application needs for discovering services registered on other Bluetooth devices and accessing available information pertinent to these services. Any service discovery application developed based on the service discovery profile requires an API to interface with the Bluetooth unit.

The service discovery protocol (SDP) specifically addresses discovering services in the Bluetooth environment. Services can include common tasks such as printing, paging, and faxing, as well as accessing various types of information via teleconferencing, network bridges, and access points. After a Bluetooth device discovers a service via SDP, the device can access that service using other protocols defined by the Bluetooth specifications. Developers can write their own APIs using the Bluetooth profiles specifications, or they can obtain application interfaces from various companies, standards bodies, and consortia.

Bluetooth profiles and APIs

To help you understand how an API corresponds to a specific profile, we use the service discovery profile as an example. The service discovery protocol (SDP) defines how to retrieve information from remote Bluetooth devices. This information then can be used to configure the Bluetooth stack to support end-user applications. SDP also can locate services on available devices, and after locating these services the user can then access them in various ways (although SDP does not define methods for accessing services). SDP supports the following types of service discovery:

✓ Searching for services by service class

✓ Searching for services by service attributes

✓ Browsing for services

To help you understand how the service discovery protocol works, take a look at a typical SDP transaction as described in the service discovery profile. In this example, an SDP client performs a service search by service class. The client is searching for an unspecified printing service. The SDP server that receives the request has only two printing services available. This SPD transaction involves the following steps:

1. The SDP client sends a message to the SDP server (SDP_ServiceSearchRequest), specifying the PrinterServiceClassID as a DataElement with a 32-bit UUID value. The code for this message might look like this:

```
/* Sent from SDP client to SDP server */
SDP_ServiceSearchRequest {
PDUID{1} {
  0x02
}
TransactionID[2]  {
  0xtttt
}
. . .
}
```

2. The SDP server returns a response to the client (SDP_ServiceSearchResponse), returning handles (unique identifiers) of two printing services. The Transaction ID is the same value as that supplied by the SDP client in the request:

```
/* Sent from SDP server to SDP client */
SDP_ServiceSearchResponse {
  PDUID[1]  {
  0x03
}
TransactionID[2]  {
  0xttt
}
. . .

CurrentServiceRecordCount [2]  {
  0x0002
}
ServiceRecordHandleList [8]  {
/* print service 1 handle */
0xqqqqq
/* print service 2 handle */
0xrrrrr
}
}
```

In this example, hexadecimal values are preceded by 0x.

In this example, the SDP has discovered and provided handles for the two print services it identified. The requesting device can proceed to establish links to one or both of these services and, through the Bluetooth API, transmit data to be printed.

Mapping API functions to SDP profile

The service discovery profile describes a generic syntax that any service discovery application can use. It is described generically because the applications being developed may be operating environment dependent — for example, specific to Windows, Linux, or UNIX systems.

The following overview indicates how developers can map API functions to the SDP profile, enabling service discovery and access to a service to occur between Bluetooth devices:

1. A device sends out an inquiry message in order to determine what Bluetooth devices are in range and available. The device sends this message as an Inquiry command, which you may implement as an API function such as GetDeviceList.

   After the inquiry is sent, remote devices can respond to the message, indicating unit address, class of device, and synchronization information.

2. After a link is established with a remote device, the initiating device can inquire about services available on the remote device. The initiating device can use an API function such as GetRemoteServices to obtain service information.

3. The device can then use the Connect API function to access the selected service.

4. The Disconnect API function closes the connection after the device accesses the service.

An application can register itself with SDP at any time. In a typical SDP implementation by Digianswer, for example, the application can register when you want to expose a service to a remote device. Applications use the API to register services, or service records, in the local database. The actual format used — for example, for database handling, or connecting SDP protocols and sending SDP requests — is necessarily implementation specific.

Salutation architecture

To give you a more in-depth look at how you can interface applications to Bluetooth systems, this section looks at the Salutation Bluetooth Profile. The Salutation Consortium developed this profile with contributions from IBM.

The open salutation architecture was created to solve service discovery and access issues among various types of equipment in mobile environments. The architecture provides a standard method by which applications, services, and devices can describe and list their capabilities for other applications, services, and devices. It also enables applications, services, and devices to search other applications, services, and devices for specific capabilities and to request and establish connections with them in order to access their capabilities. This architecture is processor, operating system, and communications protocol independent and allows for scalable implementations, even in low-cost devices.

Salutation architecture defines the Salutation Manager (SLM), which acts as a service broker for applications, services, and devices, which are referred to as a *networked entity*. The SLM enables networked entities to discover and access the capabilities of other networked entities. Networked entities can be a client, a service, or both. A service registers its capability with the SLM, while the client discovers services and requests use of them through the SLM.

The Salutation Manager provides a transport-independent interface — the Salutation Manager Application Program Interface (SLM-API) — to services and clients. The SLM communicates with other SLMs to perform its role. The salutation architecture defines this communication between SLMs, which is called the Salutation Manager Protocol. The SLM binds to a specific transport through a Transport Manager unique to that transport class.

The SLM provides the following basic tasks:

✓ Service registry

✓ Service discovery

✓ Service availability

✓ Service session management

SERVICE REGISTRY

SLM contains a registry to store information about services connected to the SLM. Optionally, the SLM registry also can store information about services registered to other SLMs. The limitation on registry implementation is the size of the storage reserved for the registry function.

SERVICE DISCOVERY

The SLM can discover remote SLMs and determine the services registered on them. Service discovery compares a required service type specified by the local SLM with the service type available on a remote SLM. The SLM can determine the following:

✓ Characteristics of all the services registered on a remote SLM

✓ Characteristics of a specific service

✓ Presence of a service on a remote SLM matching a specific set of characteristics

SERVICE AVAILABILITY

Periodically, a client application may need to check on the availability of one or more services. To do so, the application asks the Salutation Manager to request that the local LM check with the remote manager as to the availability of the services it needs.

SERVICE SESSION MANAGEMENT

When a Bluetooth client requests the use of a service identified through service discovery, a service session is created. A service session can be operated in one of three modes:

✓ **Native mode:** Messages are exchanged using a native protocol, and the Salutation Manager is not involved in the message exchange.

✓ **Emulated mode:** The Salutation Manager carries the messages between the client and the service, but the SLM does not inspect the contents of the messages.

✓ **Salutation mode:** In addition to carrying the messages between the client and the service, the Salutation Manager also defines the message formats that are used in the session.

SLM-API SPECIFICATION

The SLM-API specification provides an interface to Salutation-type applications (searching for and accessing services). This example focuses on Salutation Service Registration and Service Discovery APIs and is intended to help you understand how the APIs are mapped to Bluetooth SDP functions. The following Salutation APIs support this mapping:

✓ Service Registration:

- slmRegisterCapability()
- slmUnregisterCapability()

✓ Service Discovery:

- slmSearchCapability()
- slmQueryCapability()

Table 8-1 describes these Salutation APIs.

Table 8-1 SLM-APIs

slm-API	Description
slmRegisterCapability() Input Parameters: (Functional Unit Description Record; Callback Entry for Open Service Indication; Callback Entry for Close Service Indication; Callback Entry for Receive Data Indication; Preferred Functional Unit Handle) Output Parameter: (Functional Unit Handle)	Services call this SLM-API to register specific instances of functional units with the local SLM. The functional unit description record describes the specific instances. The calling service passes a functional unit description record describing its capability to the SLM. The SLM returns a functional unit handle that uniquely identifies the functional unit among all the functional units registered with the SLM. As long as a functional unit is registered with the local SLM, the functional unit's capability can be included in the response to a Query Capability request. The Callback entries provide an entry point into a service when the service is being used. Entry points can open and close the service as well as receive data. The service may attempt to specify a handle for the functional unit instance being registered, and this value may be assigned if it is not currently being used. Otherwise, the SLM assigns a random, unused value for the handle.

Continued

Table 8-1 SLM-APIs (Continued)

slm-API	Description
slmUnregisterCapability() Input Parameters: (Functional Unit Handle) Output Parameters: None	A service registers with the local SLM by calling the slmRegisterCapability() function; conversely, it unregisters by calling the slmUnregisterCapability() function. The functional unit handle is the value returned by the slmRegisterCapability() and used to register the service.
slmSearchCapability() Input Parameters: (SLM-ID; Service Description Record) Output Parameter: List of SLM IDs)	A client calls this function to request a search by the local SLM of remote SLMs that have a registered functional unit with a specific capability. The local SLM returns the list of SLM-IDs that can provide the requested service to the client. SLM-ID is NULL for version 2.0 of the Salutation Architecture. The service description record describes the services and capabilities that are of interest to the client.
slmQueryCapability() Input Parameters: (SLM-ID; Service Description Record) Output Parameter: (Service Description Record)	SLM-ID specifies the target Salutation Manager. If SLM-ID is NULL, the target Salutation Manager is the local Salutation Manager. The service description record describes the services and capabilities that are of interest to the client. Output service description record describes the services and capabilities available.

Here is a brief description of some of the terms and concepts used in Table 8-1:

✓ The Salutation Manager called by the client via the SLM-API is known as the local salutation manager. Any other salutation manager is known as the remote salutation manager.

✓ The functional unit description record identifies the functional unit and the capabilities of that instance of the functional unit. The functional unit maps to the Bluetooth service. Its capabilities map to the Bluetooth attributes.

✓ The service description record is a collection of one or more functional unit description records. It describes all services for which the client is searching or all services maintained by a service.

SERVICE DISCOVERY FLOW

The client and the functional unit use Salutation APIs to access their respective Salutation Managers. Salutation protocols flow between the client- and service-side SLMs, as shown in Figure 8-2.

Client	Client–side SLM	Salutation Protocol	Service–side SLM	Functional Unit
			<===slmRegisterCapability() call slmRegisterCapability() return ==>	
slmSearchCapability() call ==>				
	Query Capability call ==> <==Query Capability reply Repeated for each known SLM. Reply data may be cached for next step.			
<==slmSearchCapability() return				
slmQueryCapability() call==>				
	Query Capability call ==> <==Query Capability reply Optional step, dependent on caching capability of client's SLM.			
<==slmSearchCapability() return Repeated for each SLM found by the search capability. SLM returns the cached data.				
			<==slmUnRegisterCapability() call slmUnRegisterCapability() return ==>	

Figure 8-2: Salutation flow

MAPPING BLUETOOTH SDP TO SALUTATION APIS

Two approaches can be used for mapping the Bluetooth SDP to Salutation APIs. The first assumes that the Salutation APIs are implemented on top of the Bluetooth service discovery protocol. In this case, the mapping indicates how SDP attributes are passed in the Salutation APIs. For example:

```
Salutation APIs⇨Bluetooth SDP⇨Bluetooth Protocol
```

Here, the Salutation APIs are implemented as the entry to the Bluetooth SDP. The SDP extracts the required information from the APIs and processes it according to the mapping to SDP primitives.

The second approach assumes that the SLM can map directly to the SDP using a Bluetooth-specific Transport Manager. For example:

```
Salutation APIs⇨Salutation Manager⇨Bluetooth Protocol
```

Here, SDP is replaced by the SLM, which maps functionality to the SDP protocol. The salutation architecture makes the following mapping assumptions:

✓ **SDP is a service manager** that specifies local services and responds to requests to discover the services it manages for the remote device (RemDev). For the local device (LocDev), it enables Service Discovery (SvcDscApp) to ask RemDev if it supports specific services. These APIs enable application developers to access the functions of the SDP service manager.

✓ **LocDev service requests** are accessed through Salutation slmSearchCapability() and slmQueryCapability() API calls.

✓ Some **Bluetooth RemDevs** need to update services they support dynamically; for example, service records maintained in the service record database may need updating. Salutation slmRegisterCapability() and slmUnregisterCapability() API calls are mapped on the RemDev side to support dynamic registry of services.

MAPPING SDP PRIMITIVES TO SALUTATION APIS

Salutation APIs can be used to represent the SDP primitives. The function provided by the SDP getRemDevName, which returns the names of remote devices identified by the SDP service search, is an important component of the Salutation's slmSearchCapability() and slmQueryCapability() calls. One Salutation API can provide the function of two SDP primitives.

The mapping uses the functional definition of the Salutation APIs, but not the parameter values. The API becomes a vehicle for passing the SDP parameters to the Bluetooth SDP manager. In other words, the SLM-ID and Service Description records parameters of the Salutation APIs are replaced with the corresponding SDP parameter values. In this way, the parameters defined by the SDP primitives can be passed without modification to the Bluetooth SDP Manager via the Salutation API format. The search operation returns a list of the device names identified by the search. Table 8-2 contrasts the SDP service primitives and the Salutation primitives used in this process.

Table 8-2 SDP Service and Salutation Primitives

SDP Service Primitive	Salutation Primitive
ServiceBrowse, getRemDevName	slmQueryCapability()
	Input Parameters:
	(
	LIST(RemDev);
	LIST(RemDevRelation);
	LIST(browseGroup);
	StopRule
	)
	Output Parameter:
	(
	List of Device Names
	)
ServiceSearch, getRemDevName	slmQueryCapability()
	Input Parameters:
	(
	LIST(RemDev);
	LIST(RemDevRelation);
	LIST(searchPath, attributeList);
	StopRule
	)
	Output Parameter:
	(
	List of Device Names
	)

Continued

Table 8-2 SDP Service and Salutation Primitives *(Continued)*

SDP Service Primitive	Salutation Primitive
EnumerateRemDev, getRemDevName	slmSearchCapability()
	Input Parameters:
	(
	LIST(classOfDevice);
	StopRule
	)
	Output Parameter:
	(
	List of Device Names
	)
(No SDP Registration Primitives)	slmRegisterCapability()
	Input Parameters:
	(
	LIST(attributeList);
	Callback Entry for Open Service Indication;
	Callback Entry for Close Service Indication;
	Callback Entry for Receive Data Indication;
	Preferred Functional Unit Handle
	)
	Output Parameter:
	(
	Functional Unit Handle
	)

SDP Service Primitive	Salutation Primitive
(No SDP Registration Primitives)	slmUnregisterCapability()
	Input Parameters:
	(
	Functional Unit Handle
	)
	Output Parameter:
	None

The slmSearchCapability() call is used for the serviceBrowse and the serviceSearch SDP primitives. The difference lies in the presence or absence of the browseGroup list parameter. If this parameter is present, the Bluetooth SDP Manager performs a browse operation; if not, a search operation is performed instead.

The Functional Unit Description Record parameter of the Salutation slmRegister Capabilities API is replaced with the SDP attributeList parameter, specifying the capabilities of the service being registered. The callback parameters remain in the API definition and provide the means for defining entry points for service use. The returned value remains a handle of the registered service, which the slmUnregisterCapability API uses to identify the service to be removed from public access.

The Salutation API mapping provides the necessary means to pass SDP primitive attributes to the Bluetooth SDP Manager.

SALUTATION MANAGER MAPPING

The Salutation Manager can be accessed via the Salutation APIs and used to invoke the SDP. The SLM in both LocDev and RemDev provides management functionality of SDP. SLM exposes the existing Salutation APIs to the SrvDscApp and RemSrvApp. It generates the appropriate SDP through its Bluetooth-specific transport manager (TM) and hands it off to the L2CAP layer of the Bluetooth protocol stack. SLM also responds to SDP received from L2CAP.

Bluetooth's Compatibility with Windows, Linux, and UNIX

To reach critical mass, Bluetooth technology must interoperate with existing computer operating systems such as Microsoft Windows, Linux, and UNIX. The following sections review Bluetooth's progress toward coexistence with each of these systems.

Microsoft Windows

Microsoft has been supportive of the Bluetooth technology and has been an active participant in several Bluetooth working groups that are developing new profiles for Version 2.0 of the specification. Of course, because the Windows OS is so widespread in the computer world, Bluetooth needs to work well with it. According to the Microsoft Web site, the Windows development team is creating support in the OS for the Bluetooth technology.

Microsoft supports the Bluetooth technology as a wireless bus, complementing USB and IEEE 1394. The goal for Microsoft software support is to have Windows operating systems work with several types of devices that implement Bluetooth wireless technology, such as PC peripherals, PC companions, and devices bridged to network resources through a PC.

The scenarios targeted for support include the following:

- ✓ Device discovery and configuration
- ✓ Synchronization and file transfer using OBEX
- ✓ Dial-up networking using cell phones and null modems (also, enabling LAN access through the dial-up networking profile)
- ✓ Generic third-party RFCOMM applications written to APIs that support Bluetooth

TESTING

To further support Bluetooth efforts in the Windows OS, the Microsoft Windows OS team will test Bluetooth hardware for vendors. According to the Web site information, the team will develop and run tests that aren't included in the Bluetooth Qualifications process. The goal is to ensure that vendor products will work with the Microsoft stack and future versions of Windows. The team also will test for interoperability. This testing will eliminate the need for vendors to find bugs in their products and then send them to Microsoft to reproduce. After testing is complete, the approved product will appear on Microsoft's Hardware Compatibility List, and if the test team determines that a device works well with Windows, Microsoft will support the device in the Windows OS.

WINDOWS APIS

Microsoft cautions vendors that the APIs provided in Windows for Bluetooth technology are not based on virtual serial ports. For that reason, applications written to APIs provided by current third-party stacks won't be directly compatible with the APIs provided by the Microsoft stack. Microsoft will require samples of complete Bluetooth software solutions from vendors, including those third-party stacks, in order to plan for and address upgrade issues in the Windows OS.

You can find sample code on the MSDN (Microsoft Developer Network) Web site at http://msdn.microsoft.com/.

WINDOWS LOGO REQUIREMENTS

To use the Windows logo on devices using Bluetooth technology, third-party developers must satisfy the following requirements:

- ✓ Because Windows will use Bluetooth technology as a wireless serial bus, not as a network, NDIS drivers are not required.

- ✓ Host controller interface (HCI) devices that use Bluetooth technology must work with Microsoft-provided miniport drivers when used in conjunction with the Microsoft software that supports Bluetooth technology. These miniports must be written to support standard Bluetooth HCI specifications, which are consistent with the requirements for USB and IEEE 1394 host controllers.

- ✓ External devices must be tested in the applicable device classes (for example, audio, modem, network). Devices must support the Bluetooth service discovery protocol (SDP) and the Bluetooth Device Information Specification.

- ✓ Standard Bluetooth qualification program tests will be used where applicable for the Bluetooth HCI and for connected external devices.

Microsoft will not support Bluetooth in its Windows XP release. According to Microsoft, not enough production-quality devices conforming to the Bluetooth specification exist for Microsoft to test.

Linux

Bluetooth isn't just a closed, proprietary protocol for Windows. Linux also can run Bluetooth applications. Numerous companies are developing products to enable Linux support for Bluetooth. For example, IBM and Axis have developed Bluetooth protocol stacks for use with Linux. The IBM stack is called BlueDrekar, and the Axis stack is called OpenBT. Another Bluetooth stack available for Linux, called BlueZ, is mostly a contribution of QualComm. Each of these protocol stacks (and drivers) provides support for core Bluetooth layers and protocols and has a modular architecture. Each stack available for Linux has strengths:

- ✓ **BlueDrekar:** IBM's new Bluetooth-enabling software has three loadable modules: btstack.o, sdp.o, and rfcomm.o. These modules include support for layers from the Host Controller Interface (HCI) to RFCOMM and the service discovery protocol (SDP) layer. The stack includes an open API and an executable of the bedd daemon, which is used to provide support for SDP. Included makefiles, documentation files, and sample programs may be used to help write Bluetooth-enabled applications.

✓ **OpenBT:** The OpenBT 0.8 stack is the most mature Bluetooth stack available for Linux. This stack is currently used in many real products. It has a wider set of utilities and documentation than the other stacks. It also supports BCSP (BlueCore Serial Protocol), which is a multi-protocol communications link that adds another option beyond RS-232 and USB. OpenBT also has a wide range of hardware functions. Developers will find it easier to hook programs to the RFCOMM using this Bluetooth stack. OpenBT uses a serial abstraction to interface both to drivers and applications. OpenBT talks to the hardware either directly to the serial port or to a pseudo serial port. The applications respond to the OpenBT stack using one of the OpenBT pseudo serial ports.

✓ **BlueZ:** The BlueZ 1.2 stack is included in the standard Linux kernel. This stack has a modular design, and there is more than one Bluetooth port per stack. BlueZ 1.2 has excellent USB support. The BlueZ stack also provides support for multiple Bluetooth devices, multithreaded data processing, and standard socket interface to all layers. BlueZ uses a network abstraction to interface both to drivers and applications. BlueZ needs special network drivers for serial and USB devices, and Bluetooth devices are referenced as HCIX — for example, HCI2. The applications talk to the BlueZ stack using sockets — for example, AF_Bluetooth.

UNIX

The UNIX operating system was created by Bell Labs and is one of the more powerful, flexible, and diverse operating systems in the computer world. It is popular because it can run various machines, from micros to super computers.

The UNIX operating system is based on the concept of sharing resources. For example, at the same time a programmer is developing applications, an end user can be using a different part of the development tool that resides on the programmer's computer. The UNIX operating system's strongest point is its ability to provide real-time sharing of resources.

Although efforts are under way to incorporate Bluetooth into UNIX operating systems, UNIX is problematic because it does not allow plug-ins. However, open Object Exchange (OBEX), for both C and Python versions, can be used with UNIX systems. It can work over UNIX (BSD) sockets. The method for porting it to operate over Bluetooth would be to implement a Bluetooth socket type in the kernel, to provide L2CAP and RFCOMM sockets, and then change the socket type and address used within the OBEX code. A quicker solution would be to put a transport abstraction layer into the OBEX code, allowing it to run over APIs other than BSD sockets.

Looking ahead, SDKs and protocol stacks are in development for the UNIX environment by various companies — IBM and Axis, for example. Also, Hewlett-Packard is currently manufacturing a Bluetooth wireless printer converter cable with a 12-84C connector. With this adapter, wireless printing is possible, and products of this type would be as easy to use in the UNIX environment as any other.

Summary

Bluetooth APIs provide a programming interface for developing Bluetooth-compatible software. APIs expose objects and use methods to perform communication functions. Numerous companies have created APIs intended for use with Bluetooth technology, and these APIs enable developers to create applications for Bluetooth communication functions without having to know the technical intricacies of the Bluetooth stack and the hardware. Here are the major points we cover in this chapter:

✓ Using an API simplifies efforts to implement any of the Bluetooth functionality.

✓ Bluetooth-compatible applications can be written in various programming languages, including Visual C++, Java, and Microsoft Visual Basic, but the language must support Microsoft COM objects in order to implement the API as an out-of-process Common Object Model (COM) server.

✓ Bluetooth is an evolving, dynamic technology, so the APIs must be extensible. They must be able to accommodate changes to existing profiles and protocols as well as support the addition of new ones.

✓ Bluetooth compatibility with various operating systems is also integral to its success in the marketplace.

✓ Microsoft has been active in its support for Bluetooth technology and is a member of the Bluetooth SIG.

✓ Developers of Linux and UNIX operating systems also are incorporating the Bluetooth technology into their operating systems, with more products, developer's tools, and SDKs being targeted for both.

In Chapter 9, the focus turns to the hardware components of the Bluetooth technology.

Part III

Bluetooth Hardware and Software

IN THIS PART

Although the Bluetooth technology has many potential hardware and software applications, Bluetooth itself is nothing more than a specification. In this part of the book, we examine the hardware and software components used to implement the Bluetooth specification and we explore how the various parts of the Bluetooth standard work together so a Bluetooth device can accomplish its intended application. This part of the book also includes a comparison of Bluetooth and competing wireless technologies.

Chapter 9

Bluetooth Hardware Components

In This Chapter

Bluetooth technology integrates hardware, software, and firmware. Previous chapters in this book examine Bluetooth interfaces, including the specific elements of the Link Manager and the Bluetooth API. This chapter begins a series of chapters that focus more on the hardware and software components of Bluetooth.

This chapter examines Bluetooth hardware and how it interrelates to the other components of the Bluetooth specification, focusing on the following objectives:

✓ Reviewing the Bluetooth hardware, architecture, and integration with other devices

✓ Examining the relationship between Bluetooth hardware and firmware

✓ Considering the air interface and interoperability

✓ Exploring solution options

Bluetooth Hardware

A complete Bluetooth system requires an RF portion for receiving and transmitting signals and a module that includes a baseband microprocessor, memory for low-level protocols, and an interface to the host device. Chip solutions for the Bluetooth system can consist of one or multiple chips. Numerous manufacturers make Bluetooth chip sets, and each manufacturer chooses whether it implements functionality with one or multiple chips. Manufacturers providing Bluetooth solutions include Ericsson, Philsar, Phillips, Zeevo, TSMC, and Intel.

Taiwan Semiconductor Manufacturing Company (TSMC) recently produced an example of the one-chip solution. According to product reports, TSMC used a 0.18-micron, mixed-signal CMOS to build the first cost-effective Bluetooth wafers that combine RF, analog, and digital baseband capabilities in one integrated device.

In the multiple-chip solution, the RF portion is on one chip, while another chip contains the other portions of the system. The RF portion can be implemented in two ways: as an independent module or a single embedded chip.

Architecture

The Bluetooth system comprises the following basic parts:

- ✓ RF portion for receiving and transmitting signals
- ✓ Baseband with microcontroller that processes the transmitted or received data
- ✓ Memory for low-level protocols to manage transmissions
- ✓ Interface to the host computer for supporting software applications
- ✓ Link management software that manages the transmissions

Radio frequency

The short-distance, low-power radio — the radio frequency (RF) portion — operates in the unlicensed 2.4-GHz band and uses a nominal antenna power of 0 dBm. The range is 10 meters, with an optional range of 100 meters if the antenna power is 20 dBm. Data is transmitted at a maximum gross rate of up to 1 Mbps; however, communication overhead limits the practical data rate to a little over 721 Kbps. Interference or being out of range can increase the bit error rate (BER) and cause packets to be re-sent — which also decreases the achievable data rate.

Baseband

The baseband processes the signals from the RF block, turning the received radio signals into digital format, which the host application processes. The baseband also converts digital or voice data into radio signal format.

The baseband processor handles the tasks of checking transmitted data packets for accuracy, extracting data from the packet, and reassembling, decompressing, and filtering the packet, if necessary. The baseband function in the Bluetooth technology is called the *link controller* (microcontroller).

The link controller handles all the baseband functions and supports the link manager. Its functions include

- ✓ Sending and receiving data
- ✓ Identifying the sending device
- ✓ Performing authentication, encryption, and decryption functions
- ✓ Determining the type of frame to use on a slot-by-slot basis
- ✓ Directing how devices listen for transmissions
- ✓ Moving devices into power-saving modes

Bluetooth technology supports an asynchronous data channel, three synchronous voice channels at a rate of 64 Kbps, or simultaneous asynchronous data and synchronous voice channels. The asynchronous channel supports an asymmetric link with a data rate of 721 Kbps with 57.6 Kbps in the return direction, or a 432.6-Kbps symmetric link.

Memory

Nonvolatile memory, such as Flash Memory, is necessary for low-level protocols to manage transmissions. For example, nonvolatile memory is used for storing information such as link keys. A semipermanent link key, once defined, can be stored in nonvolatile memory and reused in a later session. Unit keys, once created, also are stored in nonvolatile memory and typically never changed.

HCI

The lower-layer protocols communicate with the host through the host controller interface (HCI). The HCI also provides an interface to the link controller and the link manager, as well as access to hardware status and control registers. HCI provides a uniform command method of accessing hardware capabilities, and the HCI link commands enable the host to control the link-layer connections to other Bluetooth devices.

The host controller transport layer enables the transparent exchange of HCI-specific information, providing the host with the ability to send HCI commands, ACL data, and SCO data to the host controller. It also enables the host to receive HCI events, ACL data, and SCO data from the host controller.

The link control commands enable the HCI to control connections to other Bluetooth devices. When link control commands are used, the link manager controls the establishment and maintenance of piconets and scatternets. Link control commands tell the LM to create and modify link-layer connections with remote devices, perform inquiries for other devices in range, and issue other LMP commands.

Link management

Each Bluetooth device has a link manager, which handles discovering remote link managers and then communicates with them to set up the link, negotiate features, authenticate QoS, and encrypt and adjust the data rate on the link.

The Bluetooth link is the method of transport used. Bluetooth supports two types of links: synchronous connection-oriented (SCO) links for voice and asynchronous connectionless (ACL) links for packet data. Each link supports the 15 different packet types used in the Bluetooth environment, depending on the application.

Chapter 6 lists the full set of 15 packet types defined by Bluetooth.

Firmware

The term *firmware* can be defined as software routines that are stored in read-only memory (ROM), which, unlike random access memory (RAM), stays intact even in the absence of electrical power. Therefore, startup routines and low-level input/output instructions are stored in firmware. Firmware falls between software and hardware in ease of modification.

HCI and L2CAP firmware are required components of the Bluetooth system. The firmware can be part of the Bluetooth module, or developers can implement protocols, including the HCI, on the microcontroller and then implement an HCI counterpart (HCI driver) and L2CAP on the host device.

You must consider firmware at an early stage of Bluetooth product development. Because the firmware plays a crucial role in how the various elements of the system work together, careful development is essential.

HCI considerations

The Bluetooth specification clearly describes the HCI protocol structure, but from an implementation point of view, the boundaries between HCI, the link manager, and the link controller are not as clear. Therefore, design these layers carefully and in parallel (if possible) in order to integrate the data structures as much as possible. Doing so also helps avoid data and code redundancy.

Carefully consider the integration of the HCI's software architecture, which consists of the data plane and the control plane, with the hardware. The data plane's components are responsible for the transfer of data across a link, and the control plane's components are responsible for link control and management activities.

A host device controls a Bluetooth network interface through a set of commands that the HCI driver supplies. The Bluetooth specification also defines a set of network interface commands that are generated from the HCI firmware and combined with data on ACL and SCO for transmission over the interface.

The HCI packet structures are wrapped with additional information relating to the transport layer above HCI. These packets include Command, Event, ACL, and SCO. The transport layer runs on top of the physical link between the Bluetooth device and its host. HCI commands don't require the same amount of processing nor do they remain in the system memory for long, so you must carefully develop the dataflow infrastructure to adequately manage HCI commands.

L2CAP considerations

The L2CAP provides protocol multiplexing, packet segmentation and reassembly, and QoS information. It serves as a liaison between the upper and lower layers of the Bluetooth stack. You must decide whether to embed L2CAP with the rest of the layers or run it as part of the host operating system. How you decide, of course, will depend on the usage model and the device that is to contain the Bluetooth unit. For example, a mobile phone needs to maintain L2CAP in embedded, nonvolatile memory, while a laptop computer doesn't.

The product design must take into account the amount of information the Bluetooth-enabled device will be able to hold in receive buffers on the host side before it fragments them into the smaller size necessary for Bluetooth packets. The maximum packet size that L2CAP can accept from the upper layers is 64KB.

Although the Bluetooth specifications define which transport layers a device can use to communicate with a host to exchange HCI packets over various physical links (UART, USB), the specifications do not designate any layers for an embedded L2CAP over the same links. The designers must determine how the interface will work. If L2CAP is on the host side, the designers must decide how to integrate L2CAP and ensure its functionality with the host's operating system. Building the L2CAP on the host side can also raise the issue of how to interface the lower part of the L2CAP with a host-side HCI driver or any other proprietary driver. In the first instance, the stack may run slower, and in the second, more programming will be required to achieve interoperability.

Interfaces and Interoperability

The Bluetooth interfaces range from the straightforward physical aspects of the RF transmission spectrum to the much more involved baseband, or logical link, aspects of the interface protocol. Because the Bluetooth unit must function in various portable and mobile products, the interfaces must interoperate between each other, and they must be easily incorporated into a host device without causing significant changes to the host system. The following sections describe how the interfaces work and explain how the design criteria guided their development.

RF (air) interface

To meet requirements for the Bluetooth air interface, a frequency band between 2.400 and 2.500 GHz was chosen. This Industrial, Scientific, and Medical (ISM) band is unlicensed and generally available for transmissions by various types of equipment and radio systems. The general availability of the band means that Bluetooth devices may encounter interference from other devices and, conversely, Bluetooth signals can cause interference as well.

Interference can be a difficult issue to resolve, especially on a global scale. For example, in most countries, the range of the ISM band is 2,400 to 2,483.5 MHz; however, due to interference issues, some countries impose national limitations. For countries with national limitations in the frequency range, Bluetooth specifies special frequency-hopping algorithms. Products implementing the reduced frequency band don't work with products implementing the full band. The SIG, of course, is working to overcome these difficulties in order to obtain global interoperability of Bluetooth products.

Each country also has out-of-band regulations. To comply with these regulations, Bluetooth uses a guard band at the lower and upper band edges. Bluetooth transmissions must avoid these guard bands so that a Bluetooth device's signals don't interfere with other transmissions. In the United States, Europe, and most other countries, the lower guard band is at 2 MHz and the upper guard band is at 3.5 MHz.

To interoperate effectively, Bluetooth devices must be configured to the same set of frequencies. But because no standards exist for negotiating use of the ISM spectrum (for example, in terms of interference issues), the Bluetooth RF interface implements frequency-hopping as the most effective means of limiting interference. And when operating in other countries that limit the use of the spectrum, Bluetooth devices only need to hop through the approved portions.

Table 9-1 lists the Bluetooth frequency allocations for several countries around the world.

Table 9-1 International Bluetooth Frequency Allocations

Location	Range	RF
U.S., Europe, and most other countries	2.400 to 2.4835 GHz	$f=2,402 + k$ MHz, $k=0, \ldots, 78$
Spain	2.445 to 2.475 GHz	$f=2,449 + k$ MHz, $k=0, \ldots, 22$
France	2.4465 to 2.4835 GHz	$f=2,454 + k$ MHz, $k=0, \ldots, 33$

After the frequency bands are established, the bandwidth and power for each individual transmission must be considered. Because it is a frequency-hopping protocol, the air interface divides the transmission spectrum in a set of 1-MHz-wide bands. Output power, however, is more complex. Table 9-2 lists the three classes of equipment, which are differentiated on the basis of power capabilities.

Table 9-2 Power Classes

Power Class	Output
Class 1	100 mW (+20 dBm) for maximum range.
	Power control is mandatory, ranging from 4 to 20 dBm.
	This mode provides greatest distance.
Class 2	2.5 mW (+4 dBm) maximum.
	0.25 mW (-6 dBm) minimum.
	Power control can be implemented, but isn't necessary.
Class 3	Lowest power.
	Nominal output 1 mW (0 dBm).

Only Class 1 requires power control, which is intended to keep devices from emitting any more RF power than necessary — which can cause interference with other signals. For Class 2 and 3 devices, power control is optional but may be useful in low-power applications. The power control algorithm is based on the interaction of devices in a piconet and on use of the link management protocol.

Data is transmitted in the Bluetooth environment over frequencies that combine standard RF schemes with the frequency-hopping algorithms of baseband. The Bluetooth technology implements an input frequency filter (IF) to simplify reception issues. Rather than tuning a receiver filter to the desired channel, a Bluetooth receiver relies on a single-frequency filter that provides a frequency that is more stable and reliable. The characteristics of the Bluetooth receiver filter emulate a "brick wall" filter, which enables many channels to share a spectrum and eliminates the need for guard bands for avoiding interference.

Baseband operation

The baseband operation covers a broad range of services, including transmission management, data encoding, frequency-hopping, error detection and correction, and framing. The Bluetooth protocols operate under the assumption that only small groups of devices actively participate in communication sessions at any given time. This assumption plays a significant role in determining how the baseband handles transmissions and connections and manages devices in a piconet or scatternet.

TRANSMISSION MANAGEMENT

The master of a piconet manages transmission using time slots. As slaves receive information from the master unit, the master determines which slots to use for transmission. Master transmissions are sent in even-numbered time slots, while slave transmissions are sent in odd time slots.

DATA TRANSMISSION

The two types of logical links used in the Bluetooth environment are, of course, synchronous connection-oriented (SCO) links and asynchronous connectionless (ACL) links. SCO links allocate fixed circuit-switched bandwidth between point-to-point connections (master and single slave) for voice transmissions. ACL links pass framed data among all members of a piconet. These two data formats enable the Bluetooth system to handle all voice and data applications. The ACL traffic is limited primarily by the transmission quality and data rate of the underlying RF transport. Up to three SCO connections can be transported in a single session.

FREQUENCY HOPPING

The air interface, as already discussed, achieves transmission goals through frequency hopping. The Bluetooth hopping scheme includes the following elements:

- ✓ **Time synchronization:** Transmissions must be on frequencies known to the transmitter and receivers at synchronized time intervals.

- ✓ **Information delivery:** Information is sent in packet formats, with each packet contained between one and five frequency hops.

- ✓ **Frequency selection:** The master unit's device address and clock determine the frequencies. In the U.S. and most of Europe, devices can choose from 79 channels. Other countries limit the spectrum to 23 channels.

- ✓ **Hop frequency:** The hop rate is 1,600 frequencies per second; time length is 625 ms.

Because of the combination of frequencies to choose from and the wide range of hopping sequences, Bluetooth transmissions are reliable and able to avoid collisions with transmissions from other piconets in physical proximity.

MULTIPLEXING DATA

Link data frames transport a range of data types, and five logical data channels can be transported in the data link payload. These frame types are all carried over the air interface, and include the following:

✓ **Link control:** Manages the flow of packets over the link interface

✓ **Link manager:** Transports link management information

✓ **User asynchronous/user isochronous:** Carries user data

✓ **User synchronous:** Carries SCO data

DATA FRAMING

The link control protocol is responsible for framing and delivery of the data elements. The frame format used for transmitting packets includes the following elements:

✓ **Access code:** The access code field is 68-bits long, consisting of 64 bits of synchronization information, and a 4-bit trailer. When a header is included in the packet, a 4-bit preamble is attached, making the access code field a total of 72 bits long. The specification defines three types of access codes: channel access, device access, and inquiry access.

✓ **Header:** This 54-bit field is used to identify the frame type.

✓ **Payload:** The payload contains the application-specific information being transported by the Bluetooth link-layer services, from 0 to 2,745 bits of data.

This information enables the link control protocol to manage the associations and delivery of information between the devices in a piconet or scatternet. The format is used for both synchronous (voice) and asynchronous (data) transmissions.

As with any wireless interface, reliable delivery of information is an issue. Noise and interference from other ISM band transmissions must be addressed. Bluetooth uses two general mechanisms to handle this issue: forward error correction (FEC) and automatic repeat request (ARQ). FEC is typically applied to SCO transmissions, while ARQ is used for data applications.

See Chapter 5 for more information on the use of FEC and ARQ.

Solution Options

The issues that affect Bluetooth product designers, as with any other designers, include supply sourcing, time to market, space constraints, and cost. With these issues in mind, designers must

---

Defining Those Pesky Networking Abbreviations

The world of networking seems like an endless stream of abbreviations, acronyms, and initials. To help you understand what they mean, as applies to Bluetooth technology, here are a few definitions:

✓ **ARQ:** Refers to automatic repeat request. An ARQN (ARQ Number) is included in each packet to communicate an acknowledgment that a packet that includes a CRC has been successfully received.

✓ **CRC:** Refers to cyclic redundancy check. A CRC is a binary value that is calculated a variety of ways. The calculation can be as complicated as a four-part algorithm or as simple as a total of the bits in a packet. The sending device places the CRC in a packet. Then, the receiving device recalculates the CRC to verify that all the transmitted bits have arrived.

✓ **FECN:** Refers to forward error correction notification or forward explicit congestion notification, depending on who you ask. FECN is used to notify devices on a network that a transmission error was received from a particular link and that an alternative link should be used until the problem is resolved.

For more definitions, see the "Bluetooth Terminology" appendix, later in this book.

---

decide whether to build Bluetooth solutions from the ground up or buy solutions from other vendors. The pressure is toward integration, while simultaneously protecting slim margins and offering product differentiation. The benefits of integration include the following:

✓ Reduced component counts shrink form factors.

✓ Integrated solutions speed time to market.

✓ Packaged RF modules require less in-house expertise.

✓ Precertified solutions avoid standards certification issues.

✓ Fewer integrated parts drive down the bill of materials.

However, increasingly, only large companies have the significant resources to build RF solutions from the ground up. The other option is to incorporate Bluetooth modules into a product design and live with whatever constraints this approach will introduce.

Module scheme

In the module scheme, object code in the baseband supports the lower-layer protocols. A host processor supports the upper-layer protocols, and the protocol software must be integrated into the host application.

The baseband processes signals from the RF portion. The link manager resides on top of the baseband and controls link setup, authentication, link configuration, and other low-level protocols. The link manager accesses the underlying link controller for services such as sending and receiving data, setting up connections, and authenticating devices. Together, the baseband and the link manager establish connections for a Bluetooth network.

The host controller interface (HCI) is the means by which the lower-layer protocols communicate with the host device. You would need to implement an HCI driver and any other necessary protocols (L2CAP, RFCOMM, or SDP) in order to use supported applications.

Embedded scheme

The Bluetooth wireless technology can be implemented on a chip as part of a tiny module. The radio frequency and logic components reside on the same chip — in other words, the RF and baseband. The module is then embedded in the host device. Under the embedded scheme, the integrated unit can run L2CAP and RFCOMM without host intervention, and the host processor can sleep while the Bluetooth chip processes the upper protocols.

In the embedded scheme, the host device receives HCI data only when necessary. The Bluetooth unit is connected to the host through a serial interface such as UART or USB, and essentially becomes an intelligent peripheral to the host. With this design, many profiles can operate without any host overhead. Also, difficulties in stack integration can be avoided. It is likely that future single-chip Bluetooth units will be manufactured specifically for a particular profile and avoid the issues introduced by generic designs.

The size of the Bluetooth unit can vary. All components, including the chip(s), the antenna, the memory, and the crystal, can be placed on a PCB about 20 mm by 15 mm. Chip thickness in this case is about 1.25 mm (minimum) or 1.55 mm (maximum).

Module versus embedded solution

The module approach has several advantages. For example, it incurs low development costs and enables products to get to market sooner. It also means the product will likely meet the Bluetooth qualification requirements more easily, require fewer RF resources, and require a low investment risk.

The module approach also has disadvantages. For example, using a module will increase unit cost. Further, the module means a fixed form factor for the product being developed — that is, the product must be able to house the module, and the interfaces and features are fixed as well.

A single-chip approach, using an embedded chip, addresses some of the disadvantages presented by the module approach by providing a more flexible form factor and offering a wider choice of interfaces and features. A single chip also keeps costs down and delivers a more complete solution. However, the development of a single chip may also require additional and specialized resources and can take longer to reach the market.

The choice to use the module or embedded approach will differ for each manufacturer, depending on resources and time-to-market requirements. Factors critical in making this decision include development investment and expertise, size constraints, interface requirements, and power consumption.

Summary

Bluetooth technology is an integration of hardware, software, and firmware. In this chapter, we examine the issues surrounding the design of the hardware elements of a Bluetooth product:

✓ The Bluetooth specification defines a system platform that includes hardware, software, firmware, and interoperability requirements. All these elements come into play in Bluetooth product design.

✓ Manufacturers must determine whether to build a Bluetooth device from the ground up or whether to use a module approach and incorporate another vendor's solution into their product. These decisions are based on various factors, including cost and time to market.

✓ Whatever approach the product designers take, they still must integrate the Bluetooth hardware, software, and firmware in a manner that allows interoperability and meets the Bluetooth certification requirements.

Chapter 10 continues this discussion of Bluetooth elements with a look at Bluetooth software.

Chapter 10

Bluetooth Software Components

In This Chapter

Although the Bluetooth radio is an essential part of the technology, many other components must work together to achieve wireless connectivity. The radio is only one element of the Bluetooth module, which includes other hardware as well as software. The hardware provides the foundation upon which the software can operate. The actual Bluetooth device can be a cell phone, a notebook computer, a PC, and so on, but in Bluetooth vernacular, the device itself is referred as the *host*, while all Bluetooth components are combined in a Bluetooth *module,* which is embedded or added on to the host device.

Communication between the host and the Bluetooth module takes place through the host controller (hardware) and link management software. After connections are established between host devices, L2CAP comes into play, providing the necessary messaging between upper and lower layers of the stack and interfacing with other communications protocols on the host device as necessary.

This chapter describes the software portion of the Bluetooth module and briefly examines how it works with the hardware and the host device to achieve wireless connectivity. This exploration of Bluetooth software has the following objectives:

✓ Reviewing Bluetooth software functions

✓ Understanding the role of firmware

✓ Examining the HCI driver

✓ Exploring planned modifications and enhancements to the Bluetooth specification

Connecting with Bluetooth Software

The link manager software, which resides in the lower layer of the protocol stack, carries out the setup and configuration necessary to establish a link between Bluetooth devices. Essentially, the link manager discovers the LM software on other devices and communicates with those devices using the link manager protocol (LMP). The link manager accesses the services of the underlying Bluetooth hardware, the link controller, which physically sends and receives data, as shown in Figure 10-1.

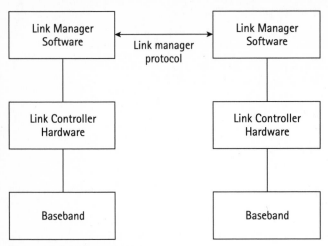

Figure 10-1: Link management

After a link has been established between LMs, the LMP controls the link establishment, manages security, and provides general control services for the connection. The LC (link controller) protocol provides sequenced, reliable data transmissions, so the LMP doesn't need to be concerned with the delivery process. The LC also takes care of retransmissions and any transmission error detection and recovery.

The LMP protocol is command/response-oriented. The messages that are transported are known as *protocol data units* (PDUs) and divided into two fields: the OpCode field, used primarily to identify the type and sequence of the packet being transmitted; and a content field, used for application-specific information. These system-level messages are essential to maintaining a link between devices, so they have a higher priority than user data or voice communications.

Several areas require link management, and to that end, LMP provides the following services:

✓ A set of mechanisms that master units in a piconet use to ensure synchronization of units in the piconet

✓ Management of link encryptors to ensure that access control and key management features are implemented for Bluetooth security services

✓ The means for exchanging capability information between devices

✓ Link state management, power management, paging control, and general supervision of units in a piconet

As you can see, numerous services can be controlled in a Bluetooth link. The link manager works with the link controller and implements the LMP to ensure reliable, secure, wireless connectivity.

See Chapter 7 for more information on the link manager and the link controller.

Examining Bluetooth Firmware

The term *firmware* refers to programming instructions stored on electronic chips, such as ROM, PROM, EPROM, and EEPROM — all of which can permanently hold their contents without a power source. Firmware plays an important role in terms of how the various elements of the Bluetooth system work together. For example, Bluetooth devices store startup routines and low-level input/output instructions in firmware.

The Host Controller Interface (HCI) and L2CAP firmware are required components of the Bluetooth system. The firmware can be part of the Bluetooth module, or on the microcontroller. If the microcontroller holds the firmware, an HCI counterpart (HCI driver) and the L2CAP must be implemented on the host device.

Host controller interface (HCI)

The HCI provides an interface to the baseband controller and the link manager. It also provides access to hardware status and control registers. In other words, it provides a uniform means of accessing the Bluetooth baseband capabilities.

The HCI is not a mandatory component of the Bluetooth module. If, for example, the Bluetooth module is fully integrated into the design of the host device, no need exists for the HCI. However, add-on devices would require the HCI to access baseband functions. An example of an add-on device is TDK's BlueM, which attaches to the back of a Palm Pilot to enable the PDA to communicate with any Bluetooth device, such as other PDAs, PCs, and printers.

The HCI runs across three sections of a Bluetooth system:

- ✓ Host controller
- ✓ Host transport layer
- ✓ Host

HOST CONTROLLER

The HCI firmware is located in the host controller, which is a Bluetooth hardware component. The host controller is the part of the module that manages communication between the module and the host device. The connection between the two elements can be built into the host's circuit board, or it can be attached to the host as an add-on. The host controller interprets data received (via the HCI) from the host, sending it to the appropriate area of the Bluetooth module; conversely, it interprets data from the module and sends the data (via the HCI) to the host.

HOST TRANSPORT LAYER

The HCI communicates with the host via the host controller transport layer. According to the Bluetooth specifications, the transport layer should enable the transfer of data without having to know anything about the data being transported. Several layers can exist between the host and the Bluetooth module, three of which have been initially defined for Bluetooth: the USB, UART, and RS-232. Regardless of which layer is being used, the host will receive notifications of HCI events.

These transporting layers enable the host to send HCI commands and ACL/SCO data to the host controller. They also enable the host to receive HCI events and ACL/SCO data from the host controller. The Bluetooth HCI specification defines the format of the commands, events, and data exchange that occur between the host and host controller.

See Chapter 11 for more information on the Bluetooth HCI and the Bluetooth protocol stack.

HOST

An *HCI driver* provides the means by which the host communicates with the HCI. The HCI driver is located on the host device. When an HCI event occurs, the host is notified via the HCI driver. After receiving the event packet, the host parses the packet to determine what HCI event has occurred. Figure 10-2 illustrates the HCI interface.

HCI COMMANDS

HCI commands are used to access the Bluetooth hardware capabilities. HCI commands are designated for specific functions. HCI commands include link commands, policy commands, status commands, and informational commands, among others:

- ✓ The HCI link commands enable the host to control the link-layer connections to other Bluetooth devices. For example, the link control commands instruct the link manager to perform inquiries and create or modify connections with remote devices.

- ✓ The policy commands direct how the LM manages a piconet. Although the LM still controls how piconets and scatternets are established and maintained, the policy commands can be used to modify the LM behavior, which can result in changes to the link-layer connections with devices in a piconet.

- ✓ Host controller and baseband commands give the host access to the Bluetooth hardware capabilities and thus enable control of Bluetooth devices, the host controller, the link manager, and the baseband.

- ✓ Status and informational commands give the host access to various registers in the host controller. The status parameters give information about the current state of the host controller, the link manager, and the baseband. The informational parameters give information about the Bluetooth device and the capabilities of the host controller, the link manager, and the baseband. The manufacturer of the Bluetooth hardware determines and sets the informational parameters. The host cannot modify these parameters.

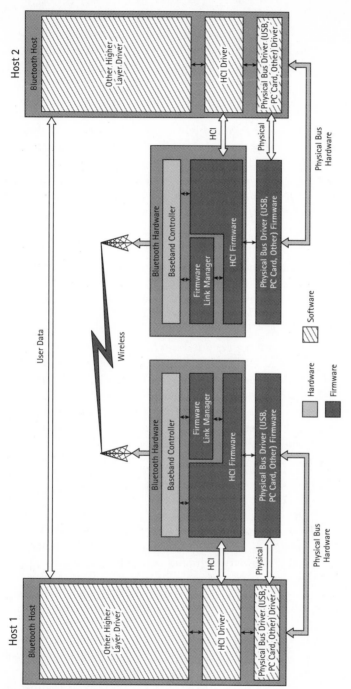

Figure 10-2: HCI interface

HCI EVENTS

Bluetooth defines numerous events for the HCI layer. These events are messages containing specific data, such as inquiry or page scan information, and they include a mechanism so a device can return any parameters or data requested. Currently, the Bluetooth technology implements 32 HCI events, including *Inquiry Complete Event* and *Page Scan Repetition Mode Change Event*.

HCI DATA PACKETS

The HCI events are sent in data packets and passed upward to the L2CAP layer of the Bluetooth stack. The L2CAP determines the channel identifier to which it routes the packet by using the HCI packet Connection_Handle field, which identifies the connection between two Bluetooth units. The L2CAP keeps track of the Connection_Handle related to each connection identifier. When the upper layer wants to send data, the L2CAP finds the corresponding channel identifier and tells the HCI layer to send data on that Connection_Handle.

L2CAP

The L2CAP is a link-level protocol that runs over the baseband and serves as a liaison between the upper and lower layers of the Bluetooth stack. Although the Bluetooth specification defines which transport layers a device can use for communicating with a host to exchange HCI packets over various physical links (for example, UART or USB), it does not designate any of them for an embedded L2CAP over the same links.

How the L2CAP interface will work depends on the design. It can be with the rest of the layers, or it can be built on the host side and integrated with the host's operating system to ensure functionality. Building the L2CAP on the host side requires determining how to interface the lower part of the L2CAP with a host-side HCI driver or any other proprietary driver.

The L2CAP layer comes into play after the initial link has been established between two devices. The L2CAP establishes the channel between devices, and the L2CAP layers in the connected units communicate, sending messages back and forth. The L2CAP receives *requests* and *responses* from the higher layers and *indications* and *confirms* of the requests from the lower layers.

Bluetooth HCI driver

The HCI driver is located on the host device and enables the host to send and receive information from the Bluetooth module. The host receives asynchronous notifications of HCI events, and when the host discovers an event has occurred, it then determines what the event is.

The HCI driver and the Bluetooth firmware communicate via the host controller transport layer. Several layers may exist between the HCI driver on the host system and the HCI firmware in the Bluetooth hardware. The Bluetooth specification defines three initial transport layers:

✓ Universal Asynchronous Receiver Transport (UART)

✓ Universal Serial Bus (USB)

✓ RS-232

UART

The HCI UART transport layer enables use of the Bluetooth HCI over a serial interface between two UARTs on the same circuit board. The UART converts parallel data into serial data for transmitting, or it converts serial data into parallel data for receiving. HCI event and data packets flow through the UART layer, but the layer does not decode them.

USB

The USB transport layer enables the use of a USB hardware interface for Bluetooth hardware — either as a USB dongle or integrated into the motherboard. By using a device class code specific to USB Bluetooth devices, it enables the appropriate driver stack to load, regardless of manufacturer. It also ensures that USB and HCI commands are differentiated.

RS-232

The RS-232 transport layer enables the use of the Bluetooth HCI over a physical RS-232 interface between the host and the host controller. The RS-232 interface is a serial communications interface. The Electronic Industries Association (EIA) defines the standards for this interface. Events and data packets flow through this layer, although the layer does not decode them.

Modifications and Enhancements to the Specification

Through its working groups, the Bluetooth SIG continues to enhance the Bluetooth specification and expand its use in new or improved applications. As is the case with most specifications, a new specification version often requires new or updated software and firmware changes as well. With that in mind, this section compares Version 1.0 to Version 1.1. (Of course, not all the specification modifications or additions require software changes or creation.)

Version 1.0 of the Bluetooth specification came out in July 1999. It consisted of the Core document and the Profiles document. In December of the same year, Version 1.0b was released with a minor revision, and in early 2001, Version 1.1 was released with further revisions. The changes from Version 1.0b to 1.1 were clarifications and corrections, relatively minor, but nonetheless affecting chip manufacturers' time to market.

The Bluetooth SIG is already working on Version 2.0 of the specification, which is projected to be more of an enhancement to the existing documentation than a modification. The projected enhancements include the following:

- ✓ **Transmission speed:** The Radio 2.0 working group is working to improve the rate at which data are transmitted, enabling transmissions of up to 10 Mbps at the current range.

- ✓ **Audio/video usage models:** Various new working groups have been formed to add to the current usage models defined in the specification. These new usage models are likely to include CD-quality headphones, speakers, microphones, wireless video displays, cameras, and wireless video conferencing.

✓ **Human interface devices (HIDs):** These products are for personal wireless systems such as personal computer systems, home entertainment systems, and various appliances. For example, the desktop computer system would incorporate one HID connected to several computers or, conversely, one computer connected to several HIDs. The home entertainment usage model involves using wireless devices such as keyboards to control remote computers or video games.

✓ **Automotive usage models:** One projected usage model involves remote car access by means of — a key replacement device such as a mobile phone or PDA that sends a coded signal to lock or unlock the car, start the engine, turn on the radio, and so on.

These are just a few of the projected usage models being considered by the SIG for Version 2.0 of the specification.

Summary

The idea of using radio frequencies to establish wireless communication between devices is relatively simple and certainly not new, but the manner in which all the elements need to work together in a Bluetooth module and interact with a host device make the technology an extremely complex one. This chapter explores the role software plays in establishing wireless communication between devices:

✓ The functions of a Bluetooth device are detailed in the Bluetooth specification, which describes and defines all aspects of the Bluetooth technology, including software and firmware.

✓ A manufacturer may decide whether to implement its applications as firmware or software, as long as those applications include the required functions.

✓ The required software or firmware elements that a Bluetooth product must include are the link manager, the link controller, and the functions defined in the host controller interface and the Bluetooth protocol stack.

Chapter 11 takes a more detailed look at the Bluetooth protocol stack.

Chapter 11

The Bluetooth Protocol Stack

In This Chapter

Bluetooth technology combines hardware and software that work together to provide wireless networks for users. The hardware consists of an embedded radio transceiver that enables the physical connections between devices. The software, which includes the functions defined in the Bluetooth protocol stack, incorporates specified protocols that enable interoperability among Bluetooth devices and applications developed by different manufacturers. This chapter describes how the hardware and software components of the Bluetooth stack interact to facilitate communications, with particular emphasis on the following topics:

✓ Examining the Bluetooth protocol stack

✓ Understanding how data is transmitted across the stack

✓ Reviewing the functions of the protocols in the Bluetooth stack

✓ Taking a look at Bluetooth communications

Overview of the Bluetooth Protocol Stack

The Bluetooth protocol stack integrates protocols specific to Bluetooth along with several existing protocols adapted from other communications and networking technologies and applications. The protocols in the Bluetooth stack provide a set of rules that define how messages are formatted and passed over a communications link and between the various layers of the Bluetooth model. The Bluetooth protocol stack also provides a prescribed framework that manufacturers and developers can use to create interoperable products and applications.

The Bluetooth protocol stack is based on existing communications and networking standards. Before we examine the layers and protocols of the Bluetooth stack, the following section reviews these standards to help you understand the logic and structure used in the Bluetooth stack.

The OSI model

The underlying generic standard and model for virtually all networking is the Open Systems Interconnection (OSI) reference model, which was developed by the International Organization for Standardization (ISO) in 1974 based on several existing models of that time. The OSI model, which is still widely accepted, was devised to separate the various network functions in order to promote interoperability among networking hardware and software from different vendors. The OSI model has been the baseline model used in the development of every open network technology since its release, including Bluetooth.

The OSI reference model consists of seven layers:

✓ **Physical layer (Layer 1):** Defines the physical and electrical characteristics of the medium over which data is transmitted.

✓ **Data link layer (Layer 2):** Provides reliable data transmission from node to node, defines physical addressing, and prepares data for transmission over the physical media.

✓ **Network layer (Layer 3):** Defines network addressing and the procedures used for sending data to its correct destination address.

✓ **Transport layer (Layer 4):** Defines the procedures used to ensure the reliable transmission of data across a communications link.

✓ **Session layer (Layer 5):** Establishes, maintains, and disconnects communications links between devices on a network.

✓ **Presentation layer (Layer 6):** Defines how data is formatted, presented, converted, encoded, and encrypted for transmission and use by application-layer protocols.

✓ **Application layer (Layer 7):** Defines the procedures and protocols that enable desktop applications to interact with the network.

Bluetooth stack layers

Like the OSI model, Bluetooth uses a layered approach to its protocol stack. And like the layers of the OSI model, each layer of the Bluetooth stack includes its own set of protocols. Table 11-1 lists the protocols included on each layer of the Bluetooth protocol stack. Figure 11-1 shows the Bluetooth protocol stack.

Table 11-1 The Layers of the Bluetooth Protocol Stack

Protocol Layer	Protocols
Core	Baseband
	Link Manager Protocol (LMP)
	Logical Link Control Adaptation Protocol (L2CAP)
	Service Discovery Protocol (SDP)
Cable replacement	Radio Frequency Communication (RFCOMM)
Telephony control	Telephony Control Specification Binary (TCS-BIN)
	AT commands

Protocol Layer	Protocols
Adopted protocols	Infrared Mobile Communications (IrMC)
	Object Exchange Protocol (OBEX)
	Point-to-Point Protocol (PPP)
	User Datagram Protocol (UDP), Transmission Control Protocol (TCP), Internet Protocol (IP)
	VCard and vCalendar
	Wireless Application Environment (WAE)
	Wireless Application Protocol (WAP)

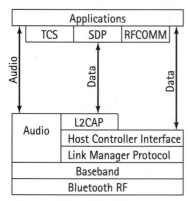

Figure 11-1: The Bluetooth protocol stack

As with the OSI model, the layered approach used in the Bluetooth protocol stack is meant to promote interoperability among applications and devices developed to the Bluetooth specification. Not every application or device uses all the protocols in the stack; some use only a slice of the stack for a particular service needed by a specific application.

The following sections, proceeding layer by layer, examine the Bluetooth-specific and existing protocols included on each layer and how they are used.

CORE LAYER

The core layer protocols provide the core of the Bluetooth functions for Bluetooth devices connected into a piconet. The protocols on this layer of the Bluetooth protocol stack are specific to Bluetooth technology. They are

✓ **Baseband:** Enables the physical link between units in a piconet and provides the different types of physical links (SCO and ACL) with the appropriate corresponding data packets. ACL packets are used for data only, and SCO packets are used for audio or a combination of audio and data.

✓ **Link Manager Protocol (LMP):** Provides link setup and control between units, including control of baseband packet size and link manager filters, and interprets LMP messages so they are never passed to higher layers. LMP messages are higher priority than user data, so they are not delayed by L2CAP traffic.

✓ **Logical Link Control and Adaptation Protocol (L2CAP):** Supports the higher levels by providing multiplexing, packet segmentation and reassembly, and Quality of Service (QoS).

✓ **Service Discovery Protocol (SDP):** Queries for device information, services, and service characteristics.

CABLE REPLACEMENT LAYER

The cable replacement layer is an application-oriented protocol layer that allows for the creation of virtual serial ports on Bluetooth devices. The primary protocol on this layer is the Radio Frequency Communication (RFCOMM) protocol, which provides for the emulation of RS-232 serial ports and the transport capabilities used by the upper layers of the Bluetooth stack.

TELEPHONY CONTROL LAYER

The telephony control layer is another application-oriented protocol layer. It includes the services and protocols used for setting up speech and data calls and controlling mobile phones and modems. The telephony control layer includes two primary protocols:

✓ **Telephony Control Specification Binary (TCS-BIN):** Defines call control signaling for data and speech calls between units and the procedures for handling groups of Bluetooth TCS devices.

✓ **AT commands:** Define a mechanism for configuring and controlling how mobile phones and modems interact in the Bluetooth usage models. These commands are defined in the Hayes SmartModem standard, which has become the de facto standard for modem configuration and control.

The Hypertext Transfer Protocol (HTTP) and the File Transfer Protocol (FTP) can be accommodated on top of the transport protocols specific to Bluetooth or on top of any of the application-oriented protocols.

Adopted protocols

The Bluetooth stack adopts many existing protocols already in use by other communications or networking technologies or platforms. Bluetooth includes these existing protocols to enable interoperability with legacy applications.

The Bluetooth stack includes these existing protocols:

✓ **Infrared Mobile Communications (IrMC):** Defines the methods used for transmitting digital voice signals over an infrared (IR) link.

✓ **Internet Protocol (IP):** The standard Internet (TCP/IP) protocol used to send data between different networks.

✓ **Object Exchange Protocol (OBEX):** Applied to control the exchange of objects between Bluetooth devices.

✓ **Point-to-Point Protocol (PPP):** Defines how data is transmitted over serial point-to-point links.

✓ **Transmission Control Protocol (TCP):** Defines the procedures used to transport data between two communicating devices using procedures that provide for the reliable transfer of the data.

✓ **User Datagram Protocol (UDP):** Sends messages to IP for delivery without the overhead required for a guaranteed delivery. UDP is useful for simple messaging between devices.

✓ **vCard:** Defines the processes used in exchanging electronic business card information.

✓ **vCalendar:** Defines a transport- and platform-independent format for exchanging scheduling information between devices.

✓ **Wireless Application Environment (WAE):** Follows the web-content delivery model, but with modifications for the unique requirements of small wireless devices.

✓ **Wireless Application Protocol (WAP):** Defines how to send and read Internet content on mobile devices.

By using existing and established protocols over its upper layers, the Bluetooth stack ensures that older applications and some legacy devices can be interoperable with both wireless technology and Bluetooth-specific applications.

Data Transmission and the Bluetooth Stack

In cabled environments, serial and parallel ports are commonly used for transmission of data between devices — for example, between computers and printers. The use of legacy applications in the Bluetooth environment requires ports for transmitting data or exchanging services across the different layers of the stack. Bluetooth devices create virtual serial ports to handle these tasks.

Creating virtual ports

Serial transmission is a means of sequentially sending and receiving information one bit at a time. Serial communication is basic for data transmission over LANs and WANs. It is used for both asynchronous and synchronous transmissions.

Parallel communication works somewhat differently. It sends multiple bits of information over a single link simultaneously. Each bit travels over an assigned wire within a cable. This type of communication generally takes place within a computer or between a computer and a locally connected device such as a printer. It's also relatively problem-free because devices do not need to place data in packets before sending.

Although Bluetooth devices send data serially over wireless connections, their internal processes use a combination of serial and parallel transmission. The encryption process, for example, uses stream ciphering to load four inputs in *parallel* to a payload key generator. The subsequently encrypted data is then sent out *serially* over a wireless link.

As already indicated, Bluetooth technology uses serial communication to transmit data in binary form. Serial data can be sent via infrared, copper, or fiber-optic links, but Bluetooth transmits serial data via radio frequency signals. When Bluetooth is implemented for cable replacement, the Serial Port Profile (SPP) is used to define how Bluetooth devices establish a virtual serial port using the RFCOMM protocol, which runs on an L2CAP channel. In this way, Bluetooth can support legacy applications that expect to communicate over a serial connection.

RFCOMM

The Radio Frequency Communication (RFCOMM) protocol provides the cable-replacement procedures in the Bluetooth protocol stack. RFCOMM is based on a subset of the European Telecommunications Standards Institute's (ETSI's) technical standard (TS) 07.10, which is also used for Global System for Mobile (GSM) communication devices.

As defined in the Bluetooth specification, RFCOMM is a simple transport protocol that provides for the emulation of RS-232 serial ports over L2CAP. RFCOMM can emulate multiple serial ports between two devices as well as serial ports among multiple devices and can support as many as 60 simultaneous connections between devices, depending upon the implementation.

RFCOMM is intended to support Bluetooth applications that use the serial ports of the devices in which they reside. To do this, RFCOMM uses port emulation to map the communication API (Application Program Interface) to RFCOMM services. In this way, RFCOMM enables any serial communications-based legacy software to operate on Bluetooth-enabled devices.

When the cable-replacement procedure is used, SPP defines how the Bluetooth devices are set up to emulate a serial cable connection, over connection-oriented channels only, and the RFCOMM protocol is used to transport the data over an L2CAP channel.

Typically, the applications on the communicating devices that require serial port emulation are legacy applications that normally would communicate over a serial cable. Although any legacy application can be operated using the virtual serial port, legacy applications are not aware of Bluetooth procedures for setting up the virtual port. Therefore, a helping application may be necessary to bridge the two environments. The Bluetooth SIG assumes the solution provider will handle this requirement.

SUPPORTED DEVICE TYPES

RFCOMM supports the following two device types:

✓ Type 1 devices: Communication endpoints such as computers and printers

✓ Type 2 devices: Communication segment devices, such as a modem or wireless network access point (NAP)

According to the Bluetooth specification, a complete communication path for RFCOMM involves two applications running on different devices (Type-1 devices or communication endpoints) and a communication segment (a Type-2 device) between the devices. In a direct connection, the communication segment is a link from one device to another. When a network is involved, the communication segment provides a link from a device to a network connection, such as a modem or NAP. Figure 11-2 shows this arrangement.

Figure 11-2: Establishing a serial connection between two devices

RFCOMM is concerned only with the connection between devices or between devices and networks. RFCOMM also can support configurations such as units using Bluetooth wireless technology as well as providing a wired interface.

SETTING UP A VIRTUAL CONNECTION
In order to access a remote device's services when legacy applications are involved, first a recognizable communications link must be established between the devices. Establishing such a link requires adding a virtual serial port to the remote device.

The Bluetooth specification describes required procedures that outline how to set up a virtual serial connection between devices. The following steps indicate how to establish the link:

1. To determine the RFCOMM server channel number of the application in the remote device, a query is submitted using the Service Discovery Protocol (SDP).

Authentication may be required at this point, or encryption may be enabled.

2. A new L2CAP channel is requested to the remote RFCOMM entity.

3. An RFCOMM session is initiated on the L2CAP channel.

4. Using the server channel number, a new data-link connection is started on the RFCOMM session.

The virtual serial cable connection is now ready for use by applications on both devices.

L2CAP
The Logical Link Control and Adaptation Protocol (L2CAP) link layer operates over an ACL link provided by the baseband-layer protocols of the Bluetooth protocol stack. L2CAP provides services

to the upper layers of the stack by transmitting data over L2CAP channels. It provides the software interface to the link controller, which enables the interoperability of Bluetooth devices. It also provides for protocol multiplexing, which supports many third-party upper-level protocols such as TCP/IP, vCard, and vCalendar.

Several protocols interface to the L2CAP layer — for example:

✓ RFCOMM provides serial data transfer using L2CAP.

✓ SDP provides service discovery specific to Bluetooth.

✓ TCS is used for voice and data call control. Point-to-point and point-to-multipoint signaling are supported on L2CAP channels — although SCO links are not supported over L2CAP.

✓ Voice-quality channels for audio and telephony applications usually use SCO links, and packetized audio data (such as IP telephony) may be sent over L2CAP — in this case, the audio is treated as another data application.

FUNCTIONS PERFORMED BY L2CAP

The functions provided by the L2CAP layer include the following:

✓ **Protocol multiplexing:** Because the baseband protocol doesn't support a "type" field that identifies the higher-layer protocols being processed above it, L2CAP provides the means for distinguishing among the upper-layer protocols.

✓ **Packet segmentation and reassembly:** L2CAP supports protocols using packets larger than those supported by the baseband.

✓ **Quality of Service (QoS):** The L2CAP connection process provides for the exchange of QoS information between devices. L2CAP monitors resources used by the protocols at each end of the connection and ensures that QoS is enforced.

✓ **Piconets:** L2CAP permits the efficient mapping of protocol groups into piconets.

The ACL link between Bluetooth devices is set up via the Link Manager Protocol (LMP). After the link is created, the channel is established.

L2CAP is based on the concept of channels and uses three types of L2CAP channels:

✓ Bidirectional signaling channels for carrying commands

✓ Connection-oriented channels for bidirectional point-to-point connections

✓ Unidirectional connectionless channels that support point-to-multipoint connections, enabling connections to a group of devices

Each endpoint of an L2CAP connection is referred to as a *channel identifier* (CID). Each connection-oriented CID must be connected to a single channel and must be configured before it can transfer data. At this point, the channel is bound to a specific upper-level protocol. QoS is negotiated for the channel during configuration, which includes dataflow parameters and transmission type.

Connectionless channels are unidirectional and used to form groups, so a single connectionless CID on a device may be connected to multiple remote devices. These channels do not require connection or configuration.

L2CAP provides a reliable channel between devices by using the baseband layer mechanisms. For example, data integrity checks are performed when requested, and the data is retransmitted until it has been successfully acknowledged or a timeout occurs. L2CAP implementations use the length field in the header of L2CAP packets to check for consistency. Any packets that fail to match the length field are discarded.

CHANNEL STATE MACHINE

An L2CAP connection-oriented channel enters various states during the interactions between the protocol layers. According to the specification, however, this applies only to bidirectional CIDs.

The L2CAP channel operational states include the following:

- ✓ **Open:** A connection has been established and configured and is ready for data flow. Data transfer is possible only in the open state.

- ✓ **Closed:** No channel is currently associated with a CID. Link-level connection does not exist, which forces all other states into the Closed state.

- ✓ **W4_L2CAP_Connect_Rsp:** A CID representing a local endpoint and a connection request message has been sent.

- ✓ **W4_L2CA_Connect_Rsp:** A connection request has been received and sent to the upper layer.

- ✓ **W4_L2CAP_Disconnect_Rsp:** A connection is shutting down, and a disconnect request message has been sent. The connection is now waiting for a corresponding response.

- ✓ **W4_L2CA_Disconnect_Rsp:** A connection on a remote endpoint is shutting down. A disconnect message has been received, and a disconnect indication message has been sent to the upper layer. The connection is now waiting for the corresponding response from the upper layer.

- ✓ **Connection:** To open a channel, the endpoint must be connected and configured. This occurs either when the local L2CAP entity requests connection to a remote device or the local entity has received an indication that a remote entity requests connection. In the first case, the request has originated in the upper-level protocol and has been passed to the remote device, and the local device enters the W4_L2CAP_Connect_Rsp state to wait for a response. In the second case, the connection request is recognized and passed on to the upper layer, and the local entity enters the W4_L2CA_Connect_Rsp state to wait for a response. In either case, when the expected response is received, the local device enters the Config state.

✓ **Config:** A connection has been established, but the units are negotiating (or renegotiating) channel parameters.

✓ **Disconnection:** To close the channel, one L2CAP entity sends a disconnection request to the other. When the expected response is received, the local device enters the Closed state.

Host controller interface (HCI)

Some link controller hardware includes a host controller interface (HCI), which is used to isolate the Bluetooth baseband and link manager from transport protocols such as USB (Universal Serial Bus) or RS-232. An HCI driver on the host serves as an interface to the Bluetooth application with the transport protocol. Supported transport mechanisms include USB, RS-232, and UART.

Using an HCI enables a Bluetooth application to access Bluetooth hardware without the need to know about the transport layer or other hardware implementation details.

RS-232

RS-232 is a serial communications interface. The name refers to a *registered standard* defined by the Electronic Industries Association (EIA). Typically, RS-232 serial ports on computers are used to make connections with external modems or other serial devices, to transmit data using serial communications.

RS-232 cables have D-type, 25-pin connectors. Table 11-2 details the pin assignments for an RS-232 cable.

Table 11-2 RS-232 Pin Assignments

Pin	Circuit Name
1	Protective Ground (Shield)
2	Transmit Data (TD)
3	Receive Data (RD)
4	Request To Send (RTS)
5	Clear To Send (CTS)
6	Data Set Ready (DSR)
7	Signal Ground (SG)
8	Data Carrier Detect (DCD)
15	Transmit Clock (from DCE)
17	Receive Clock
18	Local Analog Loopback

Pin	Circuit Name
20	Data Terminal Ready (DTR)
21	Remote Digital Loopback
22	Ring Indicator
24	Transmit Clock (from DTE)
25	Test Mode

Pins 9 – 14, 16, 19, and 23 are not used.

RFCOMM emulates the nine circuits of an RS-232 interface. Table 11-3 lists the circuits used by RFCOMM to emulate an RS-232 cable.

Table 11-3 RFCOMM RS-232 Emulation Circuits

Pin	Circuit Name
102	Signal Common
103	Transmit Data (TD)
104	Received Data (RD)
105	Request to Sent (RTS)
106	Clear to Send (CTS)
107	Data Set Ready (DSR)
108	Data Terminal Ready (DTR)
109	Data Carrier Detect (CD)
125	Ring Indicator (RI)

UNIVERSAL SERIAL BUS (USB)

The Universal Serial Bus (USB) system is a cable bus that supports the exchange of data between a host computer and a wide range of USB-compatible peripherals. USB peripherals share bandwidth through a protocol that the host computer controls. The bus enables peripherals to be attached, configured, used, and detached when the host and other peripherals are in operation.

A USB system has three elements:

- ✓ **USB interconnect:** The USB port and the services that connect and communicate with the host computer

- ✓ **USB devices:** Hubs that provide additional attachment points to the USB or functions that provide capabilities to a system (for example, ISDN connection, speakers)

- ✓ **USB host:** The host-based services that support the interface to the host computer system

USB INTERFACE TO BLUETOOTH HARDWARE

The first Bluetooth products were add-ons that enabled existing devices to function as Bluetooth devices. These products provided the consumer with a less expensive means of adding Bluetooth technology than buying a completely new device with built-in Bluetooth capability. One such add-on product is a USB adapter.

The Bluetooth USB adapter was developed for use with desktop PCs in both home and office settings. The Bluetooth adapter is used like a modem connection and supports simultaneous voice and data connections. By plugging the adapter into either a PCMCIA slot or a USB port on a PC, the user adds Bluetooth capability to the PC.

A variation of the Bluetooth adapter is the Bluetooth dongle, which is actually a small USB adapter and cable that connect into the PC's USB port. A Bluetooth dongle might connect a portable PC to a printer or scanner. A *dongle* is defined as a device that attaches directly to a port and typically contains firmware to perform a specific function.

Currently, numerous manufacturers produce either Bluetooth USB adapters or dongles. And some Bluetooth service providers are expected to distribute dongles to current and prospective customers in order to further stimulate interest in the technology.

The Bluetooth specifications provide documentation describing the USB transport layer and the requirements of the USB interface for Bluetooth hardware. The documentation provides details for implementing the USB interface as an external device (USB dongle) and for integrating it into the motherboard of a notebook computer.

Bluetooth communication characteristics

As much as possible, Bluetooth bases its technology on existing standards and incorporates existing protocols into its stack. In terms of voice and data communications, Bluetooth uses existing technologies to push forward its own development, building on what already works. Of course, this approach shortens development time and time to market, and it builds on features that already have proven track records.

CELLULAR COMMUNICATIONS

When a device can send and receive data at the same time, the two-way capability is known as a *full-duplex* operation. Providing full-duplex operation is an important consideration for voice transmissions as well as data transmissions. A system can provide full-duplex capability in two ways: Frequency Division Duplexing (FDD) and Time Division Duplexing (TDD). Bluetooth uses TDD.

FDD has been around since the 1920s and is commonly used in wireless communications systems. FDD separates transmission and reception functions to prevent interference with each other. Systems using FDD must have two antennas tuned to the different frequencies. FDD was designed to carry analog voice traffic.

TDD, on the other hand, was originally designed to carry digital data traffic. It uses a single channel for sending and receiving information. It uses one antenna, which divides its time between sending and receiving. Separation between the two is achieved in the time rather than the frequency domain. The channel is divided into time slots, each 625 microseconds long, over which data packets can be transmitted. This, of course, is the method used by Bluetooth technology. TDD can handle uploading and downloading better than FDD, and it can allocate bandwidth on an as-needed basis. (FDD requires a fixed allocation of bandwidth.)

FDD and TDD define different ways of establishing two-way communication, which is necessary for cellular systems. However, a multiple access method is also required to enable multiple users to share available bandwidth.

Bluetooth uses frequency-hopping CDMA as its multiple access method. This method has several properties that make it a good choice for ad hoc networking. For example, the signal can be spread over a large frequency range, while occupying only a small bandwidth. This avoids potential interference on the ISM band. Interference on adjacent hops can be suppressed by filtering.

The following multiple access technologies are available:

- ✓ **Frequency Division Multiple Access (FDMA):** Divides available bandwidth into a range of radio frequencies, each of which defines a channel, with one user to a channel.

- ✓ **Time Division Multiple Access (TDMA):** Divides channels into time slots for higher capacity, with one user to a channel at a time.

- ✓ **Code Division Multiple Access (CDMA):** Based on the spread-spectrum concept in which bandwidth occupied by the signal is broader than that of the information signal transmitted. Spread-spectrum systems don't use channels in frequency or time; rather, multiple conversations simultaneously share the available spectrum. The individual transmissions are distinguished by coding that allows for the detection and correction of signal errors introduced by the transmission medium and uses different coding algorithms and coding to provide QoS on different transmission channels, among other benefits.

DATA LINK LAYER FUNCTIONS

The data link layer (Layer 2 in the OSI model) establishes and terminates the logical link between nodes, controls traffic, provides error checking, and actually determines when a node can use the physical medium. Layer 2 doesn't know the contents of the packets it sends, nor where they're going. This feature is important to the flow of data in the network, because the less information the link layer must interpret, the fewer transmission delays. All communication protocols (wired or wireless), including Bluetooth, use the services defined in the OSI data link layer.

In the Bluetooth environment, the link managers in Bluetooth devices communicate with each other using the Link Manager Protocol (LMP). This layer is where the actual physical link is established so that communication can take place. True to the OSI model, the LMP does not interpret the information it sends; its task is to set up and control the link between devices. The link manager then filters out and interprets the messages so they aren't passed to the higher layers. The LMP controls and negotiates the baseband packet size and is also used for security (authentication and encryption). Further, the LMP controls power modes and duty cycles of the radio device and the connection states of a unit in a piconet.

DATA VERSUS VOICE

All Bluetooth devices must be able to transmit both voice and data signals. So, Bluetooth can be used to connect to both computing and communications devices. However, data signals travel differently from voice signals. Data signals typically use *packet-switching* technology, which means that data is divided into multiple packets before transmission. After the packets are received, the data is reassembled and put back into its original order.

Voice signals use a technology known as *circuit-switching*. In this technology, the messages are not divided into packets; instead, a dedicated channel, or circuit, is designated for each voice transmission.

CONNECTIONS AND TRANSMISSION RATES

Full-duplex transmissions allow data to flow in two directions at the same time — both sending and receiving transmissions. Half-duplex transmissions allow data to flow in only one direction at a time. A walkie-talkie is an example of a device that uses half-duplex communication; one person must stop talking before another can start. The telephone provides full-duplex capability, with transmissions being sent and received simultaneously.

In the Bluetooth specification, full-duplex, synchronous communications are referred to as SCO links. Half-duplex, asynchronous communications are called ACL links. Synchronous connection-oriented (SCO) links provide circuit-switched, point-to-point connections that are typically used for voice, data, and multimedia, using reserved bandwidth.

Asynchronous connectionless (ACL) links provide packet-switched, point-to-multipoint connections that are typically used for data communications. The value of asynchronous transmission is that each character is self-contained. If one character is corrupted during transmission, the other transmitted characters are affected, and only the corrupted character must be retransmitted.

The Bluetooth specification defines a data transfer rate of 1 Mbps. In other words, Bluetooth transmissions are faster than standard computer modems, which operate at 56 Kbps, but significantly slower than Ethernet connections, which typically operate at 10 Mbps. The 1 Mbps data transfer rate is the theoretical maximum; typically, full-duplex transmissions are at 432.6 Kbps. In asymmetric data transmissions, where signals travel faster in one direction than signals returning from the other direction, the outgoing rate is 721 Kbps, and the rate coming back is 56 Kbps. These rates are for data only.

For voice transmissions, Bluetooth requires three synchronous voice channels to operate at 64 Kbps each. A Bluetooth radio can support three synchronous voice channels and one asynchronous data channel at the same time.

Summary

The Bluetooth protocol stack includes many protocols that have been adopted from other technologies and applications. This chapter explores the following characteristics of the Bluetooth protocol stack:

✓ The Bluetooth protocols are rules that define specific ways for devices to communicate with each other, transmit data, and support applications in the Bluetooth environment.

✓ The Bluetooth stack is based on the seven-layer OSI reference model. The Bluetooth stack consists of four rather than seven layers.

✓ The layered protocol approach promotes interoperability among applications written to the Bluetooth specification.

✓ Not every application uses all the protocols in the stack; rather, applications may use a slice of the stack to obtain a particular service to support the application.

✓ The complete Bluetooth protocol stack consists of both Bluetooth-specific and existing protocols from other technologies.

Because Bluetooth uses existing protocols borrowed from other technologies, you may logically assume that Bluetooth is very similar to other technologies. Chapter 12 compares the Bluetooth technology and other cable-replacement technologies.

Chapter 12

Comparing Bluetooth and Other Technologies

In This Chapter

In the realm of cable-replacement technologies, Bluetooth is not alone. Several other existing or emerging technologies will challenge Bluetooth for the market as well as its acceptance by users. In this chapter, we examine Bluetooth in comparison to competing technologies.

This chapter explores the following topics:

✓ Reviewing the state of Bluetooth

✓ Assessing Bluetooth strengths and limitations

✓ Examining U.S. and foreign markets

✓ Sizing up competing technologies

The State of Bluetooth Development

Bluetooth has been in development for more than six years, and although the technology has yet to achieve critical mass in the marketplace, various Bluetooth products have been developed for consumers. Some of these products are currently available, and many others have been officially announced and have been demonstrated as prototypes at Bluetooth conferences.

Bluetooth product development

For the most part, the first wave of Bluetooth products has taken the form of *add-ons* — that is, products users can add to an existing device to enable Bluetooth connectivity. Examples of add-on products include

✓ PC cards

✓ USB adapters and dongles

✓ Memory adapters

✓ Phone adapters

For an up-to-date list of available or announced Bluetooth products, visit the Palowireless Web site at www.palowireless.com/bluetooth/products.asp.

PC CARDS

Bluetooth PC cards are intended for use in portable computers. Each Bluetooth PC card contains the Bluetooth radio, related electronics, and an antenna. To enable Bluetooth functionality in a portable computer, the user inserts a PCMCIA-compatible card into a slot on the side of the PC. Various manufacturers, including IBM, 3Com, and Nokia, have developed cards for use in portable computers and personal digital assistants (PDAs). Figure 12-1 shows a PC card from Nokia being installed in a portable PC.

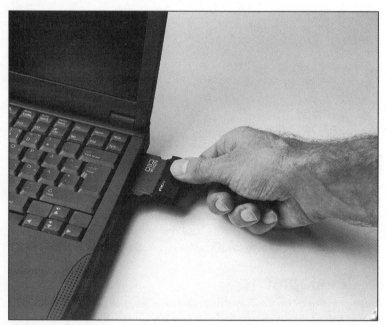

Figure 12-1: Adding a Bluetooth PC card to a notebook PC

USB ADAPTERS AND DONGLES

USB adapters and *dongles* (as some manufacturers call them) provide essentially the same function as PC cards. That is, these USB devices enable Bluetooth functionality when added to an existing device. While PC cards were developed for portable PCs, USB adapters and dongles can be used with more hardware configurations, including desktop PCs and printers.

USB adapters and dongles are easy to use; they just plug into a USB port on the back of a computer. A USB dongle designed specifically for printers also has been developed.

MEMORY ADAPTERS

Memory adapters — also known as CompactFlash, or CF, cards — are commonly used in digital cameras and handheld computing and telephone devices. To add Bluetooth functionality to a device, you simply plug the memory adapter into the device's memory slot. Various manufacturers plan to offer Bluetooth-enabling memory adapters, including Kingston, Sony, and others.

PHONE ADAPTERS

Phone adapters add Bluetooth functionality to mobile phones. One available adapter is a small module that plugs into the system connector located on the bottom of a mobile phone. Another such adapter is a special battery that replaces a phone's existing battery to give Bluetooth functionality and a Bluetooth range of up to 10 meters.

PREVIEWED PRODUCTS

At the 2001 Bluetooth Congress, manufacturers introduced various soon-to-be-released Bluetooth products. Unfortunately, the range of applications was limited, and many of the products introduced required too much proprietary functionality. However, the number of Bluetooth products displayed was promising.

One easy-to-use example came from Nokia, which introduced its Mobil Connection Kit for use with the 6310 mobile phone. The radio and aerial are embedded in the battery, and the product supports a Bluetooth headset and connects to a car kit without cables. As an added feature of this product, if the user's 6310 doesn't have the necessary firmware, the user can download it to the handset from the Nokia Web site (www.nokia.com). This product is clearly in line with the Bluetooth SIG's original vision of straight-out-of-the-box ease of use.

Plantronics introduced its M10 family of headsets, which are designed for home and office use. These headsets come with small radio add-on modules, which the user places between the desktop phone and the wall socket, enabling use of the headset at a range of up to 10 meters.

Bluetooth network access points also made an appearance at the conference. For example, Pico Communications has designed an Internet access point that enables users to connect to the corporate network. The product was developed to combine RS-232 and Ethernet ports for a range of up to 100 meters.

Growing pains

Although some Bluetooth products currently are available and more are in development, the technology still must work through some growing pains before it can succeed in the marketplace. Areas in which the technology encounters criticism include the following:

✓ Interoperability

✓ Robustness

✓ Proprietary functionality

✓ Security

INTEROPERABILITY

Concerns exist that interoperability — the cornerstone of Bluetooth technology — and compatibility may be at risk in the real world. Numerous different Bluetooth chip sets and products are available from various manufacturers, and the number likely will continue to grow. Although the Bluetooth SIG applies a qualification program that's designed to ensure interoperability, manufacturers could qualify their products and then decide to introduce their own proprietary extensions to the Bluetooth specifications. As soon as proprietary applications come into existence, compatibility is compromised. This could occur, for example, if a manufacturer wanted to incorporate features in its product that weren't available in a competitor's product. In such cases, the product may not interface correctly with similar Bluetooth devices. Technological competitiveness in this area could cause real problems in terms of compatibility — a somewhat likely scenario given the competitive climate at many high-tech companies.

ROBUSTNESS

Performance problems may mean that first-generation Bluetooth products are not ready for the marketplace. Some reports have indicated that the first Bluetooth devices are slow, lack the necessary security, and often cannot recognize other Bluetooth devices within the 10-meter range, or they connect to the wrong devices. Such shortcomings probably are to be expected in the first devices of a developing technology, and subsequent products, and especially those developed to later versions of the Bluetooth specification, probably will show significant improvement.

Bluetooth units also have been accused of being power consumers. Early adopters of the technology have indicated that battery power drains significantly faster with a Bluetooth unit added to a portable device than without the Bluetooth unit. However, manufacturers indicate that they will resolve the power consumption issue in subsequent versions of the Bluetooth units.

PROPRIETARY FUNCTIONALITY

Another goal of the SIG is to make Bluetooth products user friendly — an easy, out-of-the-box experience that requires little user interaction. The products should provide value with existing applications, using existing APIs and protocols where possible. Further, these products should be introduced with hardware that provides value, such as portable computers, phones, and handheld devices.

Judging from the products that have been previewed at the Bluetooth Congress, additional work is needed in this area. Products still require some proprietary functionality. This problem should be solved as the technology develops and designers and engineers become more comfortable with the Bluetooth specifications and begin to think more from the end-user point of view.

SECURITY

In a Bluetooth-sponsored study that was initiated to find possible problems with Bluetooth security measures, some issues were raised. For example, researchers indicated that PIN keys, device addresses, and encryption keys can be easily hacked or stolen, which would, of course, open the Bluetooth environment to potential security risks. Also, in all likelihood, computer viruses will present a problem for the Bluetooth technology. Ease of use is one of Bluetooth's selling points, and the easier a device is to operate, the more it's opened to viruses.

Whether security issues will significantly impede the progress of Bluetooth in the marketplace is questionable. The design of the Bluetooth security as it is currently specified provides the security levels required for most applications. Its limited range and use of frequency-hopping — which makes interception difficult — as well as its use of authentication and encryption would seem adequate safeguards.

Time-to-market issues

Other issues that have cropped up to slow the production of Bluetooth devices and thus increase time to market include the following:

✓ Cost

✓ Bluetooth specification revision

✓ Premature marketing hype

COSTS

The projected low cost of Bluetooth products has not yet been realized. Current prices are in the $30 to $40 range, with prices expected to fall during the next year. This high component price, however, has delayed widespread adoption of the Bluetooth chip set. Increased production and competition — which is likely over time — will help bring costs down and thus bring more Bluetooth-enabled products to market.

CHANGES TO THE BLUETOOTH SPECIFICATION

During 2000 and the first several months of 2001, companies such as Nokia and Ericsson released developer kits with Version 1.0 radios and began providing technical support for developers. In June of 2001, however, the Version 1.1 specifications came out, superseding the 1.0 specs.

The revised specifications fixed some problems in the initial specification and ultimately will enable the development of more stable products. However, the Bluetooth standards must remain fairly stable in order for developers to create robust products.

Although the changes made in the Version 1.1 specifications were not major, they were significant because they affected the Bluetooth chip design. Manufacturers had to wait for the new specifications to come out before could they move into production and begin supplying chips that are compatible with the new specs. This cycle may repeat itself in the future, as is the nature of an evolving product or technology.

The Version 1.1 specification changes that had the greatest impact were at the HCI level in the protocol stack. Of course, those developers working on products at this level couldn't complete those products because of the modifications required to meet the new specifications.

Other areas of the specifications that affect product delivery include several profiles. Developers who were using early drafts of the printer profile rather than the serial profile to write code certainly will be affected, and likely will have to rewrite code.

Problems also exist for developers producing only applications. For example, connecting to a corporate LAN is an area for which the SIG has been positioning Bluetooth. However, the Personal Area Networking profile is still months away and as yet offers no decision on how devices will move from one master to another. This is a severe limitation for companies developing applications for PANs, and likely will not have a solution until the 2.0 specification is available.

This situation puts developers in a difficult — if not impossible — position. If they move forward with current code, they take the chance that their applications will not be compatible with future versions of the Bluetooth specifications. However, if production comes to a halt, the whole issue of achieving critical mass in the marketplace becomes ever more tentative.

Timing is everything, and this is just one more delay in an already much-delayed product release.

PREMATURE MARKETING HYPE

Although it is not a limitation of the Bluetooth technology, premature marketing hype may hurt Bluetooth's chances in the marketplace. Because the Bluetooth SIG wanted to create momentum for the developing Bluetooth products and applications, it started promoting Bluetooth before the specifications were ready for release. The SIG originally thought that Bluetooth would be built into millions of devices before 2002, but this is not the case. Forecasts now indicate that Bluetooth will not achieve that kind of market saturation before 2005. One reason for this is that prices for chips must come down to approximately $5 or less before Bluetooth can reach that level of market penetration. Apparently, however, that price is still several years away.

Despite the hype and the current cost, however, the technology appears to have the industry support it needs to ensure its eventual success. Bluetooth's biggest challenge, of course, will be satisfying the end user. Ultimately, it is the end users who will decide whether the technology succeeds, and they will determine the applications for which Bluetooth is used.

U.S. and Foreign Markets

According to research projections, Bluetooth chip sets will be embedded in more than 100 million devices in the U.S. and almost 450 million devices worldwide by 2004. Another research group projects that the Bluetooth technology will be a built-in feature in more than 670 million computing and telecom products by 2005.

Bringing Bluetooth to the world

Table 12-1 shows a projected timeline for Bluetooth development and time to market.

Table 12-1 Bluetooth Development and Time-to-Market Timeline

Date	Activity
1994	Ericsson begins to study inexpensive interface between cellular phones and their accessories.
March 1998	IBM, Intel, Nokia, and Toshiba form Bluetooth Special Interest Group (SIG).
November 1999	Over 1,000 companies in the Bluetooth SIG — no products, no specifications.

Date	Activity
December 1999	SIG releases Version 1.0b of Bluetooth specifications.
End 2000	Limited product prototypes available based on Version 1.0b.
April 2001	SIG releases Version 1.1 of specifications. Bluetooth radios in $30 to $40 range. Bluetooth server products in trade shows. No products available for customers to buy.
End 2001	R&D money commitments should result in reasonable set of products at silicon level, chip level, and device adapter level.
Mid 2002	Products with integrated Bluetooth expected in the market — cost and prices still high.
End 2002	Most advanced 2.5G and 3G smart phones with Bluetooth; some PDAs with Bluetooth synchronization. Increased competition and production should bring the prices down.
2002-2003	Bluetooth probably will go through a phase in which experience will fall short of its promise. The number of 1,000-plus vendors may dwindle considerably.
2004-2005	Radio prices for vendors expected to go down to $5 to $10. Enterprise and home users may start buying Bluetooth-enabled devices. Limited replacement of fixed wiring with Bluetooth-enabled devices.
Post 2005	Bluetooth may start having major impact on short-distance networking and accessory connectivity.

Regional issues

Part of the difficulty in bringing Bluetooth to the world market is that various cellular radio standards are used throughout the global marketplace. This is particularly true in the U.S., whereas most European nations accept one standard. That's one reason why Bluetooth is expected to do well in Europe. In fact, Europe is projected as the most profitable market for vendors to target. Compared with the U.S. or Asia, European consumers are expected to have more product awareness and be more likely to purchase Bluetooth products after they hit the marketplace.

However, Bluetooth does face several areas of regional conflict in the world marketplace:

✓ Japan

✓ Spain

✓ France

Because Japan shows indications of becoming one of the larger markets for Bluetooth products, frequency restrictions could have a major impact throughout the Bluetooth industry. Currently, any Bluetooth products manufactured for the Japanese market can send and receive in only 23 1-MHz frequencies, as compared with the 79 frequencies available for use in other countries. Although companies can build country-specific Bluetooth radios, this frequency restriction means they cannot export Japanese Bluetooth devices to other countries — which somewhat hinders the idea of global interoperability.

Spain has similar issues with the Bluetooth frequencies. Devices for the Spanish market can send and receive on 23 1-MHz frequencies rather than the 79 available elsewhere. Once again, Bluetooth manufacturers must create devices specifically for Spain, and these devices will be sold only in Spain. Devices manufactured for other countries will not be distributed in Spain. Although Spain may try to extend its frequency band to the range from 2.403 GHz to 2.4835 GHz, which would put it close to other countries, its minimum band still would be 3 MHz too high.

One of Bluetooth's most publicized delays was its attempt to win the approval of the French government for Bluetooth use in the ISM band. Bluetooth's mission includes a goal of global compatibility, but because the French military uses the 2.4-GHz band, the government insisted Bluetooth would be illegal.

A similar situation occurred when Macintosh introduced its wireless AirPort product. The French government enacted a law requiring all AirPort owners to register their devices or pay a $30,000 fine. Of course, the SIG does not want that kind of arrangement with Bluetooth products.

As a result, in France, Bluetooth products can transmit and receive on only 23 1-MHz frequencies. Again, companies can manufacture Bluetooth devices specifically for France, but they can't sell those devices outside the country. Conversely, devices manufactured for use in other countries cannot be distributed in France.

Competing Technologies

Although Bluetooth technology is unique in many ways, it also borrows heavily from existing wireless standards. The standards from which Bluetooth has borrowed include IrDA, IEEE 802.11, and Digital Enhanced Cordless Telecommunications (DECT).

For example, Bluetooth's voice data transmission functionality derives from the DECT specification, while the object exchange capabilities, such as exchanging business cards, come from the IrDA technology. The IEEE 802.11 specification provides the basis for Bluetooth's frequency-hopping spread-spectrum, authentication, privacy, power management, and LAN capabilities.

Building on existing standards has enabled Bluetooth development to progress at a faster and more cost-effective pace. It also has propelled Bluetooth technology to the status of competitor to some of these technologies. The competitors closest to Bluetooth in capabilities include IrDA, HomeRF, and 802.11. These competitive technologies have the potential to impede Bluetooth success. In order to compete against them, Bluetooth must differentiate itself from the competition and offer definite advantages to the end user.

IrDA

IrDA is a cable-replacement technology that uses optics rather than radio frequency to transmit signals. IrDA has a much faster transmission rate than Bluetooth, but Bluetooth has distinct advantages in terms of range and angle of connection. IrDA also continues to face problems between PDAs and mobile phones, with users constantly having to update their drivers — a scenario that Bluetooth developers must avoid if they are to be taken seriously. On the other hand, both technologies face some of the same marketing issues — for example, marketing hype, failures to deliver on-time due to changing standards, and lack of hardware and software support. Bluetooth must clearly differentiate itself from this technology in order to avoid the pitfalls that IrDA faces.

HomeRF

HomeRF and Bluetooth have been positioned more as complementary technologies than as competitors. HomeRF serves the home-networking environment. It's faster than Bluetooth, but it is more expensive. One scenario for these technologies to work together involves using HomeRF to network home computers, while Bluetooth provides a less-expensive means for linking the peripherals to the HomeRF network. Also, Bluetooth is meant to be mobile, so users can take Bluetooth-enabled peripherals from home to the office, while HomeRF is meant strictly for the home.

IEEE 802.11

Bluetooth's most serious competitor is 802.11. This wireless LAN application also overlaps Bluetooth applications. Bluetooth has a lower price and lower power consumption, but 802.11 has faster speed and greater range. However, Bluetooth provides both voice and data transmissions, while 802.11 does not provide voice or telephony support.

Bluetooth's competitive limitations

In terms of performance, Bluetooth still must address some issues before it can match the competition in the wireless arena. Areas in which Bluetooth must improve include range, speed, and RF interference.

RANGE LIMITATIONS

The most common class of Bluetooth radios can transmit and receive signals over a 10-meter range (about 33 feet). Although this far surpasses the range of infrared connections, it may not be robust enough for use in real-world situations. In one envisioned usage model, users could compose e-mail on their laptops during airline flights and then have their messages sent automatically when they enter the airport terminal and walk past Bluetooth access points. In this case, limited range becomes a problem, because the access points would have to occur at relatively close intervals (every 60 feet or so), which would not be practical. The SIG is aware of this limitation and intends to increase the Bluetooth range as the technology develops.

SPEED LIMITATIONS

As already indicated, Bluetooth suffers compared with the other wireless technologies in terms of transmission speed. Although the theoretical transmission rate is 1 Mbps, in practical terms, asynchronous data transmission is closer to 721 Kbps, and synchronous transmissions occur at about 432.6 Kbps. This data rate falls far short when compared with existing technologies. IrDA rates are 4 Mbps, HomeRF are 10 Mbps, and 802.11 rates are 11 Mbps.

If the goal is to accommodate end users who want to download multimedia from the Internet, Bluetooth's transmission rate must be upgraded considerably. Further, the 1 Mbps rate would be unacceptable in a WLAN environment; working all day on a corporate network with Bluetooth as the gateway would be impossible at its current rate capability.

INTERFERENCE

Because the Bluetooth technology operates on an unlicensed radio frequency, some concern exists about interference from other devices operating on the same band — for example, microwave ovens. Microwaves are generated at the same 2.4-GHz frequency and have been shown to jam transmissions between Bluetooth devices operating in proximity (within a few feet) of the microwave oven. Of course, users can avoid this problem by moving away from the microwave oven when operating a Bluetooth device. Bluetooth's fast frequency-hopping seems to eliminate most interference from other devices.

Airlines also are concerned about the possibility of the radio transmitters and receivers intercepting communications or interfering with navigation. To allay this fear, the SIG specifications require that manufacturers clearly mark their products with on/off switches.

Because IrDA is an optical rather than a radio transmission, it has no issue with interference. HomeRF uses a frequency-hopping system that minimizes the possibility of interference.

The fact that Bluetooth and IEEE 802.11 wireless devices operate on the same frequency has raised concerns that the devices will interfere with each other's transmissions. Studies have shown that Bluetooth signals do interfere with 802.11 devices, but not the other way around.

Bluetooth's competitive strengths

The Bluetooth technology offers a few advantages compared with other wireless technologies. The main advantages include the following:

- ✓ Minimal hardware dimensions
- ✓ Low power consumption for connections
- ✓ Lower price of components (and expected to go lower)

The hardware dimensions and the interoperability requirements set forth by the SIG will help ensure uniformity in products and applications regardless of vendor. Unlike Bluetooth, the 802.11 wireless technology requires access points, which are expensive and at this point preclude in-home use.

In terms of power consumption, Bluetooth was specifically targeted for mobile users, so low power requirements are an important component of the technology. HomeRF, on the other hand, was intended for home use, not portable use. Power consumption is high in the HomeRF environment.

As for component pricing, although IrDA and HomeRF also are inexpensive, their limitations in terms of mobile use and ad hoc networking make Bluetooth the more cost-effective solution in this area.

Bluetooth supports both voice and data and a wide range of applications based on the Bluetooth specification. Not only does Bluetooth eliminate the need for cables, but it also enables devices to communicate with each other as soon as they come within range. Devices don't require line of sight for transmission nor any set up; the Bluetooth unit is always on and ready for ad hoc communications. Because Bluetooth eliminates cables, users can free up desk areas for more personal workspace and clear floor space, which makes for safer work environments.

The focus of Bluetooth technology on low cost, ease of use, and interoperability promises to change current mobile computing and network connectivity practices for the better. Although other wireless solutions are available, Bluetooth offers a significant advantage in its ability to allow divergent technologies to share a standard. This feature will enable interaction and increase mutual functionality and compatibility on a global scale.

Coexistence

The competition among the various technologies gave rise to the IEEE 802.15 working group. This working group is developing another wireless personal area network (WPAN) standard. The original goal of the 802.15 working group was to create 1-Mbps wireless personal area networks (WPANs) based on the Bluetooth radio specification.

The 802.15 working group has the following key requirements:

- ✓ Worldwide spectrum allocations for unlicensed bands such as 2.4 GHz
- ✓ Up to 10-meter range
- ✓ Low cost, relative to the target device
- ✓ Small size — for example, approximately .5 cubic inches (excludes antenna and battery)
- ✓ Power management: Very low current consumption, averaging 20 milli-amps or less at 10 percent Tx/Rx (transmit/receive) load
- ✓ Asynchronous or connectionless data links
- ✓ Synchronous and connection-oriented links
- ✓ Allow coexistence of multiple wireless PANs in the same area (20 within 400 square feet)
- ✓ Allow coexistence of multiple wireless systems such as P802.11 in the same area
- ✓ Delivered data throughput at the physical or MAC (Media Access Control) address level (one device to one device)

The working group's original focus has changed, however, and 802.15 now intends to develop standards for WPANs, in an attempt to deal with the issues of coexistence and interoperability with other wireless network technology — specifically, Bluetooth, 802.11, and HomeRF.

Summary

Bluetooth has several competing technologies, all of which are trying to gain market share and the acceptance of users. This chapter raises the following points regarding Bluetooth and its competition:

✓ The Bluetooth technology is still in its infancy, but it promises to change the future of mobile computing and communication.

✓ Although Bluetooth has fallen behind in its projected market share goals, it is nevertheless making strides toward global standardization, interoperability, and ubiquity.

✓ The Bluetooth concept offers various benefits compared with other technologies.

✓ Bluetooth requires minimal hardware dimensions, low-cost components, and low power consumption for mobile devices.

✓ Bluetooth's competitive advantages will make it possible to support many types of devices at a low price.

✓ Bluetooth has diverse product offerings — including mobile phones, PDAs, computers, and headsets — in development by many companies, whose broad support will continue to help create a unique market position for Bluetooth technology.

Building on the information in this and the previous chapters, Chapter 13 looks at Bluetooth applications.

Part IV

Applying Bluetooth

IN THIS PART

The Bluetooth world really has only two types of participants: users and developers. For current or potential users, Chapter 13 describes the usage models and scenarios under development within the Bluetooth specification. If you are a developer, or a potential developer, you should read Chapter 14, which describes the process required to get a Bluetooth product approved.

Chapter 13

Bluetooth Applications

In This Chapter

From the wide diversity of the Bluetooth SIG's working groups and the profiles and scenarios they produce, you can sense a great deal of optimism in the Bluetooth world. However, Bluetooth's ultimate success will be measured in terms of the products and the applications that companies develop to fit those profiles and scenarios, as well the acceptance of those products in the marketplace.

As we explain in this chapter, each working group is charged with the definition and development of a specification that defines the application of Bluetooth in one or more vertical technologies, such as automotive, telephony, and imaging, to name only a few. This definition is published as a Bluetooth profile. In many cases, the working groups also will create a description of a possible scenario in which the Bluetooth technology can be applied. These profiles and scenarios guide developers in their quest to produce a Bluetooth-enabled product.

In this chapter, we describe the function-definition bodies of the SIG and their work products. This chapter has the following objectives:

- ✓ Detailing the various Bluetooth working groups

- ✓ Explaining Bluetooth profiles and scenarios in general

- ✓ Examining specific product and application profiles and scenarios

- ✓ Understanding the mobile marketplace

The Bluetooth Working Groups

The Bluetooth SIG has identified various usage models for the Bluetooth environment. A specific profile supports each usage model, defining the protocols and features necessary for implementation. The Bluetooth SIG has established various working groups to oversee the development of standards for these usage models.

Each working group is responsible for defining specifications that control the development of Bluetooth-enabled products within a particular technology or application area. The areas assigned to the working groups vary, but still overlap, which requires a great deal of cooperation between the affected working groups. Here is a brief overview of the charter and responsibilities of the Bluetooth SIG working groups:

✓ **Audio/Video (AV):** The Audio/Video (AV) working group is charged with defining AV protocols and profiles that position Bluetooth as the low-cost, low-power, globally available wireless audio/video standard for consumer electronics. Manufacturers must not compromise these values for performance issues such as quality and range. The goal is to provide interoperability within defined application profiles.

✓ **Car Profile (CAR):** The Car Profile (CAR) working group is responsible for ensuring device interoperability in the car environment using the Bluetooth specifications.

✓ **Coexistence at 2.4 GHz (Coexist):** Because Bluetooth operates in an unlicensed radio spectrum throughout the world, Bluetooth products must be able to work despite the presence of other radio spectrum products. The Coexistence at 2.4 GHz (Coexist) working group is responsible for ensuring that Bluetooth products that come into the range of wireless LANs, cordless telephones, and other radio products, whether at home or the office, continue to operate successfully.

✓ **Extended Service Discovery Profiles (ESDP):** The responsibilities of the Extended Service Discovery Profiles (ESDP) working group include developing profiles that provide mappings of industry Service Discovery Protocols over Bluetooth. The mappings are discovered using the Bluetooth Service Discovery Protocol (SDP). The ESDP working group also is responsible for SDP extensions.

✓ **Human Interface Device (HID):** The Human Interface Device (HID) working group ensures that Bluetooth-enabled HID devices such as keyboards, pointing devices, gaming devices, and monitoring devices are compatible with each other, easy for consumers to use, and affordable. The group is responsible for developing an operational profile for Bluetooth HID devices, giving manufacturers an unambiguous set of rules for including Bluetooth connectivity into their HID devices.

✓ **Imaging (Imaging):** The Imaging working group defines the minimal requirements and generic functions necessary for the identified imaging usage models, which will enable the exchange of digital images between devices. On the destination end, the images will be displayed, stored, printed, or sent to another location via a Bluetooth data access point.

✓ **Local Positioning (LP):** The responsibility of the Local Positioning (LP) working group is to develop a location descriptor in order to provide information that other applications can use to determine location.

✓ **Personal Area Networking (PAN):** The Personal Area Networking working group (PAN) is concerned with the issues surrounding the creation of ad hoc, mobile IP (Internet Protocol)-based personal area networks (PANs), including the security of these networks.

✓ **Printing (Printing):** The responsibilities of the Printing working group include developing specifications to ensure that Bluetooth printers will always interoperate with other devices to some level of negotiated printing capability. This working group considers such issues such as connection establishment, security, pairing, and capability negotiation.

According to the Printing charter, typical usage scenarios may include printing from a mobile phone, a PDA, a camera, or a PC. The scenarios also include Bluetooth-enabled control of the printer, with printable content accessed via other physical connections. Typical printing capabilities may include simple text printing and document-quality and image printing.

✓ **Radio 2.0 (Radio2):** The Radio 2.0 working group (Radio2) has the responsibility to recommend improvements to the original Bluetooth radio specification (Radio 1.0) in the development of a new and expanded radio standard, Radio 2.0. The original Bluetooth radio specification, which was announced in July 1999, includes a common set of specifications for wireless voice and data transmission at up to 10 meters (about 33 feet). Radio 2.0 will not replace the Radio 1.0 specification but will add a set of optional extensions to the older specifications.

✓ **Unrestricted Digital Information Extension for Japanese 3G Handset (UDI):** The responsibilities of the Unrestricted Digital Information Extension for Japanese 3G Handset working group include providing a Bluetooth standard profile that enables the UDI transfer service of the 3G cellular phone system to external devices connected to the 3G cellular phone handsets via Bluetooth. UDI is a synchronous data transfer interface defined in the 3GPP technical specification as an unrestricted digital data transfer service. The UDI working group is concerned with the methodology for achieving UDI communication using Bluetooth and describing the profile specification especially targeted at the Japanese market, which strongly requires UDI transfer service. Based upon the 3GPP guideline, ARIB (Association of Radio Industries and Businesses, the Japanese regional standardization body) has defined the interface between the 3G handset and external devices. The UDI working group will adopt this ARIB definition document as one of the references for the UDI profile.

See Chapter 2 for more information on the SIG working groups.

Profiles and Scenarios

The profiles defined by the Bluetooth specifications describe how to implement usage models. The usage models in turn describe various user scenarios in which Bluetooth performs radio transmission.

Each profile defines messages and procedures for a specific service and use case. It also defines features that are mandatory for each profile, and it defines parameter ranges. The profile concept is intended to ensure interoperability between similar products developed by different vendors.

The Bluetooth specifications define four general profiles on which usage models and all other profiles are based:

✓ **Generic Access Profile (GAP):** GAP is the bedrock upon which all other profiles are based.

✓ **Serial Port Profile (SPP):** This profile defines how devices can be set up for serial port emulation.

✓ **Service Discovery Application Profile (SDAP):** SDAP defines the procedures used to retrieve information from and discover services on other devices.

✓ **Generic Object Exchange Profile (GOEP):** GOEP defines how Bluetooth units are to support the object exchange usage models such as the file transfer, object push, and synchronization profiles.

For every usage model, there are one or more corresponding profiles.

Generic Access Profile (GAP)

The Generic Access Profile (GAP) defines the general procedures for discovering other Bluetooth units and the link management procedures for establishing a connection between them. It defines generic operations that other profiles can use, and if devices implement multiple profiles, the GAP defines the procedures for handling all of them. The GAP also describes how devices behave in standby and connection states, which ensures that links and channels can be established between devices. Figure 13-1 shows the relationship of the GAP to other profiles.

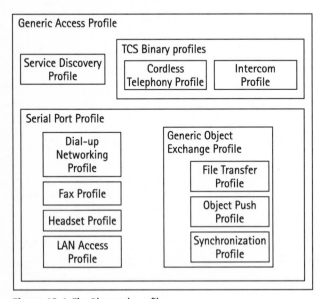

Figure 13-1: The Bluetooth profiles

Bluetooth devices that don't conform to any other profile must conform to the GAP. This requirement ensures that any Bluetooth units, regardless of manufacturer or application, can exchange information to discover which applications or services are supported. Bluetooth devices that conform to another profile can adapt procedures specified by the GAP but must be procedurally compatible.

Common parameters defined by the GAP at the user interface (UI) level include the following:

✓ **Device names:** The GAP specifies that Bluetooth devices can have user-friendly names up to 248 bytes in length. If a device cannot handle the maximum number of characters (for example, in the case of a cell phone, which has limited display capacity), it can allow only the first 20 characters.

✓ **Bluetooth PIN:** The GAP specifies when the PIN is used (to authenticate a device) and how it is to be used. The PIN can be entered at the user interface level or stored in a device that doesn't have sufficient resources for entering and displaying numbers.

✓ **Class of device:** The GAP specifies that this parameter should be transmitted during device discovery to indicate device type and supported services. The UI representation of device class is implementation specific.

GAP-defined modes include the following:

✓ **Discovery modes:** The GAP specifies that, for purposes of inquiry, devices are either in discoverable or nondiscoverable mode. The specifications describe two discoverable modes: limited and general. In limited discoverable mode, a device makes itself available for a limited period of time. In general discoverable mode, a device is continuously available for discovery by other inquiring devices. In nondiscoverable mode, however, a device does not respond to inquiry by other devices.

✓ **Connectivity modes:** The GAP specifies that, for purposes of paging, devices are in either connectable or nonconnectable mode. In connectable mode, devices enable *page scan* — the means by which a connection is established between devices. In nonconnectable mode, a device doesn't allow page scan and is not available for connection with another device.

✓ **Pairing modes:** The GAP specifies that pairing is initiated when devices are communicating for the first time and need to create a common link key. The devices use the link key in subsequent communications. A device is either in pairable or nonpairable mode. In pairable mode, a device enables creation of a bond for purposes of communication. In nonpairable mode, creation of a bond is not allowed.

✓ **Security modes:** The GAP specifies three security modes. In mode 1, a device does not initiate any security procedure. In mode 2, security is enforced when a channel is established (L2CAP) between devices. And in mode 3, security is enforced at the link level.

Idle mode procedures described by the GAP include the following:

✓ **General inquiry:** Provides the inquiry initiator with information about remote devices and is used to discover devices on a continuing basis.

✓ **Limited inquiry:** Provides the inquiry initiator with information about remote devices that are available for only a limited time.

✓ **Name discovery:** Provides the inquiry initiator with the device name of devices in range and responding to paging.

✓ **Device discovery:** Provides the inquiry initiator with the address, clock, class of device, page scan mode, and device name of the units within range.

✓ **Bonding:** Creates a relationship between Bluetooth devices based on a common link key. The key is created and exchanged during the bonding procedure. The devices can store the key and use it during future authentication procedures.

The GAP defines three establishment procedures:

✓ **Link establishment:** How a physical link (asynchronous connections) is to be established between devices.

✓ **Channel establishment:** How a channel is to be set up between devices. A channel can only be established after a physical link is created between devices.

✓ **Connection establishment:** The procedure used to establish a connection between applications on Bluetooth devices.

Serial Port Profile

The Serial Port Profile (SPP) is based on the GAP and defines how Bluetooth devices are set up to emulate a serial cable connection using RFCOMM. RFCOMM is a simple transport protocol that emulates a virtual serial port between Bluetooth devices using RS-232 control signaling. The profile ensures data rates of up to 128 Kbps. Typically, legacy applications are connected using this protocol.

The Bluetooth specification describes three application-level procedures that are required for establishing a virtual serial port connection between devices:

✓ **Establishing a link:** When this process is complete, the virtual serial connection is ready for use by both devices.

✓ **Accepting a link:** After the initiating device establishes the link, the remote device needs to accept it and provide any security information required by the initiator.

✓ **Registering a service record in the local SDP database:** Each service using the RFCOMM transport protocol must have an SDP (Service Discovery Protocol) service record. This record indicates the parameters needed to access the corresponding service or application.

INTEROPERABILITY WITH L2CAP

According to the specification, the SPP is only for connection-oriented channels, and only the initiating device can issue an L2CAP connection request. The SPP provides three configuration options:

- ✓ **Maximum Transmission Unit (MTU) size:** Refers to the largest possible unit of data that can be sent over the link. The size should be set as large as possible based on the device's physical constraints. The default size is 672 bytes; minimum size is 48 bytes.

- ✓ **Flush Timeout:** Refers to the amount of time the sending LM attempts to transmit before ending transmission and flushing the packet. The receiving device is informed of the length of the flush timeout interval.

- ✓ **Quality of Service (QoS):** Refers to any performance guarantees required. If such guarantees are required, a QoS request must be sent, indicating performance parameters. These parameters can include delay variation, peak bandwidth, and latency. If the request does not include QoS, best-effort service is assumed.

INTEROPERABILITY WITH LM

Because LM is involved in transmitting data between devices, the SPP must comply with LM requirements when implementing its own requirements. The specifications overlap in the following areas:

- ✓ The SPP requires support for encryption in connected devices. This is in addition to any requirements defined in the LM specification.

- ✓ The SPP also requires that Bluetooth units be able to handle rejection of requests for optional features. If one unit tries to use a feature not supported by the other device, the initiating unit must send a detach message indicating *unsupported LMP feature*.

- ✓ The SPP does not have any requirements about low-power modes or when to use them. Each device's LM determines this requirement, issuing requests as necessary.

- ✓ Most features at the link control level are activated by the LMP, and errors are usually caught at that layer. Inquiry and paging procedures, however, are independent of the LMP layer, and errors in use can be difficult to detect. Currently, no method is defined in the SPP to guard against or detect improper use of these features.

Service Discovery Application Profile (SDAP)

This profile defines the procedures used to discover services registered on other Bluetooth devices. SDAP handles the search for known, specific services as well as a general service search. In this profile, only connection-oriented channels are used, and no L2CAP broadcasts are used.

A Bluetooth unit requires a Service Discovery User Application for locating services. The SDAP describes how this application should interface with the Service Discovery Protocol (SDP) to send and receive service inquiries between Bluetooth units. The SDP supports searching for services by the following means:

✓ **Service attributes:** Used when searching for a specific service.

✓ **Service browsing:** Used when services are unknown; searches for any services available.

✓ **Service class:** Used when searching for a specific service.

The SDAP details the features required in the service discovery application. These features can be summarized as follows:

✓ The Bluetooth inquiry is activated when the user requests a search for services.

✓ After the inquiry finds a remote device, the service discovery application needs to finish service discovery and terminate the link with one device before connecting to another device.

✓ If a remote device is already connected, the local device will not disconnect after service discovery.

✓ The service discovery application enables the user to select a trusted or untrusted mode of operation. In other words, the user can designate devices as trusted and only allow connections with devices so designated.

Generic Object Exchange Profile (GOEP)

This profile defines the requirements Bluetooth devices must meet to support object exchange (OBEX) usage models. Several usage models are based on this profile, including file transfer and synchronization. The GOEP depends on the Serial Port Profile for object exchange.

The GOEP describes the following object exchange functionality:

✓ Establishing an Object Exchange (OBEX) session between client and server

✓ Pushing a data object to the server using the PUT operation of the OBEX protocol

✓ Pulling a data object from the server using the GET operation of the OBEX protocol

Product Profiles and Scenarios

The Bluetooth SIG has identified various usage models for developing Bluetooth products, and each usage model has a supporting profile that defines protocols and features required for implementation. The SIG has defined the following product profiles:

✓ Intercom profile

✓ Cordless telephony profile

✓ Headset profile

✓ Dial-up networking profile

✓ Fax profile

✓ LAN access profile

✓ File transfer profile

✓ Object push profile

✓ Synchronization profile

Intercom profile

The intercom profile supports usage scenarios requiring a direct speech link between two devices such as a telephone and a computer, with the link established using telephony-based signaling. This is popularly referred to as the *walkie-talkie* usage model.

Figure 13-2 depicts the typical example cited by the profile: cell phone users engaging in a speech call on a direct, phone-to-phone connection using Bluetooth only.

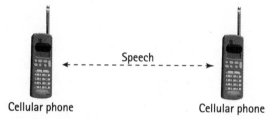

Cellular phone   Speech   Cellular phone

Figure 13-2: Intercom profile scenario

The procedure for establishing an intercom call works as follows:

1. The call initiator must obtain the Bluetooth address of the call acceptor — for example, by using the device discovery procedure.

2. If either device user wants to enforce security, this must now take place to create a secure connection.

3. The initiator then establishes a link and channel. (Only connection-oriented channels are used in this profile.) Authentication and encryption are performed at this point, if required.

4. The intercom call is established.

5. The channel and link are released when the intercom call is cleared.

According to the Bluetooth specification, circumstances can occur that will result in call request failure — for example:

✓ Normal call clearing

✓ User busy

✓ No user response

✓ No answer from user

✓ Call rejected by user

✓ No circuit or channel available

✓ Temporary failure

✓ Requested circuit or channel not available

✓ Bearer capability not presently available

✓ Bearer capability not implemented

✓ Requested facility not implemented

✓ Timer expired

Cordless telephony profile

The cordless telephony profile defines the protocols and procedures to be used by devices implementing the usage model known as the 3-in-1 phone, which incorporates a cell phone, a pager, and a personal digital assistant (PDA) in one device. This usage model can support cordless-only telephony or cordless telephony available through a PC.

The specification defines two roles for this profile:

✓ **Gateway (GW):** A terminal endpoint, which handles all network communication.

✓ **Terminal (TL):** The wireless user terminal — for example, a cordless phone.

Typical call scenarios might include the following:

✓ Connecting to the gateway so incoming calls can be routed to the TL and outgoing calls can be originated at the TL

✓ Calling from a TL to a user on the network

✓ Receiving calls from the network

✓ Calling directly between two terminals

Reasons for call establishment failure include the following:

✓ Unassigned number

✓ No route to destination

✓ User busy

✓ No user responding

✓ Number changed

✓ Invalid number format

✓ No circuit or channel available

✓ Requested circuit or channel not available

✓ Bearer capability not presently available

✓ Bearer capability not implemented

✓ No answer from user

✓ Call rejected by user

Headset profile

The headset profile defines protocols and procedures to be used by devices that implement the usage model known as the *ultimate headset*. Common examples of such devices include headsets, personal computers, and cell phones.

According to the specification, the headset can be connected wirelessly in order to act as the device's audio input and output mechanism with full-duplex audio. This usage model gives the user mobility while maintaining call privacy. Figure 13-3 shows how the headset profile is applied.

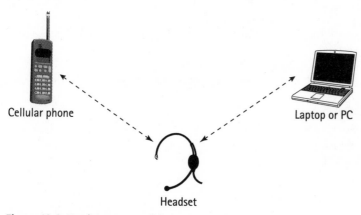

Cellular phone

Laptop or PC

Headset

Figure 13-3: Headset usage model

The headset profile specification defines the following roles:

✓ **Audio Gateway (AG):** Typically, cell phones and personal computers act as gateways.

✓ **Headset (HS):** This device acts as the AG's remote audio input and output mechanism.

The specification defines the following restrictions for this profile:

✓ The ultimate headset is the only usage model active between two devices.

✓ This profile mandates the use of Continuously Variable Slope Delta (CVSD) for audio transmission. CVSD is a voice coding method that enables transmissions even where high bit-error rates are present.

✓ Only one connection at a time is supported between the headset and the audio gateway.

✓ The audio gateway controls SCO link establishment and release, while the headset directly connects or disconnects the internal audio streams upon SCO link establishment or release.

✓ The profile offers only basic interoperability, which means it does not support multiple-call handling.

✓ The profile assumes that the headset's user interface can detect user-initiated action such as pressing a button.

Dial-up networking profile

The dial-up networking profile defines protocols and procedures to be used by devices implementing the Internet Bridge usage model. Common examples of this model include devices such as modems and cell phones. Possible scenarios for this usage model include:

✓ A cell phone or modem used by a computer as a wireless means of connecting to a dial-up Internet access server

✓ A cell phone or modem used by a computer to receive data calls

Figure 13-4 shows examples of these usage models.

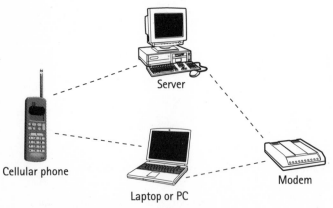

Figure 13-4: Dial-up networking usage models

The specification defines the following roles for this usage model:

✓ **Gateway (GW):** Device that provides access to the public network; typical gateways are cell phones and modems.

✓ **Data Terminal (DT):** Device that uses the dial-up services of the gateway; typically, laptop and desktop computers function as data terminals.

The specification defines the following restrictions for this profile:

✓ The modem does not require the capability to report or discriminate between different types of incoming calls.

✓ Support is provided for one-slot packets only, ensuring data rates of up to 128 Kbps. Support for higher rates is optional.

✓ The profile supports one call at a time.

✓ The profile supports only point-to-point configurations.

✓ The specification does not define how to discriminate between two SCO channels originating from the same device. Device manufacturers determine how to deal with this situation.

✓ Initialization must be performed before a cell phone or modem can be used with a PC or a laptop for the first time.

✓ The profile does not support multiple instances of its implementation in the same device.

The specification describes the following fundamental requirements for implementing this profile:

✓ Before the DT can use the GW services for the first time, initialization must take place between the devices. Initialization includes exchanging a PIN code, creating link keys, and performing service discovery.

✓ Before devices can initiate or receive calls, they must establish a link. The DT always initiates this task, which requires paging a device.

✓ This profile has no fixed master or slave roles.

✓ The GW and the DT provide serial port emulation.

✓ An SCO link transports audio signals.

✓ Authentication and encryption are employed for security purposes, and the baseband and LMP are the mechanisms used to support it.

Fax profile

The fax profile defines the protocols and procedures used by devices implementing the fax portion of the usage model known as Data Access Points, Wide Area Networks. Devices that may be used as a wireless fax modem include cell phones and modems.

The Bluetooth specification defines the following roles for this profile:

- ✓ **Gateway (GW):** The device, such as a cell phone or modem, that provides the fax services.

- ✓ **Data Terminal (DT):** The device that uses the fax services of the GW. Typically, laptop and desktop computers serve as data terminals.

The fax profile specification defines the following restrictions:

- ✓ GW does not require the capability of reporting or discriminating between different incoming call types.

- ✓ This profile requires support for one-slot packets only, ensuring data rates up to 128 Kbps. Higher rate support is optional.

- ✓ One call is supported at a time.

- ✓ Only point-to-point configurations are supported.

- ✓ The profile does not specify how to discriminate between two SCO channels originating from the same device. Device manufacturers determine how to handle these situations.

- ✓ The profile doesn't support multiple instances of its implementation in the same device.

The following procedure takes place when a DT wants to use a GW's fax services:

1. To obtain the Bluetooth address of the GW, the DT uses device discovery.

2. The devices must establish a secure connection using authentication and encryption.

3. The DT initiates link establishment. (The profile has no fixed master or slave roles.)

4. The fax call is established.

5. The GW and the DT provide serial port emulation.

6. An optional SCO link can be used to transport fax audio feedback.

7. The channel and link are released after the fax call is cleared.

LAN profile

The LAN profile defines how to access LAN services using point-to-point protocol (PPP) over RFCOMM. The PPP over RFCOMM method was chosen for providing LAN access to Bluetooth devices because of the number of devices equipped with PPP software. Although PPP can support various network protocols, such as IP and IPX, the profile doesn't mandate the use of any particular one.

The profile defines how PPP networking is supported for the following scenarios:

✓ LAN access for a single Bluetooth device

✓ LAN access for multiple devices

✓ PC-to-PC communication

The specification defines the following roles:

✓ **LAN Access Point (LAP):** The device that provides access to the LAN — for example, Ethernet, cable modem, or USB. LAP provides services of a PPP server. PPP connection is over RFCOMM, and RFCOMM transports the PPP packets. LAP also can be used for flow control of the PPP data stream.

✓ **Data Terminal (DT):** The device that uses the services of the LAP — typically, laptop and desktop PCs and PDAs. The DT is a PPP client and forms a PPP connection with a LAP to gain LAN access.

The profile describes the following usage scenarios and requirements:

✓ As shown in Figure 13-5, a single DT can use a LAP as a wireless connection to a LAN. Once connected, the DT operates as if it were connected via dial-up networking. In this way, the DT can access all services provided by the LAN.

✓ Multiple DTs can use a LAP as a wireless connection to a LAN, as shown in Figure 13-6. After connection, DTs operate as if they were using dial-up networking. DTs can then access all LAN services and communicate with each other via the LAP.

✓ PC-to-PC connections involve two Bluetooth devices forming a single connection with each other, as shown in Figure 13-7. In this scenario, one of the devices takes on the role of a LAP, and the other assumes a DT role.

LAN ——— LAN Access Point · · · · · · · Data Terminal

Figure 13-5: Single DT

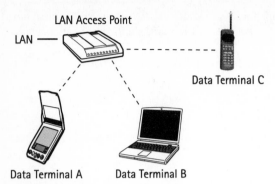

Figure 13-6: Multiple DTs

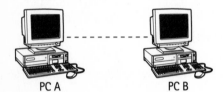

Figure 13-7: PC-to-PC communication

The following procedure takes place when establishing LAN access between a DT and an LAP:

1. The DT must discover an LAP that is available, in range, and capable of providing PPP, RFCOMM, and L2CAP services. For example, the DT user may use an application to find and select a suitable LAP.

2. The DT requests a baseband physical link with the selected LAP. After the physical link is established, the devices perform mutual authentication, and each device uses encryption.

3. The devices establish a PPP/RFCOMM/L2CAP connection.

4. An IP address is negotiated between the LAP and the DT, and then traffic can flow across the PPP connection.

5. The DT or the LAP can terminate the PPP connection at any time.

File transfer profile

The file transfer profile defines the protocols and procedures used by applications implementing the file transfer usage model. Typically, devices using file transfer are PCs, notebooks, and PDAs. The file transfer profile describes the following scenarios:

✓ Using a Bluetooth device to browse the file system of another Bluetooth device

✓ Transferring objects such as files and folders between two Bluetooth devices

✓ Using a Bluetooth device to manipulate objects on another Bluetooth device — for example, deleting objects or creating new folders

The profile defines the following roles:

✓ **Client:** The device that initiates the operation. It pushes and pulls objects to and from the server.

✓ **Server:** The device that provides the object exchange server and folder browsing capability.

The file transfer profile describes the following scenarios:

✓ If file browsing is supported, the client can browse the file system of the server device. Servers should have a root folder that is not the root directory of the file system, but a designated public folder for browsing.

✓ The client can transfer files and folders to and from the server. Servers are allowed to have read-only folders, so they can restrict object pushes.

✓ The client may create and delete folders and files on the server, although the profile does not require that the client support these capabilities. Servers can support read-only folders and files so they can restrict folder and file creation and deletion by the client.

✓ Devices adhering to this profile must support client or server capability or both.

This profile requires the following capabilities:

✓ Link-level authentication and encryption support are required, but their use is optional.

✓ OBEX support for authentication is required, but use is optional.

✓ Neither server nor client are required to enter any discoverable or connectable modes automatically, although they may have that capability.

✓ Initiating file transfer typically requires end-user intervention on the client side.

✓ Support for bonding is required, but use is optional.

Object push profile

The object push profile (OPP) defines the protocols and procedures used by applications implementing the OBEX usage model known as *object push*. Typically, the devices used for this model are notebook PCs, PDAs, and mobile phones. As shown in Figure 13-8, the following scenarios are indicated for this usage model:

✓ Using a Push Client, such as a mobile phone, to push an object, like a business card or appointment, to a Push Server

✓ Using a Push Client to pull an object from a Push Server

✓ Using a Push Client to exchange objects with a Push Server

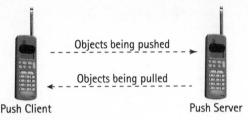

Objects being pushed →

← Objects being pulled

Push Client   Push Server

Figure 13-8: OBEX usage model

All three functions are activated by the user and not performed without user interaction. When the user elects to initiate one of these functions, the user must first perform an inquiry to obtain a list of available devices in range. Then, the desired function can be performed.

The profile defines the following roles:

✓ **Push server:** The device that provides an object exchange server.

✓ **Push client:** The device that pushes and pulls objects to and from the push server.

Restrictions applying to this profile are the same as those defined in the GOEP. The following profile fundamentals are required:

✓ Support for link-level authentication and encryption is mandatory, but use is optional.

✓ Support for bonding is mandatory; use is optional.

✓ OBEX authentication is not used.

✓ Neither server nor client are required to enter any discoverable or connectable modes automatically, although they may be capable of doing so. End-user interaction is always required to initiate the object push.

Synchronization profile

The synchronization profile defines the protocols and procedures used by applications implementing the synchronization usage model. Typically, the devices using these models include notebook PCs, PDAs, and mobile phones. As illustrated in Figure 13-9, the following scenarios are indicated for this usage model:

✓ Use of a mobile phone or PDA by a computer to exchange Personal Information Management (PIM) data, including phonebook and calendar items.

✓ Use of a computer by a mobile phone or PDA to initiate exchange of PIM data.

✓ Use of a mobile phone or PDA by a computer to start synchronization automatically when a mobile phone or PDA enters RF range.

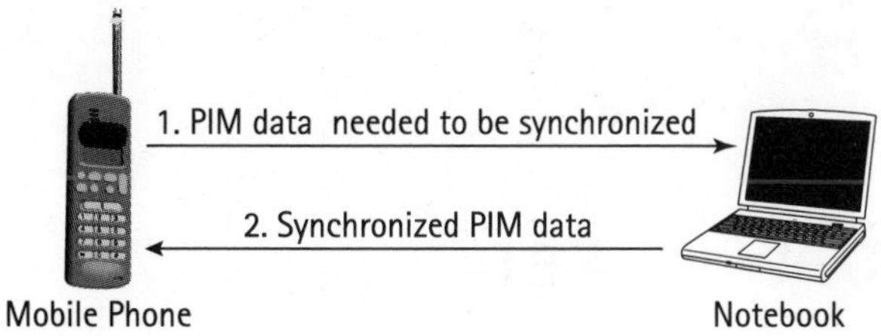

Figure 13-9: Synchronization usage model

The synchronization profile defines the following Infrared Mobile Communications (IrMC) roles:

✓ **IrMC Server:** The device that provides an object exchange server; typically, a mobile phone or PDA.

✓ **IrMC Client:** The device that contains a sync engine and pulls and pushes PIM data from and to the IrMC server.

Functionality requirements include the following:

✓ Bonding, link-level authentication, and encryption must always be used.

✓ Because both the IrMC client and server can act as a client, both can initiate link and channel establishment.

✓ Neither IrMC client nor server are required to enter any discoverable or connectable modes automatically, although they may be capable of doing so. End-user action is required to initiate synchronization.

The IrMC specification describes the requirements for IrMC synchronization. Support of synchronization with IrMC level-four functionality is mandatory for both clients and servers. The Bluetooth synchronization function is required to support one of the following:

✓ Synchronization of phonebooks

✓ Synchronization of calendars

✓ Synchronization of messages

✓ Synchronization of notes

Content formats are defined for Bluetooth synchronization in order to ensure application-level interoperability. The content format requirements vary depending upon application class:

✓ Phonebook applications must support data exchange using vCard 2.1.

✓ Calendar applications must support data exchange using vCalendar 1.0.

✓ Messaging applications must support data exchange using vMessage.

✓ Notes applications must support data exchange using vNote.

Mobility in the Global Market

The SIG hopes that the wireless connectivity solutions promised by the Bluetooth technology will change the shape of mobile communications, mobile networking, and mobile e-commerce. The Bluetooth SIG intends to evolve the technology to provide greater bandwidth and distances and increase the potential platforms and applications used in the emerging global marketplace.

Mobile communications

The communications platforms that are projected for the future combine various technologies and features in a single device. For example, one device could enable mobile Internet browsing, messaging, imaging, location-based applications and services, mobile telephony, and so on. Using such integrated mobile devices will allow full mobile Internet and multimedia access, including voice, data, and images.

Ericcson plans to offer an integrated communicator platform that supports high-speed data transmission, triple-band voice, and Internet access. The platform incorporates a built-in GPS receiver for positioning information, as well as Bluetooth and infrared components for wireless connections with other devices and networks. The device has a color touch screen, enabling easy navigation, pen input, and handwriting recognition.

Mobile networking

Bluetooth and IEEE share the common goal of creating a global standard for wireless personal area networks (PANs) that will provide the foundation for a broad range of interoperable consumer devices. The IEEE 802.15 wireless PAN in conjunction with the Bluetooth technology intend to provide mobile users with global networking solutions, ad hoc networking capability, wireless connectivity for voice and data, and coexistence with other wireless technologies.

M-commerce

Bluetooth is set to play a key role in electronic commerce. The Bluetooth specification adds a new dimension to e-commerce that has the potential to change how portable and wireless devices are used.

For example, mobile phones and Palmtops may be used to access the Internet and pay for goods and services anywhere. Bluetooth components will enable mobile phones with smart cards to be read without having to remove the smart card from the device.

Another payment solution envisioned for wireless mobile e-commerce is Ericsson's wireless wallet. The wireless wallet would serve as a replacement for a conventional wallet, and instead of containing currency, it would contain multiple smart card readers. The smart card inserted into the wallet could communicate with a Bluetooth-enabled mobile device such as a cell phone. When shopping on the Internet with the mobile phone, the appropriate smart card in the wallet would be accessed and used for payment.

Using Bluetooth technology in ways similar to these examples, the retail, banking, and financial industries will be able to generate increased revenues via mobile e-commerce. New business opportunities will open up to companies of all types and sizes, and they'll be able to realize the market potential of mobile e-commerce.

Summary

In an effort to guarantee the success of Bluetooth products, the Bluetooth SIG has created a variety of working groups, each charged with defining specific usage models and application scenarios in certain technology areas. To this end:

✓ The Bluetooth SIG has identified various usage models intended for the Bluetooth environment.

✓ Each usage model is supported by a specific profile.

✓ The profiles define the protocols and features for the designated usage model, ensuring that the same feature works the same way for similar products regardless of manufacturer.

✓ The working groups oversee the continued development of the profiles and usage models in order to promote the goals of the SIG.

✓ These goals include product interoperability on a global scale, wireless networking for mobile users, and low cost for the end user.

Now that you have some idea of the profiles and usage models in which Bluetooth products can be developed, take a look at Chapter 14 for a review of the steps used to create a Bluetooth product.

Chapter 14

Creating a Bluetooth Device

In This Chapter

Developing an official Bluetooth product, whether hardware or software, is not something that any company can do on a whim. Ericsson, the original Bluetooth developer, has assigned to the Bluetooth SIG both the Bluetooth trademark and the authority to grant a license for the use of the trademark. In order to control which products, software, and services carry the Bluetooth logo and trademark, the SIG has developed a rigorous procedure that any company wanting to make a Bluetooth product must follow. To help you understand that procedure and the requirements a new Bluetooth product must meet, this chapter covers the following topics:

✓ Reviewing the qualification process and its relationship to Bluetooth specifications

✓ Understanding the process for developing Bluetooth systems: hardware and software

✓ Completing product qualification and testing

✓ Testing radio and lower-layer protocols

✓ Validating test results

The Bluetooth Qualification Process

The Bluetooth SIG has implemented a testing and qualification process that all products must undergo in order to become licensed as official Bluetooth products. After a product passes the qualification process, the SIG grants a license to use the Bluetooth technology, brand, and logo at no charge. In addition, the qualified product (and its producer) is listed on the official Bluetooth Web site (www.bluetooth.com) as an official and licensed product.

This prescribed qualification process (see "Bluetooth Qualification and Testing," later in the chapter) helps ensure that all products and applications comply with the Bluetooth specifications. The Bluetooth SIG's qualification process requires filing product documents and manufacturer declarations as well as the results of the required product testing performed by the manufacturer and an official Bluetooth Qualification Test Facility (BQTF).

All proposed Bluetooth products must go through the qualification process, but the qualification requirements may differ depending on the type of product. For example, much of the testing process is waived for products developed specifically as development tools or demonstration kits. In some cases, qualification is as simple as filing a declaration of conformance. Also, end products that integrate a prequalified Bluetooth component may be exempt from testing, depending on the areas covered by the integrated component's qualifications.

Adherence to the Bluetooth specification

The Bluetooth specification is divided into two parts: Volume 1, Core, and Volume 2, Profiles. The Core specification deals with the standards that govern the operation of the Bluetooth technology. The Profiles specifications prescribe the use of the Bluetooth technology in a variety of intended applications.

The Core section of the Bluetooth specification details the Bluetooth technology, including information about the following elements:

✓ Protocol stack

✓ Bluetooth radio

✓ Link manager

✓ Transport layer

✓ Interoperability between communications protocols

✓ Testing and compliance

The Core section is the most technical part of the Bluetooth specification. It specifies the components and protocols for Bluetooth hardware and software (firmware).

Volume 2 of the Bluetooth specification includes usage models (profiles) for specific types of Bluetooth applications. These profiles detail the technology and procedures that are required to implement the various applications.

Together, the Bluetooth specifications and the Bluetooth Qualification Program (BQP) are intended to ensure interoperability of Bluetooth products, regardless of manufacturer. The specifications describe in detail the hardware and software requirements for Bluetooth products and applications. The BQP describes the rules with which new products and applications must comply in order to use the Bluetooth name.

Developing Bluetooth systems

Essentially, a Bluetooth system comprises a radio unit, a baseband link controller, and link management software. However, a Bluetooth system also includes an antenna, a microcontroller (MCU, or microcontroller unit), a host controller interface (HCI), and higher-level software that handles interoperability and functionality. Each component and its operations must meet the Bluetooth Core specifications.

Alternatively, however, developers can implement proprietary or licensed systems that integrate two or more of these components as a single entity. For example, the HCI can be included on the MCU, and the HCI driver and L2CAP can be placed on a machine (such as a PC) that hosts the Bluetooth chip set. Regardless, the product must include all the required elements. The manufacturer determines exactly how to meet the requirements.

MEETING THE HARDWARE SPECIFICATIONS

When designing a Bluetooth processor, the developer must keep several key issues in mind. Because the baseband has rigorous timing requirements, the processor must provide for minimal power consumption and cost-effectiveness. The developer also must decide whether to use dedicated link controller hardware or whether to implement link control in the MCU.

Under the Bluetooth specification, the MCU must provide three basic features:

✓ **Little Endian operation:** This data-formatting operation orders the bits within a byte of data. Within a 16-bit or 32-bit computer word, the bytes at the lower addresses are assigned lower significance and the data is stored or transferred using a "little-end first" approach.

✓ **Multibyte vectors (32-bit device preferable):** The MCU should support instruction code that is multiple bytes in length — either 16 bits or 32 bits. This feature is especially needed if security features are included.

✓ **Dense object code:** Because of program space and timing considerations, the instruction set of the MCU should be compact, yet powerful.

The Bluetooth radio unit implements a frequency-hopping spread spectrum (FHSS). Using FHSS, signals can jump quickly from one frequency to another and thus reduce interference and increase security. However, using FHSS places some timing constraints on the baseband.

The baseband-layer processing must be assigned one-half of a Bluetooth timing slot because some access procedures produce two packets per slot, and FHSS inquiry response packets may start at a half-slot boundary. Also because of timing issues, link control functionality must be implemented as a finite state machine running in interrupt mode, and link control code must be synchronized with slot boundaries.

Because of rigid timing constraints, developers may want to replace some of the Bluetooth firmware with dedicated hardware. For example, developers may prefer this design for time-consuming and time-critical procedures such as error correction, cyclical redundancy checks, and testing the bit sequence. If these procedures are implemented in the hardware, packet type and current field can be traced during transmission to decide which transformations should be enabled or disabled. By implementing these functions in hardware rather than the MCU, you speed up firmware execution.

Reduced power consumption is another reason to implement some baseband functions in the hardware. Because most Bluetooth-enabled devices will be battery operated, power consumption is an important issue. By implementing some baseband functions in the hardware, you can slow the MCU clock and thus reduce power consumption.

MEETING FIRMWARE SPECIFICATIONS

Developers must carefully design the HCI, link manager, and link controller layers and possibly develop them in parallel, to integrate data structures and avoid data and code redundancy. The HCI packet structures must contain information that relates to the transport layer above HCI.

This transport layer runs on top of the physical link between a Bluetooth device and the host device. Because HCI commands don't require the same amount of processing, nor do they remain in the system memory for the same amount of time, developers must carefully construct the data flow structure.

In terms of the L2CAP layer, developers need to decide whether to embed L2CAP with the rest of the layers or run it as part of the host operating system. This decision depends on the usage model and the type of device. For example, a cell phone needs to maintain L2CAP in embedded nonvolatile memory.

Developers must address two problems if L2CAP is built on the host. First, they must integrate this layer into the host's operating system to ensure that protocol multiplexing can take place with minimal alteration to the host's driver stack. Second, they face the problem of creating an interface between the lower part of the L2CAP and a host-side HCI or other proprietary driver. The first design could cause the stack to run slower, and the second will need more programming to achieve interoperability requirements.

Bluetooth Qualification and Testing

To bring a Bluetooth product to market, a manufacturer must fulfill two requirements:

✓ The manufacturer must be a member of the SIG.

✓ The manufacturer must participate in the Bluetooth Qualification Process (BQP) and show that the product complies with Bluetooth specifications.

Membership in the SIG at the adopter level is free. As a member of the SIG, the company becomes a partner to the licensing agreement, which gives the member the right to develop and manufacture products and software using the Bluetooth specification at no charge.

The Bluetooth qualification requirements are independent of and in addition to any regulatory requirements defined by various national or international regulations, such as the regulations of the Federal Communications Commission (FCC) in the United States.

By understanding the requirements necessary for the type of Bluetooth product they plan to develop, manufacturers may avoid delays in the qualification process. A manufacturer needs to perform the following tasks to facilitate qualification of a product:

1. Read the Bluetooth Qualification Program Reference Document (PRD), which is the primary reference document for Bluetooth qualification.

2. Use qualified Bluetooth components in your product.

3. Involve the Bluetooth Qualification Body (BQB), which will assign a Bluetooth Qualification Administrator (BQA), well before product launch so you can resolve any issues early in the process, and to schedule interoperability testing, ensure conformance testing is complete, and file necessary documentation. The BQA tracks all required documents and maintains the Qualified Products List (QPL) database.

   The Bluetooth Qualification Test Facility (BQTF) may perform the testing, or the product manufacturer may do so. The Bluetooth Technical Advisory Board (BTAB) is a resource for discussing problems related to testing and qualification and for exchanging information.

4. When the product is ready for testing, complete the Bluetooth Implementation Conformance Statement (ICS), which describes the Bluetooth functionality built into the product. Also, complete the Profile ICS and Implementation eXtra Information for Testing (IXIT) documents.

Figure 14-1 shows the qualification process and the Bluetooth SIG organizations involved in this process.

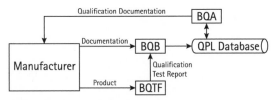

Figure 14-1: The qualification and testing process used for a new Bluetooth product

Test structure for Bluetooth products or applications

The Bluetooth qualification process requires product testing by both the manufacturer and a BQTF. The BQTF issues the test reports to be reviewed by the BQB. Any hardware or software modifications must be documented and reviewed by the BQB that issues the certificate qualifying the product.

Testing for a new Bluetooth product is conducted on two levels:

✓ **Conformance testing:** Requires testing against a reference test system.

✓ **Interoperability testing:** Requires functional testing performed against another operational Bluetooth product.

The test specifications designate certain areas for conformance and interoperability testing. Testing applies to the following areas of any Bluetooth product seeking qualification:

✓ Radio link quality

✓ Lower-layer protocols

✓ Profiles

Any information (documentation, user manual, and so on) that will be included with the product and intended for the product's end users also must meet Bluetooth requirements for end-user documentation.

TEST DOCUMENTATION

The Bluetooth Qualification Program Reference Document (BQPRD) covers the policies that govern how the test requirements are to be satisfied. Conformance and interoperability test requirements are included in the Test Case Reference List (TCRL).

The Bluetooth product requirements contained in these documents continue to be further defined as testing is performed on more mature products and as a result of the maturation of the measurement and test equipment.

TESTING CATEGORIES

The TCRL describes four test categories (A @nd D) that qualify a product at different levels. Before a product can be released for commercial sales, it must complete the Category A testing. However, during a product's development, testing may only be done as far up as Category B or lower. Table 14-1 lists the testing categories.

Table 14-1 Test Case Reference List (TCRL) Categories

Category	Type of Testing
A	Must be tested by a BQTF on validated and commercially available qualification test equipment.
B	Bluetooth products can be tested by member or BQTF using standard test equipment, and any testing results must be supported with evidence.
C	Bluetooth products can be tested by member or BQTF using standard test equipment, but test results do not require supporting evidence.
D	Preliminary test case; no official qualification value. Purpose is to inform manufacturer of upcoming test case.

As the testing procedures in each category grow, new tests will be announced three to six months before becoming mandatory. The Bluetooth SIG publishes new testing requirements on its Web site (www.bluetooth.org). A manufacturer can perform its own testing for categories B and C (and D, of course), but a manufacturer can only perform Category A testing if it is an approved Bluetooth Qualification Test Facility (BQTF).

The "Official Bluetooth Website" at www.Bluetooth.com is intended for the general public, whereas www.Bluetooth.org is for the use of the Bluetooth SIG's membership.

The Bluetooth Unit Test specification details the interoperability tests performed for the base-band and link manager layers of the Bluetooth protocol stack. Conformance testing of the radio (link quality) and lower-layer protocols is described briefly in the next section.

Testing the radio and lower-layer protocols

The Bluetooth RF Test Suite Structure defines the tests that are to be performed for certification of the Bluetooth radio layer. Tables 14-2, 14-3, and 14-4 list the specific areas to be tested and the structure of the testing within each function area.

Table 14-2 Bluetooth Radio Frequency Transmitter Testing Requirements

RF Test Area	Test Type
Output power	Transmitter test, capability test, conformance test
Power density	Transmitter test, capability test, conformance test
TX output spectrum — frequency range	Transmitter test, capability test, conformance test
TX output spectrum — 20 dB bandwidth	Transmitter test, capability test, conformance test
TX output spectrum — adjacent channel power	Transmitter test, capability test, conformance test
Modulation characteristics	Transmitter test, capability test, conformance test
Initial carrier frequency tolerance	Transmitter test, capability test, conformance test
Carrier frequency drift	Transmitter test, capability test, conformance test

Table 14-3 Bluetooth Radio Frequency Transceiver Testing Requirements

RF Test Area	Test Type
Out-of-band spurious emission	Transceiver test, capability test, conformance test

Table 14-4 Bluetooth Radio Frequency Receiver Testing Requirements

RF Test Area	Test Type
Sensitivity — single-slot packets	Receiver test, capability test, conformance test
Sensitivity — multislot packets	Receiver test, capability test, conformance test
C/I (Carrier-to-Interference) performance	Receiver test, capability test, conformance test
Blocking performance	Receiver test, capability test, conformance test
Intermodulation performance	Receiver test, capability test, conformance test
Maximum input level	Receiver test, capability test, conformance test

TRANSMITTER TESTING

As indicated in Table 14-2, various transmitter tests are used on Bluetooth components and systems to ensure that they meet the specification requirements. Three different types of payload data are required in each test case. Each pattern provides different stress mechanisms and is chosen for each bandwidth measurement. Use of different patterns also helps identify any problems with modulation schemes.

Frequency hopping is generally turned off for many tests in order to reduce the number of test variables and to identify individual performance characteristics. However, transmission and reception channels can be set at extreme ends of the band in order to force switching frequency. The requirements of the test determine the method used. (Test requirements are documented in the RF Test Specification.)

TEST MODES   A Bluetooth device can operate in the following modes:

✓ **Normal mode:** This test mode measures the RF performance in a standard Bluetooth communication, in which the tester acts as a master, the device acts as a slave, and Poll packets are sent between the two.

✓ **Transmitter (TX) mode:** This test mode verifies that the Bluetooth device is operating in a specific state. In this test mode, the device is required to transmit a packet according to the tester's specific instructions.

✓ **Loopback test:** This test mode requires the Bluetooth device to decode packets sent by the tester and then send back the payload using the same packet type.

SETUP   Depending on the type of device being tested, one of the following transmitter test setups can be used:

✓ Setup to test performance of a fully functional Bluetooth device

✓ Setup to test performance of a complete Bluetooth transmitter

✓ Setup to test performance of RF components of a Bluetooth transmitter

POWER TESTS   Power measurements include output power, power density, and power control. Power is a critical parameter in digital communication, and these tests ensure that levels are high enough to maintain links but low enough to minimize interference and prolong battery life.

TRANSMITTER OUTPUT SPECTRUM TESTS   The transmitter output spectrum measurements are intended to analyze the power levels in the frequency domain in order to ensure that out-of-channel emissions are minimal. This helps reduce system interference as well as ensure regulatory compliance of the Bluetooth device.

MODULATION TESTS   Modulation measurements reflect the performance of modulation circuitry and the stability of the local oscillator. Verifying modulation requires that a device have the ability to demodulate a signal so that frequency of each bit can be determined.

TIMING TESTS   Although not required in the Bluetooth specification, timing tests can be performed on Bluetooth signals. Testing may include analysis of the burst profile, phase lock loop, settling time, and all other timing characteristics.

TRANSCEIVER TESTING

Testing transceivers, as indicated in Table 14-3, consists of performing some out-of-band spurious emissions tests. These tests verify that the Bluetooth radio will operate within regulatory requirements. Separate standards are required for the U.S. and Europe. The U.S. follows the Federal Communications Commission (FCC) standard, while Europe follows the European Telecommunications Standards Institute (ETSI) standard.

RECEIVER TESTING

Various receiver tests, as listed in Table 14-4, are required to ensure the integrity of the Bluetooth receiver's performance. The Bluetooth specification requires the following measurements:

✓ Sensitivity — single-slot packets

✓ Sensitivity — multislot packets

✓ Carrier-to-interference (C/I) performance

✓ Blocking performance

✓ Intermodulation performance

✓ Maximum input level

Bit error rate (BER) is the criterion used in evaluating receiver performance. It is determined by comparing transmitted and received payload data and then noting the differences in bits.

Different setups can be used to perform BER measurements. The measurement can be performed using a Bluetooth standalone tester or a test system. When performed with a standalone tester, a link is established, the tester sends a packet, the device returns the packet, and the tester then performs the BER measurement. The RF test specifications require analyzing a minimum of 1,600,000 bits when performing the receiver measurement.

Using a basic test system to perform the BER measurement consists of using a signal generator with BER analysis capability and a signal analyzer with FM demodulation capability. For this type of setup, a special internal Test Facilities utility is implemented in the device. This utility asks the device to retransmit packets it receives. After the signal is demodulated and resent to the signal generator, the BER measurement is performed.

In each of these measurement setups, the Bluetooth device must be able to retransmit recovered data from a received signal.

SENSITIVITY — SINGLE-SLOT PACKET TEST   Bluetooth receiver sensitivity measures the minimum signal level that is required by the receiver to produce the maximum BER allowed. In order to meet Bluetooth specification requirements, the BER must not exceed 0.1 percent.

SENSITIVITY — MULTISLOT PACKET TEST   The multislot packet test is similar to the single-slot sensitivity measurement, with the main difference being that multislot packet sensitivity uses impaired DH3 or DH5 packets rather than impaired DH1 packets.

CARRIER-TO-INTERFERENCE (C/I) PERFORMANCE TEST   The C/I test requires sending co-channel or adjacent channel signals in parallel with the desired signal and then measuring the receiver's BER. The test is performed at the lowest, middle, and highest operating frequencies with the interfering signals at all operating frequencies in the band. The BER must be no more than 0.1 percent.

BLOCKING PERFORMANCE TEST   The BER measurement is taken after sending a continuous wave (CW) interfering signal with the desired signal. The desired signal is transmitted at 3 dB over the reference sensitivity level, while the interfering signal ranges from 30 MHz to 12.75 GHz in

1-MHz increments. The Bluetooth RF Test Specification defines different power levels for the interfering signal. The BER measurement must be no more than 0.1 percent to validate the receiver's performance when a blocking signal is present.

INTERMODULATION PERFORMANCE TEST The intermodulation performance test measures unwanted frequency components that result from the interaction of two or more signals passing through a nonlinear device. BER greater than 0.1 percent indicates a problem in receiver performance.

MAXIMUM INPUT LEVEL TEST   The maximum input level test measures the receiver's BER performance when the input signal is at a maximum power level, which is specified at –20 dBm. This test is performed at the lowest, middle, and highest operating frequencies.

POWER SUPPLY MEASUREMENTS

The Bluetooth specification requires testing power source voltages that are extreme for some Bluetooth devices. Measuring power versus time and monitoring the frequency error measurements are good ways to discover power-related problems.

PROFILE CONFORMANCE AND INTEROPERABILITY

All manufacturers trying to qualify products must perform conformance testing for the lower layers of the protocol stack (described in the previous section), and for the Generic Access Profile (GAP) and Service Discovery Protocol (SDP). Interoperability testing is performed for all remaining profiles:

- ✓ Radio frequency (link quality)
- ✓ Protocol conformance (lower-layer protocols)
- ✓ Profile conformance
- ✓ Profile interoperability

See Chapter 13 for more information on the GAP and SDP.

AVAILABLE TEST TOOLS

Various Bluetooth testing tools are available for companies developing new Bluetooth products. Here are some of the currently available test tools:

- ✓ **Bluetooth Protocol Analyzer:** This product tests the protocols and bandwidth between Bluetooth devices. CATC (www.catc.com) and Tektronix (www.tektronix.com) have protocol analyzer products.

✓ **Bluetooth Application Tool Kit:** Software development tool includes Ericsson's Bluetooth module that connects to a PC for development and testing purposes. For more information, visit Ericsson's Web site at www.ericsson.com.

✓ **Bluetooth HCI Toolbox:** Software tool for testing the HCI module, available from and licensed by Ericsson.

✓ **Bluetooth Script Engine:** Software tool that verifies application porting, available from and licensed by Ericsson.

✓ **Bluetooth Log Analyzer:** Software tool that enables viewing the internal signaling of a Bluetooth application, available from and licensed by Ericsson.

Testing validation

Because the testing process required for Bluetooth qualification is open to various implementations from different test equipment manufacturers, validating the test system is an essential part of the qualification process. Validation of the testing system ensures that test results are comparable and reliable.

According to the Bluetooth specification, testing validation must be done on all conformance testing systems. The validation process determines whether the testing system provides

✓ Comparable results

✓ Reliable and traceable results

✓ Test system-independent results

✓ Conformance to Bluetooth core and test specifications

VALIDATION SPECIFICATIONS

The criteria for the validation of a conformance test system differ for radio frequency, protocol, and profile characteristics, and the validation specification must detail each set of criteria.

The test system validation specification is an implementation-specific description of the validation activities of a particular product. This specification covers in detail all aspects of the validation guideline and how it has been applied to the test system. The test system validation report summarizes the results of the validation process when it's finalized and must include the following information:

✓ Date of validation

✓ Identification of the test system (hardware, software)

✓ Reference identification to the Bluetooth implementation samples

✓ Who performed the validation

✓ Validation specification used

✓ Detailed results of validation activities

According to the guidelines, the test system validation process is divided into RF test system validation and protocol test system validation, each of which is further divided into these parts:

✓ **Test platform validation:** The hardware and software that provide the capabilities for performing a series of test cases in accordance with the Bluetooth core requirements.

✓ **Test case implementation:** The software that provides the capabilities for the test platform to perform test cases as prescribed in the test specifications.

VALIDATION DOCUMENTATION

In order to validate the testing on a potential Bluetooth product, specific types of documentation and equipment are required and must be furnished to the Bluetooth test and interoperability (BTI) working group. Table 14-5 lists these requirements.

Table 14-5 Bluetooth Test Validation Documentation

Validation Requirement	Description
Test system conformance statement	Official document delivered by test equipment manufacturer.
	Indicates the capabilities of the test system.
	Contains information about the scope of test cases that are to be performed on the test system.
	Indicates which Bluetooth capabilities were implemented, which versions of the Bluetooth test specifications were used, and the limitations and deviations of the test systems with respect to the Bluetooth test and core specs.
Test platform documentation	Verifies whether the specified capabilities match the specifications.
	Typically contains technical documentation.
	Indicates which versions of the Bluetooth core and test specs were used, including used errata.
	Describes the hardware and software.
	Describes configuration management (procedure and status).
	Includes user manuals.

Continued

Table 14-5 Bluetooth Test Validation Documentation *(Continued)*

Validation Requirement	Description
Test case documentation	Describes the software.
	Indicates which versions of the Bluetooth core and test specs were used, including used errata.
	Describes the configuration management (status).
	Describes measurement equipment used and configuration.
	Includes user manuals.
	Describes measurement uncertainty budgets.
Equipment for validation	Typically contains test platform, test case implementations, analysis and monitoring tools, and Bluetooth implementation samples.

When testing is completed on a potential Bluetooth product, the applicant must send the validation specification and the report for a particular test system to the BTI for review. After the BTI checks to see if all the requirements for Bluetooth validation are fulfilled, it sends a notice to the BQRB, which has the authority to announce new validated test systems.

Completing the qualification process

After all product testing is complete and verified by the validation process, the qualification process should be in the final stages. Completion of the qualification process requires the following steps:

1. BQB checks product declarations in the ICS and relevant supporting documentation (Profile ICS and IXIT documents).

2. BQB reviews test reports filed in the compliance folder.

3. BQB must approve the product.

4. Declaration of Compliance (DoC) must be completed and filed with the Bluetooth specifications by the BQB.

5. After passing the qualification process, products go to the Bluetooth Qualification Administrator (BQA) for official listing and certification.

Products

At the end of 2001, nearly 450 products had been qualified, including the following:

- ✓ Bluetooth-enabled mobile phones
- ✓ Wireless headsets
- ✓ PC cards for portable computers
- ✓ Bluetooth network access points
- ✓ Add-ons to enable handheld devices for Bluetooth capabilities

Summary

The Bluetooth SIG set up the qualification process to ensure that products comply with the Bluetooth specifications:

- ✓ The qualification process entails testing by the product's manufacturer and a BQTF.
- ✓ The test facility issues a report to the BQB, which reviews this and all hardware and software documentation about the product.
- ✓ If the documentation and testing are acceptable, the BQB issues a qualification certificate for the product.
- ✓ When a product successfully passes the qualification requirements, the Bluetooth brand mark can be used to let customers know the product is an approved product that is interoperable with other Bluetooth devices, regardless of manufacturer.

Part V looks at Bluetooth as a networking tool, and Chapter 15 details the network topologies used by Bluetooth piconets and scatternets.

Part V

Networking with Bluetooth

IN THIS PART

Bluetooth is, first and foremost, a cable-replacement technology. However, inherent in its specification is its ability to transparently create links and networks with both Bluetooth and non-Bluetooth devices. This part of the book looks at Bluetooth as a networking technology and explains how it establishes wireless personal networks, piconets, and scatternets, and how it connects to local and wide area networks. And because security plays such a large role in any network, this part of the book also assesses the strengths and limitations of Bluetooth networking.

Chapter 15

Bluetooth Network Topologies

In This Chapter

This chapter presents an overview of the networking topologies used to implement Bluetooth applications. Briefly, it examines how Bluetooth networks differ from conventional cellular networks, and how the differences both enhance and complicate communications.

Further, this chapter describes how Bluetooth networks are formed, the relationships among the Bluetooth units in a network, and how communication is maintained without the aid of base stations and terminals to promote interconnectivity. This chapter addresses the following objectives:

- ✓ Examining the Bluetooth networking environment
- ✓ Understanding mobile ad hoc networks (MANETs)
- ✓ Establishing a piconet
- ✓ Establishing a scatternet
- ✓ Understanding master-slave switching

The Bluetooth Networking Environment

Bluetooth radio technology is based on ad hoc peer network communications, which simply means that the network has a different *topology* (the location of the network nodes) each time a node connects to the network. Typically, ad hoc networks are mobile networks in which the nodes (police cars, radio-dispatched trucks, and so on) are constantly moving from one location to another. The mobile ad hoc network, or MANET, is the underlying model for the Bluetooth network model.

What is a MANET?

There is nothing new about ad hoc radio systems; the walkie-talkie system used by the military and police departments is an example of such a system. The Bluetooth difference, however, lies in the scope of the networking capability. Members of the Bluetooth SIG envision widespread commercial acceptance of the Bluetooth technology, with Bluetooth networks becoming ubiquitous.

With the anticipated proliferation of Bluetooth devices, numerous ad hoc networks would exist in the same area. However, unlike a radio dispatch network, a Bluetooth ad hoc network does not have a central controller that the units can rely on for interconnectivity. In other words, Bluetooth units share the same medium for communication in the same general location without mutual coordination. This differs from conventional cellular environments in which a wired infrastructure with terminals coordinates and maintains communications among mobile units.

A MANET is a wireless, multi-hop network that differs significantly from a wired network, a cellular network, and even a wireless local area network (LAN). A MANET has the following characteristics:

✓ **Autonomous mobile users:** Each mobile terminal serves as both a host and a router.

✓ **Decentralized structure:** The network control is spread among the mobile terminals, with each device acting as a link relay when needed.

✓ **Dynamic topology:** The connectivity of the mobile terminals varies with time, which requires the use of efficient routing protocols to maintain the multi-hop routing paths.

✓ **Radio communications interference:** One of the problems with radio communications channels is that the mobile terminals using them are subjected to noise, fade, and interference, not to mention less bandwidth than is available on a wired network.

In addition to the Bluetooth working groups that are diligently trying to take advantage of — or solve, as the case may be — these issues, the MANET working group of the Internet Engineering Task Force (IETF) is developing standards for mobile ad hoc networks that connect to the Internet.

Background on MANET

All Bluetooth developers hope that the next generation of wireless communication systems will provide for rapid increases in the number of independent mobile users, all using Bluetooth devices. However, mobile wireless networks very likely will be deployed in other areas, including emergency and rescue operations, disaster relief efforts, military networks, local police and fire departments, plumbers, and others. These networks are perfect applications for a MANET because ad hoc networks can do a better job addressing their changing needs, as well as those of the communities they serve, than the fixed-base mobile networks they now use.

Because the nodes on a MANET are mobile, the network's decentralized topology may and will change rapidly and unpredictably. The mobile devices themselves have the responsibility for discovering the topology and delivering messages directly, including such tasks as routing.

A MANET faces as many implementation issues as it has applications, which range from small, static networks constrained by power sources, such as a Bluetooth network, to large-scale, mobile, highly dynamic networks. The issues facing mobile wireless networks include the varying quality of wireless links, propagation path loss, signal fade, multi-user interference, power sources, and the dynamics of an ever-changing topology.

The Challenge of the Bluetooth Topology

Although all communications networks must address the following issues, they have different implications for Bluetooth developers because of the differences in the Bluetooth networking environment:

✓ Applied radio spectrum

✓ Interference

✓ Multiple access scheme

✓ Channel allocation

✓ Power consumption

✓ Service priority

✓ Available unit discovery

✓ Connection establishment

We discuss these issues in the following sections.

Applied radio spectrum

If Bluetooth communications are to be widely used by the public, the choice of radio spectrum becomes extremely important. It must be open to the public without the need for licensing. Also, it must be global in nature, because Bluetooth is set to capture the worldwide market of mobile business people. For these reasons, the unlicensed, globally available Industrial, Scientific, and Medical (ISM) band was selected as the most appropriate radio band for Bluetooth use.

Interference

Using an unlicensed, globally available radio band necessarily makes interference an issue. Developers must consider interference from external sources, as well as interference from other Bluetooth users. The Bluetooth technology addresses this problem by means of frequency avoidance. In frequency avoidance, a desired signal can be transmitted at points where interference is low or absent. The 2.45-GHz ISM band provides about 80 MHz of bandwidth. Because most radio systems are band-limited, a high degree of probability exists that Bluetooth devices can use a part of the spectrum in which no dominant interference exists.

Multiple access scheme

A primary design concern involves avoiding interference and the bands on which interference is expected. However, designers cannot easily predict where interference may occur in any specific market, so some scheme must be developed to facilitate interference avoidance.

The solution is to select a multiple access scheme. Perhaps the most viable option is frequency-hopping code-division multiple access (FH)-CDMA. It can deal with uncoordinated communications systems, and the signal can be spread over a large frequency range while occupying only a small bandwidth. Thus, it avoids a lot of potential interference in the ISM band. It further provides for a time division scheme for alternately transmitting and receiving signals. This scheme effectively prevents cross-communication in the radio transceivers. Also, multiple ad hoc links make use of different hopping channels with different hopping sequences to further accommodate multiple accesses.

Channel allocation

Bluetooth has been designed so multiple ad hoc networks can maintain communications in the same area at the same time. To do this, Bluetooth uses several independent channels, with each channel serving a limited number of participants. Each channel is associated with one specific network. No more than eight units can participate on this channel.

Power consumption

Because Bluetooth was conceived as a technology for mobile users, power consumption is an important consideration in Bluetooth networks. Special attention has been paid to current consumption. In idle modes, a unit's scanning duty cycle is well under 1 percent. Different modes require different duty cycles, so the percentage can go down even farther. In the connection state, current consumption is also minimized. If no useful information needs to be exchanged, transmission does not take place.

Service priority

Bluetooth supports two types of traffic: synchronous and asynchronous. The synchronous — or voice — traffic has priority over asynchronous — or data — traffic. Synchronous connection-oriented (SCO) and asynchronous connectionless (ACL) links, respectively, support the different transmissions.

Unit discovery

The Bluetooth technology handles the discovery of units within range and available for connection via inquiry procedures. This method requires that the radio units in different devices wake periodically to listen for inquiry signals. A unit must be within the 10-meter range to receive the signal.

Connection establishment

Bluetooth implements page and page scan procedures to establish connections between available units. After a unit responds to an inquiry signal, the page procedure comes into play. The unit initiating the connection enters page mode and sends signals that can only be received by a unit in page scan mode. In page scan mode, a unit wakes up periodically to scan for incoming pages. When the paging unit receives a response, it can establish a connection with the responding unit.

Establishing a Network

Any two devices that come within range of each other can establish an ad hoc connection. In Bluetooth communications, one unit initiates contact with another unit. The initiating unit is said to be the *master* unit. The responding unit is said to be the *slave*. Any unit can be a master or a slave in any given connection. Remember, the ad hoc capability provides for peer-to-peer communications in the Bluetooth environment. Therefore, the master and slave designations only indicate which unit initiates the connections. A unit can be a master in one network and a slave in another.

The Bluetooth networks are referred to as *piconets*. This word is derived from *pico*, which means very small (actually one-trillionth, which certainly infers small), and *network*. Figure 15-1 shows a very simple example of a piconet in which a computer has built a very small network with its keyboard and printer.

Figure 15-1: A basic Bluetooth piconet

In each piconet, one Bluetooth device serves as the master unit. In other words, this unit initiates the connections with the other units in the piconet, which are the master's slaves. Any given piconet can have as many as seven active slaves, but only one master unit. The master unit controls all traffic on the channel — with all transmissions between units flowing through the master.

A Bluetooth unit can participate in more than one piconet at a time. If multiple piconets cover the same area, a Bluetooth unit can participate in two or more of the piconets. When a unit participates in multiple piconets, the unit serves as a communication bridge, enabling the piconets to form a larger network. A set of piconets interconnected by such a bridge is known as a *scatternet*.

Overlapping communications among piconets enable the formation of scatternets, as shown in Figure 15-2.

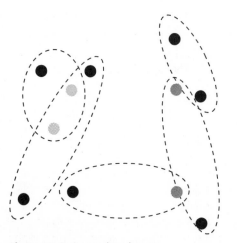

Figure 15-2: Connecting piconets

One of the strengths of the Bluetooth network environment is that it focuses on low power consumption. For example, before a connection is made with another device, a Bluetooth unit is in standby mode. In this low-power mode, the device wakes up intermittently (every 1.28 seconds) to listen for transmissions.

The devices that share a piconet can implement three other power-saving modes. Although you can have only seven active slaves on any given piconet channel, you can have many more slaves on the channel if they are in one of these three power-saving modes:

✓ Hold

✓ Sniff

✓ Park

Hold, sniff, and park modes can only apply to ACL links — not SCO links — because SCO links transmit time-bound data, which is a priority transmission. If the unit temporarily withdraws from communication in a piconet, it can no longer guarantee the priority necessary for an SCO link.

See Chapter 5 for more information on the Bluetooth ACL and SCO links.

Hold

In hold mode, only a device's internal timer is running in order to remain synchronized to the master. The unit does not transmit any data. This mode can be used when connecting units in several piconets. When a unit moves out of hold mode into active mode, data transmissions restart right away.

Sniff

In sniff mode, a device participates in network traffic at a reduced rate. It listens for message and packet transmissions, but only at "sniff intervals." This lowers the device's duty cycle, so it saves power.

Park

The main difference between sniff and park mode is that a device in sniff mode keeps its active member address (AM_ADDR). A device entering park mode gives up its AM_ADDR.

Park mode offers some advantages over sniff mode. Park mode has an even lower duty cycle, which means even less power consumption; it allows more than seven devices to be connected to a master; and it allows more time for the parked slave to participate in different piconets. In this mode, a device remains synchronized to the channel but cannot send or receive data until it once again enters active mode. This mode enables the device to consume much less power while at the same time opening the bandwidth to other units in the piconet.

Figure 15-3 illustrates the units in a piconet and their various roles and modes.

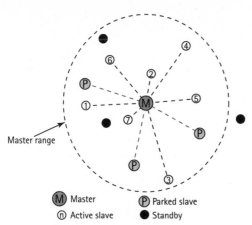

Master range

Ⓜ Master	Ⓟ Parked slave
ⓝ Active slave	● Standby

Figure 15-3: Master-slave modes

Making the connection

A Bluetooth device initiates a connection with another device by moving into page mode. However, a device can only make a connection from a page message if it already knows the address of the other unit. If it does not know the address, it must discover the other device (and its address) via an inquiry message and then send a page message to actually establish the connection.

The master unit initiates the connection by sending a page message to another unit. To send the page message, the master needs to know a slave's identity and its system clock to calculate the channel access code (CAC) and wakeup sequence and to predict the slave's wakeup sequence phase. A slave unit's system clock determines the phase in its wakeup sequence.

The slave unit listens for activity. It listens for 18 timeslots and compares any incoming signals with its access code, which is derived from its own identity. If the unit finds a match, it wakes up, and the connection setup procedure is implemented.

More About Piconets

A piconet can consist of one master and one slave, or one master and many slaves. As already indicated, each piconet has its own master, and each piconet hops independently with its own channel-hopping frequency and phase — which the master unit determines. The hop channel is determined by the hop sequence and by the phase in the sequence. The master's identity determines the sequence, and the master's clock determines the phase. The slave units in the network synchronize with the master unit's clock and the master unit's identity on the same channel. This process creates a unique connection among the units in this network, as shown in Figure 15-4.

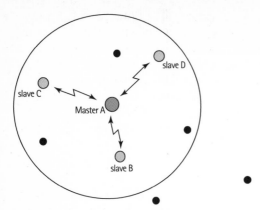

Figure 15-4: Establishing a piconet

The master unit controls all traffic on the network, allocating capacity for SCO links and handling the polling scheme for ACL links. So, every slave unit is addressed in a specific order and with a specific polling scheme. A slave can only send packets after being addressed. This method avoids packet collisions among sending units.

A Bluetooth unit can be a slave in several piconets, but master of only one. This makes sense because the piconet is based on the master's clock and address. Because "two" piconets with the same master both would be synchronized to that master, this would constitute essentially one piconet.

More About Scatternets

Scatternets enable transmission between devices that are not directly connected and perhaps cannot be directly connected because the physical distance between them is too great. Instead, another device that is in range of both units can bridge this distance gap. As shown in Figure 15-5, scatternets consist of multiple, independent piconets in which connections among them overlap.

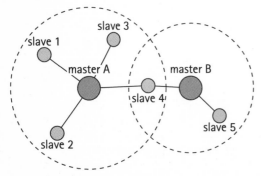

Figure 15-5: Establishing a scatternet

Within a scatternet, all units share the same frequency range. The Bluetooth specifications define ten different types of hopping frequencies — five each for the 79-hop and the 23-hop systems. Only one of these types is used in piconet communication: the channel-hopping sequence. The other four types are used for paging, page response, inquiry, and inquiry response. Each piconet, however, uses a hop sequence for transmitting packets that is based on its own master unit. This ensures that each piconet hopping sequence will be unique. All transmissions across piconets must pass through the master unit in each individual piconet. One system constraint in the Bluetooth network environment is that a unit can transmit or receive data in only one piconet at a time.

A unit can switch between two or more piconets by using time multiplexing, a protocol managed in the logical link control and adaptation protocol (L2CAP) layer. In ACL links, a unit can enter either hold or park mode in one piconet in order to join another piconet. The unit simply changes its channel parameters. In sniff mode, enough time may exist between sniff slots for a unit to join another piconet. In SCO links, a unit can only join another piconet in the nonreserved slots between packets, and this can only occur with a single SCO link using high-quality voice (HV3) packets. Units that join more than one piconet must synchronize their clocks with more than one master. For a unit to switch from one piconet to another, it must save all important parameters, such as FLOW, ARQN, and SEQN.

The formation of piconets and scatternets involves a few performance issues. One such issue involves traffic collisions. One or more piconets may use the same channel simultaneously, which creates the probability of collision.

The baseband specifications indicate that a channel is defined by a unique hopping sequence. Even though two piconets cannot have the same hopping sequence (because the hopping sequence is based on the master's device address), each hopping sequence does use the same 79 hop frequencies at different times. This can inevitably lead to collisions when two devices temporarily have the same hop frequency selected.

Some packet collisions are to be expected. But depending on the number of piconets in a network, collisions could occur too often and thus slow down the transmissions to a great degree. The more piconets that exist in a small area, the greater the chance of collisions. Collisions are handled by retransmission of the message.

Another performance issue involves a unit that serves as master in one piconet and as a slave in another. The performance of the piconet in which the unit is master will necessarily suffer somewhat when the unit responds as a slave in another piconet. When the unit is in active mode as a slave in another piconet, it must listen to the master of that piconet, and it can't predict when it will be polled. This performance issue could be circumvented by having the unit remain in active mode in only one piconet at a time. The unit would then have to be in hold or park mode in the other piconet(s). Hold mode would be preferable because the unit retains its active member address (AM_ADDR). Also, in hold mode, an SCO link is still supported. However, if a unit has an SCO link in one piconet, it may be able to form an SCO link in another piconet.

Device scheduling brings up another performance issue. When a unit participates in more than one piconet, it must determine which piconet it should listen to or service. Depending on whether a unit is in active mode or parked, it would spend different amounts of time with different piconet masters. Park mode, of course, would have the lower priority. Hold and sniff modes would have higher priority than park mode, but lower than active mode. Further, because the units need to synchronize radios from one piconet to another in order to maintain signaling in each piconet, a unit loses some time during the switch. However, this can be seen as a performance constraint when building scatternets.

For good performance, decrease bridging overhead as much as possible. That is, allow fewer units to overlap piconets. Also, carefully control the number of Bluetooth links in any scatternet formation. Smaller is better, and this is, in fact, what Bluetooth was originally designed for — small personal area networks.

Master-Slave Switching

In some cases, an existing master or slave may want to change from one piconet to another, and in the process, the unit takes on the new role of master or slave. This process is known as a *master-slave switch*. This section outlines several scenarios in which a master-slave switch may be necessary.

A master or a slave can become a part of another piconet by being paged. The slave becomes master of a new piconet by initiating paging. However, if the paging unit prefers a slave role, a master-slave switch can take place. This might happen, for example, if a unit is paging the master of an existing piconet because it wants to join that piconet.

A master-slave switch also may occur if the slave of an existing piconet wants to set itself up as master of a new piconet and wants the current piconet master to join the new piconet as a slave. In this situation, the master unit takes on a double role — becoming slave in the new piconet while remaining master of the old piconet.

A third possibility involving role switching occurs when a slave needs to take over an existing piconet. This switch essentially involves transferring slaves from an existing piconet to a new one. This can be done, of course, via the paging procedure, but that could take a long time. A faster method involves letting the new master use the timing knowledge of the old master to simply "take over" the existing piconet.

Here's an overview of the master-slave switch process:

1. The master-slave switch requires a reversal of the transceiver (TX) and receiver (RX) timing. This is a TDD switch. Changing the clock and device address of the master essentially means a piconet switch, as well.

2. The piconet switch is enforced on each slave separately.

3. After a unit acknowledges the reception of an FHS packet, the unit uses the new piconet parameters, as defined by the new master, and the piconet switch is complete.

Some transfer issues lack support in the Bluetooth specifications (such as transferring security information to a new master), so designers must handle some functionality of the master-slave switch at the application level.

Summary

Bluetooth networking is designed to operate in an ad hoc, or on-the-fly, manner:

✓ Mobile ad hoc networks (MANETs), including Bluetooth networks, face numerous connectivity and communications issues.

✓ Bluetooth builds its networks into piconets and scatternets, both of which apply solutions to overcome the constraints typical to a mobile and dynamic network topology.

Chapter 16 continues the discussion of Bluetooth networking with a look at how to go about implementing Bluetooth in a networking environment.

Chapter 16

Implementing Bluetooth in Network Environments

In This Chapter

Cabling always has been one of the larger roadblocks to installing home or office networks. You must install cable to connect the computers and peripheral devices you want to attach to the network. So, in many cases, home and small office users opt to continue using their "sneaker-net" to avoid the expense and hassle of installing cable throughout their home or building.

Wireless technologies, and especially Bluetooth, provide a means with which home and office users can network their computers without the fuss and bother of cabling. Imagine your home office with your peripherals, such as your printer, scanner, and video camera, spread out conveniently around the room (or even in another room) and connected to your network without cabling. This arrangement creates what is called a Wireless Personal Area Network, or WPAN (or PAN for short). In small or large office settings, wireless network technology can connect a company's computers and peripherals, forming what is called a wireless local area network (WLAN), regardless of where they are located, and without cabling.

To help you understand the benefit of these technologies, this chapter has the following objectives:

- ✓ Examining wireless personal area networks (WPANs)
- ✓ Taking a look at wireless local area networks (WLANs)
- ✓ Interfacing with Bluetooth
- ✓ Reviewing application examples and usage models

Connecting to Wireless Personal Area Networks (WPANs)

A wireless personal area network (WPAN) connects mobile, wireless devices to other wireless devices, as well as some stationary, wired devices. Typically, a WPAN connects a computer and its peripherals together via wireless technologies, with its emphasis on the devices within a user's personal area.

These devices typically offer a communications range of around 10 meters (or about 33 feet). At this relatively small distance, these small portable devices can conserve their limited battery power and reuse their bandwidth.

To be defined as a WPAN, a personal area network must meet the following requirements:

✓ Allow devices to share information and resources

✓ Enable low power consumption and frequently make and break connections for mobility

✓ Allow resource discovery and use

✓ Incorporate international regulations for global interoperability

A WPAN also incorporates the idea of *ubiquitous computing* — that is, connecting a wireless personal digital assistant (PDA) to a desktop or portable computer, connecting mobile phones to the Internet, or accessing voice and digital data communications.

Physical connections

Because of the relatively short distance required for WPAN communications, a WPAN can use various communications channels, including electric, magnetic, optical, and electromagnetic channels.

ELECTRIC FIELD

Research has demonstrated that the human body can be used as a conduit for information to create a WPAN. It works in this way: Electronic devices are placed on or near the body. These devices modulate an electric field that sends small currents through the body. This electric field enables the devices to establish data connections by touch or proximity (within two meters). The devices radiate only a negligible amount of energy, so global, unlicensed operation is possible. A drawback to this system, however, is that the body also acts as a shield. When a part of the body is placed on a device, it blocks electric fields from entering or leaving the device.

IBM has done research in this area and envisions this type of technology being used to pass simple data between electronic mobile devices. For example, two people could exchange electronic business cards via a handshake.

MAGNETIC FIELD

Magnetic fields also have been implemented for WPAN computing. The system enables the bandwidth to be allocated in cells that match a single user's space (such as the length of an arm). It uses a 5-MHz carrier for 240 Kbps, and consumes only 10 milliwatts of power. Because the magnetic field is unimpeded by bodies, human shielding is not an issue.

INFRARED

Infrared (IR) is another means of connecting WPANs. It offers a low-cost, moderate-range method for enabling low-data-rate wireless communication. Television remote controls, for example, use this technology. Laptop computers use faster IR transceivers to exchange data.

The biggest problem with IR communication is that signals are blocked by opaque or solid objects. IR requires a clear line-of-sight, so it is not practical for many applications, particularly mobile devices worn or carried by a person.

Table 16-1 compares the performance of the various physical channels discussed so far.

Table 16-1 Physical Channel Types

Channel	Range	Advantages	Problems	Use
Electric field	2m	Data transmitted by touch; international use	Signals blocked by body	Individual identification
Magnetic field	6m	Signal goes through body, international use	Antenna size	Data messaging
Optical infrared (low data rate)	10m	Simple, inexpensive, no regulations	Directional, line-of-sight	Home remotes
Optical infrared (high data rate)	1m	Simple, inexpensive, no regulations	Directional or high power	IrDA for laptop computers

RADIO FREQUENCY

Radio frequency (RF) is perhaps the most viable physical connection for WPANs. The short-range WPAN requirements enable the use of low-power, high-bandwidth connections, depending on device proximity. Limitations of radio WPANs are international emission regulations and standardization of the physical and data link layers. The ISM bands (particularly 2.4 GHz) offer the following advantages:

✓ Unlicensed global support (with some restrictions)

✓ High bandwidth capability

✓ Maturing technology

✓ Emerging standards

The most promising radios for widespread WPAN usage are in the 2.4-GHz ISM band because of this frequency's bandwidth and international availability. Several groups are developing radio specifications operating at 2.4 GHz, including, of course, the Bluetooth SIG. Another group is the Home Radio Frequency (HomeRF) working group, which is a consortium of several major consumer electronics and computer companies. (Many of these companies also belong to the Bluetooth SIG.) This group is working to develop an open industry specification for wireless communications in the home in order to interconnect PCs, peripherals, and remote displays.

The HomeRF aims for PC-card implementation, while the Bluetooth specification uses the embedded radio model. Also, the Bluetooth SIG continues developing a global specification for wireless technology, with the intended goal of Bluetooth-enabled devices becoming globally ubiquitous.

The HomeRF and Bluetooth specifications are incompatible, segmenting wireless operation into home and business markets. The radio technologies are similar, but they differ in terms of range (distance) and power capability, as shown in Table 16-2.

Table 16-2 Comparison of HomeRF and Bluetooth Technologies

Parameter	HomeRF	Bluetooth
Distance	50 meters	10 meters
Hop rate	50 Hz	50 Hz
Power transmission	100 milliwatts (North America)	1 milliwatt

Like the Bluetooth SIG, the HomeRF group has developed specifications to define support for voice as well as data transmissions. The HomeRF specification is based on the shared wireless access protocol (SWAP). It defines a common interface to support voice and data networks in the home environment.

Although these developing standards are currently incompatible, some justification exists for developing a system that will enable devices to switch dynamically between HomeRF and Bluetooth. The Bluetooth technology holds a clear advantage with its aim of becoming a global wireless standard, and it continues to make progress toward that goal.

WPAN networking

The Open Systems Interconnect (OSI) model explicitly defines how to incorporate devices into computer network systems. It describes the functions of multiple layers that can be developed independently but still function cohesively. The OSI is a seven-layer model, but only four of its layers are important in personal area networking:

✓ Physical layer, which transfers unstructured bits across a communication channel.

✓ Data link layer, which establishes connections and provides for reliable data transmissions.

✓ Network layer, which provides logical addressing and data transmission services to the upper layers independent of the physical and data link methods used.

✓ **Application layer**, which provides services, such as file transfer, to the software running on the user's computer.

See Chapter 11 for more information on the OSI model and how its layers relate to the Bluetooth architecture.

On the physical layer, the medium most commonly used for WPANs is the 2.4-GHz radio. This medium effectively takes care of the lower layers by establishing the link and channel over which information flows from one device to another.

Embedding a radio in a device establishes the physical connections, but the devices also need an acceptable format for transmitting the data so they can share data, applications, and resources. This requirement involves the upper layers. Because mobile devices are small, portable, and wireless, they have unique requirements for data formatting and transmission.

DATA FORMAT FOR WIRELESS DEVICES

Just as the World Wide Web provides a working model of how text and graphics are exchanged, there is also such a specification designed for small mobile devices. The wireless access protocol (WAP) is an open specification for sending and reading Internet information on wireless devices with text displays (for example, cell phones, PDAs, and handheld computers). The specification defines scripting, telephone functionality, some content formats, transport, and security.

Because of the small screens on mobile devices, the data format must be optimized for delivery to smaller screens. To provide information in this format, Web sites are built with a "light" version of Hypertext Markup Language (HTML), called Wireless Markup Language (WML). WML not only optimizes use of small screens, it also enables easy, one-hand navigation without the use of a full keyboard. It has built-in scalability, ranging from two-line text displays to the full graphic screens used by some mobile devices.

DATA TRANSPORT AND SERVICE DISCOVERY

Although the Web was intended for desktop users to view and link to multimedia, WAP will enable similar functionality in mobile devices such as cell phones. More ambitious uses of wireless devices also are envisioned, such as sharing an office printer or automatic synchronization of a user's devices when they are in proximity. To accomplish these tasks, a mobile device requires a means by which it can discover and use the services of another device. The Bluetooth specifications have already established several protocols for service discovery and access to services, but more are being developed by the Bluetooth SIG. However, various other research projects are under way by other groups and companies for the purpose of addressing network service issues for WPANs. Table 16-3 describes a few of these projects.

Table 16-3 WPAN Research Projects

Project	Description
Jini	Started in 1994 by Sun Microsystems, Inc.
	Enables devices to create spontaneous networks when plugged in to each other. ("Plugging in" can include wireless proximity.)
	Network infrastructure running on top of Java.
	Enables devices running Java Virtual Machines (JVMs) to share services.
	Java code consists of class library forms and conventions.
	Intended to eliminate device configuration and driver installation.
JavaSpaces	Java event-driven system.
	Uses remote method invocation (RMI) to allow buy/sell requests to be fulfilled.
	Allows negotiated use of resources, commits to a set of operations, and notifies objects of state changes.
	Intended for reservation and trading services.
Hive	MIT project.
	Enables construction and operation of distributed systems through networked computing.
	Uses RMI and object serialization to call and move Java objects running on other JVMs.
GinJo	Geographical interaction network for jumping objects (GinJo).
	IBM project.
	Ad hoc wireless network in which messages and code hop from one device to another when they meet in public areas.
	Intended to interact with, for example, billboards. Billboards would "jump" an electronic coupon to a mobile device for restaurants, free parking, and so on.
Tspaces	IBM project.
	Written in Java.
	Provides group communication, databases, URL-based file transfer and event notification.
	Provides means for client application to be downloaded by proximity.
	Intended to be used as a universal print, e-mail, and pager service.

A PAN EXAMPLE

Bluetooth technology soon will make an impact on the video industry. Japan's Sony Corporation recently presented two networked video cameras that feature Bluetooth short-range wireless technology. The video cameras — the digital video (DV) format DCR-PC120 and the new MICROMV format DCR-IP7 — can communicate with each other without cable connections, sending still digital images directly to personal computers, or using a mobile phone, to the Internet.

Sony calls the DCR-IP7 the Network Handycam IP. It uses new MICROMV technology that converts moving images and sound to the MPEG2 format, enabling devices to store and transfer videos more efficiently because it takes up less memory space. The other Bluetooth-enabled camera (DCR-PC120) uses the more common DV (digital video) format.

Working with Wireless Local Area Networks (WLANs)

WLANs have been around for several years but are just beginning to gain favor because of lowered costs and improved standards. WLANs transmit data using radio frequencies instead of cables. They can reach a radius of 500 feet indoors and 1,000 feet outdoors. The use of antennas, transmitters, and other access devices can broaden that range.

Unlike the Bluetooth networking environment, WLANs require a wired access point that connects all the wireless devices in the network to a wired infrastructure. Although WLANs do minimize the need for cables, they are not intended for interconnecting a range of mobile devices that require low power consumption.

WLAN is described by the 802.11b standard, issued by the Institute of Electrical and Electronics Engineers (IEEE). WLANs using these specifications are intended for applications different from those using the Bluetooth specifications. While Bluetooth devices use little power and transmit only small amounts of data over short distances, 802.11b connections range from 1 Mbps (million bits per second) to 11 Mbps in the 2.4-GHz radio band. The next version is expected to transmit data at even higher speeds of up to 54 Mbps in the 5-GHz band.

Although Bluetooth and HomeRF also can be seen as WLAN technologies, Bluetooth works in smaller areas than 802.11b. And in its current development, Bluetooth is still more clearly in the WPAN domain. HomeRF, on the other hand, hasn't become as popular as 802.11b.

The speed and range of WLANs make them useful for large corporate offices or for areas where configuration flexibility is required — without dependency on cables. For example, WLANs can be set up in homes, thus enabling multiple users Internet access on one connection. Resorts, apartment buildings, and airports also may offer WLAN access. Starbucks and Microsoft are teaming up to equip Starbucks coffee shops with WLANs in order to provide laptop users access to the Internet.

In a typical WLAN configuration, one or more access points connect to an EtherNet hub in order to connect to a wired network. Think of these access points as bridges that are equipped with transceivers providing the interface between wired and wireless networks.

The access point receives, buffers, and transmits data between the wireless local area network and the wired network infrastructure. So, wireless and wired technology come together to support mobile connectivity.

WLANs use the direct sequence spread spectrum for higher data rates (up to 11 Mbps), or the frequency-hopping spread spectrum for lower rates (up to 1 or 2 Mbps). Direct sequence provides a higher data rate, but it is more expensive and uses more power than the frequency-hopping sequence. Also, frequency-hopping is more resistant to interference.

Apparently, the 802.11 and 802.11b standards have some security flaws. A report by researchers at UC-Berkeley states that they were able to intercept transmissions over the wireless network. Although the transmissions were encrypted, the researchers were able to decrypt the data.

WLANs also have problems with interference. If too many devices in the same area use WLANs, the band that's used for transmissions can become overcrowded. Problems with signal interference have already occurred, and the airwaves may become overloaded. Interference also may come from the proliferation of Bluetooth units on the airwaves.

These interference problems exist because the two standards operate in the same 2.4-GHz radio band, and they both use the frequency-hopping spectrum. Interference can occur when Bluetooth and 802.11 devices transmit in proximity and at the same time. This can cause the destruction of data bits and consequently the need to retransmit data, and thus slow down the respective systems and provide poor service to the end user. Bluetooth devices probably will interfere with the operation of 802.11 devices, rather than the other way around, because the hopping frequencies for Bluetooth transmissions are 600 times faster than those of 802.11. And a barrage of Bluetooth signals could significantly degrade the quality of 802.11 network operations.

The FCC doesn't mediate frequency issues between products on the unlicensed radio bands; therefore, the Bluetooth SIG and IEEE must resolve these differences. In order to do this, the IEEE has formed the 802.15 Coexistence Task Group 2, which is developing practices for coexistence with WPANs that operate in the 2.4-GHz spectrum.

Before Bluetooth can move from the WPAN arena to become competitive with WLANs, the SIG must address a few issues — for example:

✓ Compared with the amount of data that may be transported through WLANs, the 2.4-GHz band offers limited transport capacity.

✓ The 2.4-GHz signals may be intercepted by the use of equipment such as parabolic antenna amplifiers. Even if the frequency-hopping scheme provides some built-in security, confidentiality could be compromised by the sophistication of current decryption technology.

✓ Significant interference issues may exist on the 2.4-GHz band.

✓ Alternative technologies are already available and currently realizing more efficient WLANs.

However, Bluetooth probably will make strides in these areas in the months to come. For example, personal hubs may become available to handle wired and wireless communication in the Bluetooth environment. Also, Bluetooth is making advances in terms of signal range. A new antenna already in development will boost a device's range from 10 to around 50 meters — putting Bluetooth on par with 802.11b. Cost is another factor that can work in favor of Bluetooth devices. Although WLAN prices have gone down, Bluetooth devices are already low cost, and set to push costs down even further.

WLAN application examples

Bluetooth can enable users to interact easily with a wide range of network applications. The type of information exchanged over a network can include both voice and data. The equipment used to access the network can include PDAs, voice headsets, and cellular phones. Users will access similar devices in point-to-point connections, as well as LAN access points, or access units designed to provide connectivity to a variety of facilities.

The following sections offer a few application examples of how Bluetooth can be integrated into a WLAN. These examples reflect the applications, usage models, and profiles defined in the Bluetooth standards. The Bluetooth standards are intended to meet the needs of a range of users and applications, including networking. Whenever possible, the Bluetooth SIG has pointed developers toward using standard and existing protocols and services, including PPP, AT-style commands, and the object exchange (OBEX) protocols, which ensures both interoperability with existing networks and ease of implementation.

For more details on Bluetooth applications, usage models, and profiles, see Chapter 13.

CONNECTIONS TO LANS

You are in your favorite coffee shop, discussing a proposal with a customer, and you need to access a document stored on the local area network in your office. You have your PDA with you, and your cell phone is in your briefcase in the trunk of your car, which is parked outside the coffee shop.

In the past, provided you had access to a phone connection, you could dial up your LAN and download the document you need to your portable computer. However, using the ad hoc networking capabilities of Bluetooth, you can connect your PDA to your cell phone and connect to your LAN via dial-up access. In this same scenario, you also can access information on the Internet by connecting from your PDA through your cell phone, even though the phone is locked in the trunk of your car. Of course, the cell phone and the PDA must be within the 10-meter range of the Bluetooth radios, but given that requirement, Bluetooth and its ad hoc networking capabilities provide a flexible and convenient way to access information.

SMALL OFFICE LANS

A growing small business cannot always predict the floor plan of its offices too far into the future. Installing a network using traditional copper cabling can fix the location of employee work areas or require additional cabling when new people are added to the firm. A wireless approach to networking enables you to locate workstations anywhere inside the range of the wireless network access points (NAPs) and thus provides the flexibility a small business needs.

By placing Bluetooth-enabled NAPs strategically around the office space and equipping user workstations and portable computers with Bluetooth network adapters, the result is almost an instant network. The drawbacks are, of course, based in the 10-meter range of the Bluetooth radios. But with careful planning, employees should be able to connect to the network in an ad hoc fashion, wherever they are inside the offices, or even if they are walking around.

LARGE OFFICE LANS

Because of its limited range, Bluetooth may not seem applicable to a large office network, with HomeRF or 802.11 wireless solutions seemingly more appropriate. However, using the same scenario that we describe in the preceding section on "Small office LANs," Bluetooth may have its place in the large office environment as well.

Bluetooth's ability to create ad hoc networks and to query for available services provides a flexibility that can help to make employees more efficient. For example, if you are scheduled to give an important presentation to a new customer in a conference room located across the building from your office, you need to get your slides into the conference room. If the conference room does not have a network connection (meaning a network wall-jack), your choices are either to "sneaker-net" your slides or to move your computer into the conference room. But what if you had a Bluetooth-enabled projector and could access your slide presentation from your desktop computer via the wireless network? Or, should you need to access the Internet, what if you could connect a computer via a Bluetooth link to your cell phone (which could be back on your desk) to access the information you wanted to display?

Bluetooth may not be the networking medium of choice for a large office network, but it still has applications and can provide the flexibility that only a wireless service can provide.

MOBILE NETWORKS

Intransit Networks of Seattle, WA is developing a system that provides for tracking mobile assets. The system combines RF ID tags, Bluetooth radios, wireless Internet connections (using public carriers), and proprietary software to enable companies to track their high-value assets that may be located away from the company's main locations.

The technology, which the company calls "geo-fencing," consists of low-power Bluetooth radios attached to mobile equipment that provides for the tracking and status reporting of one or a collection of deployed assets. For more information about the system, visit the Intransit Web site at www.intransitnetworks.com.

Another example of a WLAN in a mobile environment comes from Sweden's national Board of Health and Welfare. By using multiple types of wireless communications between hospitals and accident sites, the Swedish system hopes to be able to provide better quality care for a patient in transit to the hospital. IS Swede is currently testing this mobile WLAN in two counties, with 51 ambulances and 7 hospitals involved in the pilot. Over the next two years, the board of health intends to expand the system to all hospitals and ambulances in the country.

To perform this type of care, IS Swede combines various wireless technologies, including WLANs, a global positioning system (GPS), and mobile computing. When the ambulance arrives at an accident scene, the paramedics collect critical information about the patient, such as blood pressure, pulse, and overall condition. Then, using a bar-code scanner and WLAN radio, the paramedic enters the information, which is transmitted to an access point in the ambulance. This information is then transmitted in real time to doctors and the patient database at the hospital. After a doctor analyzes the information, instructions are transmitted back to the paramedic for treating the patient.

The access point in the ambulance has a range of 200 feet, and it connects to a wired Ethernet LAN that interconnects with a radio in the ambulance. The radio completes the link to the hospital, providing continuous connectivity whether the ambulance is mobile or stationary.

The success of this WLAN in Sweden provides a model for other countries to follow. And the blueprint can be expanded to cover similar applications in other fields, such as parcel tracking between delivery trucks and delivery stations, or evidence tracking between crime scenes and police stations.

Summary

Wireless technology is in its early stages of development. Here are the key issues we raise in this chapter:

- ✓ The various wireless networking strategies currently involve some incompatibilities.

- ✓ The various manufacturers and standards groups should move toward a global standard because communication demands compatibility. By establishing and implementing compatible systems, manufacturers can have a much bigger impact on the worldwide marketplace and their customers' lives.

- ✓ WPAN and WLAN have many potential applications, and if the IS Swede example is an indication, the impact of Bluetooth technology in wireless networking should be beneficial.

Any discussion of networking — for either a personal or a local area network — must address security. Chapter 17 looks at the security features and issues of the Bluetooth technology.

Chapter 17

Bluetooth Security

In This Chapter

The Bluetooth specification requires the use of built-in security to maintain the integrity of Bluetooth data. Further, Bluetooth security must prevent leaking information to unauthorized users as well as prohibit network blocking. Bluetooth provides for security in the lower and the upper layers of the protocol stack. In the lower layer, at the link level, Bluetooth security enables the implementation of authentication and encryption. In the upper layers, Bluetooth provides for more public-oriented security usage models, such as discovering services or exchanging virtual business cards.

This chapter takes a look at security at the link level as well as the service level, focusing on the following objectives:

✓ Examining security provisions in the Bluetooth specification

✓ Detailing security in the Bluetooth protocol stack and describing the security protocols defined in the Bluetooth profiles

✓ Assessing the strengths and limitations of Bluetooth security

✓ Protecting a Bluetooth device

✓ Applying Bluetooth security

Security in the Bluetooth Specification

The Bluetooth specification defines different security levels for Bluetooth devices and for their services. The Bluetooth specification includes security features that are to be implemented at the link level, and it also indicates how security can be implemented in an interoperable way, at the service level. To help you understand why and how Bluetooth security works, this chapter first takes a look at security as described in the part of the Bluetooth specification known as *profiles*.

The profiles describe how user models are to be implemented. You may view a profile as a vertical slice through the protocol stack. It defines features in each protocol that are mandatory for the specific profile. It also defines parameter ranges for each protocol. Bluetooth profiles are intended to decrease the risk of interoperability problems among products developed by different manufacturers.

The various profiles in the specifications use different parts of the protocol stack as needed to support specific functionality. The Generic Access Profile (GAP) — the profile on which all others are based — defines common requirements that are to be used by transport and application profiles. In this section, we look at the GAP in terms of how it relates to link-level and service-level security protocols.

The GAP describes security in terms of three different modes:

✓ Security mode 1: Nonsecure data transfer

✓ Security mode 2: Service-level security

✓ Security mode 3: Link-level security

Mode 1 — Nonsecure

In security mode 1, a device is not secure. In this mode, the device never initiates any security procedures. Examples of nonsecure data transfer include the automatic exchange of business cards and calendars (that is, vCard and vCalendar).

Mode 2 — Service-level security

In security mode 2, a device doesn't initiate any security procedures until a channel establishment request has been sent or a channel establishment procedure has been initiated. Security, in this case, takes place at and above the logical link and adaptation protocol (L2CAP) level — that is, in the higher layers of the stack. This enables more versatility for running parallel applications with different security requirements.

In mode 2, according to the GAP, a device must classify security requirements for different services (for example, file transfer or dial-up networking), using at least the following attributes:

✓ **Authentication:** Enables one Bluetooth device to verify the identity of another device before allowing connection establishment.

✓ **Encryption:** Ensures the integrity of transmitted data by systematically encrypting each data packet transmitted to other devices.

✓ **Authorization:** Enables one Bluetooth device to grant another device access to a specific service.

Mode 3 — Link-level security

In security mode 3, a device initiates security procedures before a link is established — at the link set-up level (the lower layers of the stack). Link-level security is easier to implement than mode-2 security. Link-level security procedures can include the following:

✓ Creating and using keys

✓ Authenticating devices

✓ Encrypting packets

Link keys are used to initiate authentication. Or, if a link key has not yet been created, a *pairing* procedure takes place in which a passkey is created. An encryption key is used for the encryption process.

Authentication is the process of verifying the identity of a device with which a connection is to be established. *Encryption* is the process of encoding data for transmission between devices to ensure its integrity.

Security in the Bluetooth Protocol Stack

As we explain in the previous section, Bluetooth enforces different security protocols at different levels of the Bluetooth stack. When a device is in security mode 2, the protocols are enforced in the upper layers of the stack, at the service level. In security mode 3, the protocols are enforced in the lower layers, at the link level. Each security mode uses a slice of the protocol stack to support the security procedures specific to its requirements, as indicated in Figure 17-1.

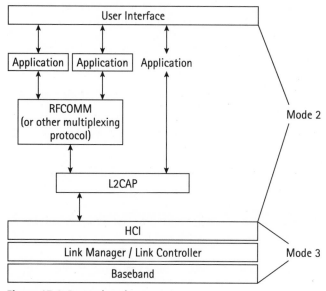

Figure 17-1: Protocol stack

First, take a look at how the link-level protocols in the lower layers are implemented when a device is in security mode 3.

Link-level protocols

Mode-3 security enforces authentication and encryption. The security protocols defined in the Bluetooth specifications use the following four elements for device authentication and data encryption:

✓ Bluetooth device address (BD_ADDR): A 48-bit address unique for each Bluetooth device.

✓ Private link key: A 128-bit random number used for authentication purposes.

✓ Private encryption key: 8–128 bits, used for encryption of data.

✓ Random number (RAND): A frequently changing, 128-bit, random or pseudo-random number created by the Bluetooth device itself.

AUTHENTICATION PROTOCOLS

Authentication is a link manager protocol (LMP) that verifies the identity of a remote device before establishing a connection. This two-part protocol is a challenge-response strategy in which one device challenges another to determine whether it has the correct, shared secret key required to establish a connection. If authentication is successful, a link is established between the devices. Also, during the authentication process, the LMP generates an authenticated ciphering offset (ACO) value, which is stored in each device. This ACO value will later be used to generate an encryption key.

Secret, or link, keys are exchanged during the initialization phase of the procedure, which must be carried out separately for each two units that want to implement authentication.

The following four types of link keys can be used for authentication:

✓ Unit key: Derived at the installation of the Bluetooth device.

✓ Combination key: Derived from two units. This key is generated for each pair of devices and is used when more security is needed.

✓ Master key: Used when the master device wants to transmit to several devices at once. It overrides the current link key for the current session.

✓ Initialization key: Used in the initialization process and protects the initialization parameters when they are transmitted.

All the link keys are 128-bit random numbers and are either temporary or semipermanent. Here's an overview of how the authentication procedure is enforced:

1. The verifying unit sends the claimant (remote device) a random number (RAND) to be authenticated.

2. The verifier and the claimant use the authentication function (outlined in the Bluetooth specification) with the RAND, the claimant's BD_ADDR, and the current link key to produce a response.

3. The claimant sends a response to the verifier.

4. If the verifying unit determines that the responses match, authentication is successful.

Because each application can indicate which unit is to be authenticated, the master unit might not be a verifier. Some applications may only require one-way rather than mutual authentication.

If the authentication fails, a certain time interval must pass before a new attempt at authentication can be made.

PAIRING PROCEDURE   If no link key exists, the pairing procedure is used to authenticate two devices based on a Bluetooth security code, referred to as a PIN. Subsequently, a common link key is created. The user does not have to memorize the PIN, because it is used only once to create the link key. If by some chance the link key is deleted, and pairing must be repeated, the user can enter another PIN. However, some devices may have an embedded PIN, in which case no user interaction is required.

The pairing procedure can be used for a single secure connection, or it can be the basis for creating a trusted relationship — a *bond* — between devices.

The GAP specification defines two pairing modes: pairable and nonpairable. In pairable mode, a device accepts pairing initiated by a remote device. In nonpairable mode, pairing is not accepted when initiated by a remote device.

The pairing protocol works as follows:

1. An initialization key is created based on a random number and a PIN (up to 16 characters in length) entered by the two devices.

2. Initialization generates a common link key, which the devices then exchange.

BONDING   According to the GAP, bonding is used to create a relationship between two devices based on the common link key (the bond). The link key is created, and the pairing process, or exchange of keys, takes place during the bonding procedure. Both Bluetooth devices then store this link key. In other words, creating a bond between devices enables the permanent exchange of keys; thus, it can eliminate the repetition of exchanging link keys on each subsequent communication attempt with the bonded device. The bonding procedure also can involve higher layers of the protocol, if a device is to be designated as trusted.

The GAP defines two types of bonding:

✓ **Dedicated bonding** occurs when two devices only want to create and exchange a common link key.

✓ **General bonding** is a link establishment procedure carried out in both devices under specific conditions, which is then followed by an optional higher-layer initialization process (establishing a trusted relationship).

According to the specification, bonding is a procedure that performs the first authentication, during which a common link key is created and stored for future use. Pairing, as in LMP-pairing, is a procedure that authenticates two devices using a PIN but also creates a common link key that is used as the basis for a trusted relationship or a single secure connection.

ENCRYPTION PROTOCOLS

Encryption is the process of encoding user data for protection in packet payloads to ensure its integrity during transmission. Authentication must take place before encryption can be implemented. Encryption depends on an encryption key, which is derived from the current link key (exchanged during authentication). Each time encryption is needed, the encryption services of the LMP automatically change the encryption key. Making the authentication key and the encryption key separate entities means the Bluetooth devices can use a shorter encryption key without weakening the authentication procedure.

The encryption key size can vary from 8 to 128 bits; therefore, the size of the encryption key used between the two devices must be negotiated. Either master or slave can propose or reject the other device's key size suggestions.

The Bluetooth specification places some limits on the negotiation, however. Each device has a defined maximum allowed key length. Also, every application defines a minimum acceptable key size. If either party in the key size negotiation fails to meet this minimum key size requirement, the application stops negotiation and the devices cannot use encryption. This is a necessary requirement because of the possibility of a malicious device forcing a lower encryption setting in order to do harm.

The encryption procedure performs the following steps:

1. Authentication is successfully established between two devices.

2. An encryption key is negotiated between the devices, derived from the link key.

3. After the devices agree upon a key size, the encryption key is created.

4. If a semipermanent link key is used, broadcast transmissions are not encrypted — only point-to-point transmissions. If a master key is used, all transmissions can be encrypted, depending on the unit's encryption mode.

5. Encryption is systematically implemented for user data transmissions.

Service-level protocols

Whether a security procedure is initiated or not depends upon the security requirements of the requested channel or service. In other words, if a device requests a channel from another device that requires authentication and encryption, the requesting device must supply the necessary information. Similarly, if a device requests access to the service of another device, appropriate security procedures must be applied.

In security mode 2, a device cannot initiate any security procedures before either a device has received a channel request or the device itself initiates a channel request. This security is enforced at the L2CAP layer and above.

AUTHENTICATION AND AUTHORIZATION

Two key concepts in Bluetooth security are authentication and authorization. As we explain in the section "Mode 3 — link-level security," earlier in this chapter, *authentication* is the process of determining and verifying the identity of a remote device before connection is established. *Authorization* is the process of granting one device access to another device's services. Authorization always includes authentication.

According to the GAP, a device in mode 2 should classify security requirements of services as follows:

✓ Authentication only required

✓ Authentication and authorization required

✓ Neither authentication nor authorization required — services available to all devices

DEVICE-LEVEL SECURITY DESIGNATIONS

Different security levels can be defined for devices and services. This feature provides further flexibility to the security architecture, enabling one device to grant access for different services based on another device's security designation.

According to the Bluetooth specification, devices can be designated as follows:

✓ **Trusted:** A trusted device can be given unrestricted access to all services of another device. A device can be designated as trusted after successful pairing (or bonding) has occurred. Services that a device may have available can include file transfer, synchronization, or dial-up networking.

✓ **Untrusted:** An untrusted device has only limited access to services or can be denied service altogether.

✓ **Unknown:** An unknown device is a Bluetooth device for which no information (such as name, address, and passkey) is available. It is essentially an untrusted device.

SERVICE-LEVEL SECURITY DESIGNATIONS

For services, the requirements for authorization, authentication, and encryption are set independently. The access requirements specified by the GAP allow defining three security levels:

✓ **Authorization required:** This security level also requires authentication in order to verify that the remote device is, in fact, the one it claims to be. After the authorization procedure, access to a service is granted automatically to trusted devices. However, because an untrusted device doesn't create fixed relationships, it may be granted access to a service on a limited basis.

✓ **Authentication required:** A remote device only needs to be authenticated before it can connect to the application.

✓ **Encryption required:** The link must be changed to encrypted mode before access to the requested service is granted.

Service discovery and application-specific services

The service discovery application profile (SDAP) defines the features that devices use to discover services on other Bluetooth devices and gather information about these services. In this profile, only connection-oriented channels are used.

A Bluetooth device implements the service discovery protocol (SDP) to locate available services on remote devices. The SDP does not access the services. After a link is established, services can be located and selected via the user interface. Although SDP is not directly involved in accessing a specific service, it prompts the stack to access the service.

The SDAP doesn't require authentication or encryption for SDP transactions. However, if any involved devices use these security measures, service discovery takes place only on the devices that pass the authentication and encryption requirements. The SPD does not impose any pairing requirements. It performs discovery only when a device can establish a baseband link with another device. However, the service discovery application must enable a user to choose whether connections will be permitted with trusted or untrusted devices.

SERVICE DISCOVERY APPLICATION PROFILE (SDAP)

The service discovery application profile (SDAP) is the Bluetooth specification that defines the procedures to be used by a service discovery application to locate services on other Bluetooth-enabled devices. To do this, the SDAP implements the Bluetooth service discovery protocol (SDP). The L2CAP layer transports the PDUs defined in the SDP, enabling the service discovery application to search for available services.

In the SDAP, devices can search for services by class, by service attributes, and via browsing. In the first two cases, a search is conducted for known and specific services. In the third case, however, the search is more general. Further, these searches can be made on a specific device on which a connection already has been established, or the search can be directed toward discovering devices in the general area that may have the desired services. In either situation, the following procedure must take place:

1. A device must be discovered.

2. A link is established, which may require the implementation of authorization or encryption, depending on the security mode invoked.

3. Inquiry can be made about supported services. If the service discovery application wants access to a service, authorization may be required, depending on security requirements previously established.

Any security restrictions for SDP transactions are dictated by the security requirements in place for the link or channel on which connection is established. Even though the discovery of services is based on its own set of protocols and has its own profile, it is still subject to the GAP requirements. Whatever security mode is in effect will determine whether services can be discovered on remote devices, and, once discovered, whether they can be accessed.

Security enforcement for authentication, authorization, or encryption may differ for client and server roles. So, peer units running an application may not have symmetric security levels because a server probably has a higher security level requirement than a client. For example, as shown in Figure 17-2, the initiator (A) of the connection may be in mode 3 while the respondent (B) is in mode 2.

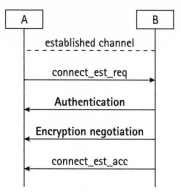

Figure 17-2: Asymmetric security modes

SERVICE DISCOVERY PROTOCOL (SDP)

The service discovery protocol (SDP) is the Bluetooth protocol that enables an application to discover what services are available on a remote device as well as the characteristics of the available service.

The SDP has the following requirements:

- ✓ Discovering services based on class of service
- ✓ Browsing for services without having prior knowledge of the services
- ✓ Discovering new services on devices when they become available
- ✓ Determining when services become unavailable based on RF proximity of a device
- ✓ Using L2CAP as the transport protocol

Service discovery takes place between an SDP server and an SDP client. The service discovery protocol enables client applications to discover services on a server application and to discover attributes of the services. An attribute, in the Bluetooth system, identifies the class of service and the protocol needed to use the service.

Each service is an instance of a class of service. Service classes must define all the attributes of services that represent instances of the class. Further, each service class is assigned a unique identifier so service discovery based on class of service can take place.

If a client wants to use a service, it must open another connection to the service provider. SDP only allows discovery of service and information about the service — not the means to use the service.

In the Bluetooth specification, the SDP protocol is defined as a request/response model. Each transaction consists of a request PDU and a response PDU. When used in conjunction with the L2CAP transport protocol, a client must get a response to a request before it can send another request on the same connection. This feature enables flow control on the channel. Figure 17-3 shows the simplicity of the SDP mechanism.

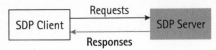

Figure 17-3: SDP client-server protocol

SERVICES APPLICATIONS

According to Bluetooth specifications, a *service* is an entity that provides information, performs an action, or controls a resource for another device. Services can be implemented as software, hardware, or a combination of the two (for example, a printer, file transfer, and so on). Further, each service is an instance of a service class. According to the Bluetooth specifications, for two Bluetooth devices to be interoperable, they must use the same set of protocols for each class of service. And, as previously indicated, each Bluetooth profile defines the specific protocols to be used for the service class.

Services that can be offered between devices include file transfer and exchange of electronic business cards. Each service application must include the required protocols to ensure interoperability.

FILE TRANSFER   A file transfer application, for example, must include protocols defined in the File Transfer profile. The file transfer usage model enables the transfer of data objects between Bluetooth devices. Such devices include PCs, smart phones, or PDAs. The object types for transfer include Excel spreadsheets, audio files, image files, or Microsoft Word files.

The FTP requires application-level support for authentication and encryption, although actual use of these security features is optional. Similarly, authentication support is required, though use is optional.

A file transfer application has three main features:

✓ **Folder browsing:** Displaying folder contents and setting the current folder from a remote device.

✓ **Object transfer:** Transferring items in a folder from one device to another.

✓ **Object manipulation:** Deleting and creating folders and files on a remote device.

Figure 17-4 shows client-server interaction for the file transfer protocols.

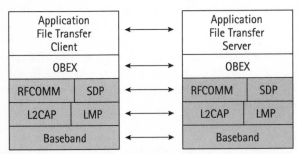

Figure 17-4: File transfer protocols

OBJECT EXCHANGE   An application that enables a Bluetooth device to push or pull an object such as a business card to or from the inbox of another Bluetooth device will be based on the Object Push profile. Devices that would use the Object Push profile include notebook PCs, PDAs, and mobile phones.

This profile requires support for link-level authentication and encryption, but their actual use is optional. Support of bonding also is required, but use is optional.

Such an application has the following main features:

✓ **Object push:** Initiates the process that pushes an object from a push server.

✓ **Business card pull:** Initiates the process that pulls a business card from a push server.

✓ **Business card exchange:** Initiates the process that exchanges cards with a push server.

These three functions are user-activated, never automatic. Figure 17-5 shows client-server interaction for the object exchange protocols.

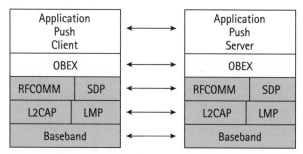

Figure 17-5: Object exchange protocols

Bluetooth Security Strong Points

Two criteria for measuring the strength of a security system are flexibility and usability. A system must be flexible in order to accommodate various situations in which security issues might arise. And a system's security features must be easy to implement in order to ensure use. The Bluetooth architecture provides for both criteria.

Bluetooth provides security at the link level (in the lower layers) as well as the service level (upper layers). Users can require security either before a link is established between devices or before a channel is established. At the link level, authentication and encryption of data can be implemented. At the service level, authorization for access to specific services is required.

The architecture also allows for choice among three different security modes. Users can choose the level of security they consider most appropriate for each connection attempt. Users that require more security, for example, can use security mode 2, the most stringent level, which requires authentication, authorization, and encryption of data.

Bluetooth specifications define different security levels for devices and services. If users want to restrict service access to other devices, they can implement security so that access is granted only on a per-service basis. On the other hand, if users want to allow certain devices unrestricted access to services, they can designate such devices as trusted and thus eliminate repetitive security procedures.

Devices that implement different security levels can still communicate with each other. This feature is important in a client-server situation, which typically has stringent security on the server side, while still allowing access by clients with lower security levels. In any given connection, the higher security settings would override the lower settings.

Examining the Limitations of Bluetooth Security

Whether in traditional or ad hoc networking situations, the very existence of a network opens the system to attack from unauthorized parties. The areas in which computer networks may face threats fall into the following general categories:

✓ **Disclosure:** Information leaked to an unauthorized party.

✓ **Integrity:** Unauthorized change to information.

✓ **Denial of service:** Access to network blocked by unauthorized party.

In terms of data integrity and disclosure, Bluetooth networks are vulnerable to attack in the following specific areas.

✓ **Entering and storing the PIN:** As we describe earlier in this chapter, the PIN code can be used in combination with other variables to generate a link and encryption key. To do this, users enter a four-digit PIN and transmit it to each other. The fact that it's transmitted over the air makes it vulnerable. Further, because users on both ends need to enter this number to initiate a secure connection, they may want to store the PIN in both devices to avoid repeatedly entering the number at each connection attempt, or they may use an easy number to remember (for example, 1111). If the device is lost or stolen, the stored number could be a problem. Also, easily remembered numbers are easily discovered by unauthorized parties. Both situations pose a risk to the integrity of the data being transmitted.

✓ **Using the link key:** Authentication and encryption are based on the link key, and only units participating in a connection should share the link key. However, a link key can be based on a unit key, which never changes. If devices A and B communicate using A's unit key, and A subsequently communicates with C using A's unit key, then device B can use A's unit key to decrypt communications between A and C because B already knows A's unit key code. To do this, B would simply fake a BD_ADDR to calculate the encryption key.

✓ **Bluetooth device address:** Each unit has a unique device address that distinguishes it from other units. The very uniqueness of this address, however, makes it vulnerable. After this address is associated with a person, the person can be traced, activities can be monitored, and the device address in question stolen.

Bluetooth networks also may be vulnerable to denial-of-service attacks because all the devices in an ad hoc network are dependent on each other to relay messages, and because all information is transmitted over the air. An unauthorized party could try to jam the network and thus prevent the flow of information among units. Also, because Bluetooth units rely on battery power for operation, an unauthorized party could attempt to increase the power consumption in a unit, and thus prematurely drain battery life.

Several problems still must be worked out in the Bluetooth security procedures, particularly if Bluetooth is to be expanded to accommodate wide area networks. The original Bluetooth concept was for personal area networking, not for wide area networks. For personal area networks, in which the range is only up to 10 meters, security is desirable but not necessarily essential. However, because the SIG hopes to make Bluetooth a higher-end wireless standard, security functions will need to be re-addressed as use changes.

Protecting a Bluetooth Device

Within the current architecture, you have several ways to protect your Bluetooth device from security threats. Users who need to transmit sensitive information should invoke the more stringent security mode. This means using security mode 2 and requiring authentication, encryption, and authorization when communicating with other devices.

Users also may want to create trusted relationships between select devices. That way, when data is transmitted, users will be assured that only the trusted device is allowed to receive the information.

When creating ad hoc networks among devices, keeping the networks small and in a secure area — for example, in a conference room — will provide protection from unauthorized parties gaining access. The range for Bluetooth connections is only up to 10 meters. Most hackers prefer to be farther away from their victims.

You also can protect data transmissions by using specific keys to encrypt traffic. For example, when a combination key is used, the master unit creates a combination key with each slave in a network. So, information from a slave is sent to other slaves only by the master unit. In this way, the master unit has more control over where data originates as well as where it is sent.

Requiring two-way authentication is another means of protecting information (but not the device, remember). In this situation, both devices must enter the secret key as well as verify that the correct key information was received. Mutual authentication decreases the likelihood of an unknown device being able to establish a connection.

Users need to refrain from selecting PINs that are too easy to remember or too short. The longer the number and the more unique, the less likely it will be discovered by an unauthorized party.

Applying Bluetooth Security

Security continues to be the area on which Bluetooth developers must place greater emphasis to gain greater acceptance in the marketplace. Of course, security is a big concern in all wireless communications. However, because Bluetooth authenticates devices and not users, the possibility exists for security breaches.

For example, if you use your Bluetooth cell phone to call a friend on her Bluetooth cell phone, the authentication process uses a secret encryption key known only to participants on a connection. Because you want to keep the conversation secure, you use your friend's secret key. Later that day, another friend calls and you use your key again. Your friend now has your key and, using a faked device address (which is commonly 0000) and the standard encryption method, can now listen to your cell phone conversations or masquerade as you to place calls.

Safe communications with Bluetooth

In most cases, and especially those that involve WPAN uses for the Bluetooth technology, the security features in Bluetooth provide the level of security required. Bluetooth security does have its weaknesses, like the scenario we describe in the preceding section, but in many applications, when Bluetooth is used in areas where it is most applicable, there should be little concern for security issues.

The applications in which security is not likely to be an issue include:

✓ Bluetooth peripheral devices for computers, such as a mouse, keyboard, printer, or scanner.

✓ Accessing e-mail from a mobile phone or PDA connected via a Bluetooth link to your portable PC, even if it is in your briefcase.

✓ Finding a suitable printer in a hotel lobby or convention hall and printing a document from your portable PC without the need for a cable. The same goes for finding fax machines and other devices.

✓ Giving someone your business card electronically from your PDA or PC to the other person's Bluetooth-enabled device.

Dealing with ad hoc issues

When an ad hoc network is created in an office space such as a conference room, two methods are available to secure the connections so that someone outside the conference room cannot eavesdrop on your meeting. The first method is to use combination keys to encrypt data sent between devices. In this method, the master creates combination keys with each slave device on the ad hoc network, which allows any information sent by one slave to be sent to all other slaves by the master.

The second method of securing an ad hoc network is using a master key, which allows all devices on the network to use the same key to encrypt information and transmit to the network, without the need for the master relaying it. Beyond these two approaches, Bluetooth ad hoc networks must be protected using application-level programs.

Summary

Security is an evolving part of the Bluetooth specifications. In this chapter, we discuss the following key points:

- ✓ The Bluetooth technology uses discovery processes that enable Bluetooth devices to identify each other, establish appropriate connections, access each other's services, and run common applications.

- ✓ Various security requirements exist to ensure data integrity and secure connections in a Bluetooth peer-to-peer network.

- ✓ Bluetooth has some security issues to be resolved before it is ready for use to secure networks in a large company or mobile environment.

Bluetooth is not the only wireless, cable-replacement technology available. Chapter 18 takes a look at competing wireless technologies.

Part VI

Bluetooth in the Marketplace

IN THIS PART

Bluetooth is not without competing technologies that provide many of the same benefits. This part of the book looks at the competing technologies and how they compare to Bluetooth in terms of features, limitations, and benefits. We also take a look at the future of Bluetooth by anticipating future Bluetooth products and usage scenarios, evaluating Bluetooth compatibility with 3G, and assessing Bluetooth's potential for success.

Chapter 18

Competing Technologies

In This Chapter

Bluetooth is only one of a variety of cable-replacement technology specifications that are available today. Each of these technologies has its strengths and weaknesses and is better suited for certain applications. Actually, most of the wireless technologies that we discuss in this chapter aren't all that different. Many use the same transmission modes and protocols and provide application support in many of the same areas.

This chapter focuses on the following topics:

✓ Comparing Bluetooth and competing and complementary technologies

✓ Exploring best-use scenarios for wireless technologies

✓ Examining third-generation (3G) wireless technology

Wireless Technologies

Bluetooth is only one of several technologies that support wireless communications, including some that can compete for the wireless market and possibly impede the success of Bluetooth. Others can complement the Bluetooth environment, potentially coexisting and working well together. This chapter describes some of the other wireless technologies that are currently available and offers a comparison of their features and capabilities with those of the Bluetooth technology.

Bluetooth and infrared

Infrared communication is accomplished through an optical connection, which uses an 850-nanometer infrared light between devices for transmitting voice as well as data. The signal needs line-of-sight and a straight path from one device to another, and devices must be positioned close to each other. The connection distance is 1 meter or less. Because the devices are positioned close together when exchanging data, infrared offers a secure method for transmission. Infrared is intended for point-to-point links between two devices for simple data transfers and file synchronization.

Although infrared and Bluetooth technologies support many of the same applications, each technology has its advantages and disadvantages. In the exchange of electronic business cards, for example, infrared performs better. Infrared users easily make the exchange by pointing one device at another. And because people exchanging business cards typically are in physical proximity of each other, the limited range of infrared data exchange is not an issue.

Although Bluetooth also supports the exchange of electronic business cards, the exchange is neither as direct nor as easy. One Bluetooth device must first discover the other device, perform any necessary security requirements, access services, and finally exchange business cards. A process that's quick and easy using infrared is time-consuming and somewhat tedious with Bluetooth devices. (However, once the connection is made, data transfer is fast.)

However, Bluetooth does not require line-of-sight for communication with other devices, and this facilitates communication with other devices in a piconet. Exchanging data with multiple devices is not possible with infrared. It only offers point-to-point links between two devices.

The Bluetooth technology's omnidirectional capability allows synchronization with other devices to occur automatically when devices are in range of each other. Bluetooth technology also enables synchronization to occur while the user is moving. This cannot happen with infrared, which requires that both devices remain in a fixed location for synchronization to take place.

In terms of data transfer, infrared does provide a faster rate than Bluetooth, which is a big advantage. Bluetooth moves data between devices at about 721 Kbps, while infrared transmits data at a rate of 4 Mbps.

Both Bluetooth and infrared can make wireless connections between portable devices and a wired network. But because Bluetooth has no line-of-sight requirement, it can do this more easily than infrared. Bluetooth users have more flexibility in the placement of access points than infrared users. (An access point accepts wireless signals from portable devices while providing a wired connection to the LAN.) Also, the Bluetooth device does not have to remain stationary while connected to the LAN (within a 33-foot range), but an infrared device does.

Both infrared and Bluetooth target dial-up connections to the Internet. And both work well for this connection, with Bluetooth gaining a small advantage in terms of device placement. The Bluetooth user does not have to position one device next to another when making the connection, but the infrared user does.

Using infrared technology certainly has advantages and disadvantages, as summarized in Table 18-1. Although it has more advantages than disadvantages, the disadvantages are significant in terms of how they impact the usability of an IR device.

Table 18-1 Advantages and Disadvantages of IR Technology

Advantages	Disadvantages
Speed	Limited range
Inexpensive	Limited connection angle
Low power consumption	
Secure	
No RF interference	

Bluetooth and HomeRF

Home Radio Frequency (HomeRF) is another wireless technology that uses the unlicensed 2.4-GHz ISM band. This technology is supported by a 100-member consortium of companies, many of which also belong to the Bluetooth SIG. The HomeRF consortium has created an open-industry specification for wireless digital devices and PCs in a home environment, so its focus differs slightly from the Bluetooth PAN.

HomeRF supports both voice and data transmission using frequency-hopping spread-spectrum radio. HomeRF transmission rates are from 2 to 10 Mbps. Because of the difference in hop rates used by Bluetooth and HomeRF devices, the chance of interference between devices is slight.

The HomeRF specification is based on Shared Wireless Access Protocol (SWAP), which provides the following channels for transmission:

✓ Six voice channels, based on the Digital Enhanced Cordless Telephone (DECT) standard

✓ One data channel, based on the IEEE 802.11 specification

HomeRF technology offers a low-priced alternative to the 802.11 wireless networks because it doesn't require dedicated access point hardware. Instead, point-to-point connections are made between devices. HomeRF connections are good for as much as approximately 50 feet but are not as robust as Ethernet networks. That makes HomeRF fine for the home environment, but not for a corporate setting. HomeRF is not intended for portable devices or ad hoc connections, giving Bluetooth a clear advantage in this area.

HomeRF and Bluetooth technologies can easily coexist and in some cases complement each other. For example, to create a viable home network, you could use HomeRF to connect all PCs to each other, with Bluetooth connections between peripherals and the PCs. Because both systems use frequency-hopping, this type of home network shouldn't experience any interference problems.

Clearly, HomeRF provides many advantages for creating a network in the home, but in any other environment, it has distinct disadvantages. Table 18-2 lists the advantages and disadvantages of HomeRF.

Table 18-2 Advantages and Disadvantages of HomeRF Technology

Advantages	Disadvantages
Speed	Limited range
Inexpensive	Integration with wired networks difficult
Easy to install	Not as stable as Ethernet-based networks
Access points not required	High power consumption, so not good for portable use
Allows up to 127 devices per network	
Allows multiple networks in same location	
Frequency hopping reduces interference	

Bluetooth and wireless LANs

Another wireless connection option is the IEEE 802.11 standard, or Wireless Fidelity (Wi-Fi), as it's also known. Like Bluetooth, this technology uses RF signals broadcast in the 2.4-GHz frequency band. This technology is strictly for data transmissions and doesn't handle voice signals or offer telephony support. It can be used for ad hoc connections, but it basically replicates an Ethernet network without wires.

 Technically, you can transmit voice signals over a data line using the same technology implemented for voice communication over the Internet, but the quality of communication suffers compared with traditional voice calls.

The 802.11 specification uses a direct-sequence, spread-spectrum (DSSS) technology. This differs from the Bluetooth use of frequency-hopping spread-spectrum (FHSS) technology. DSSS signals are fixed within a 17-MHz channel, as opposed to the 79 different hop frequencies used by Bluetooth. As a result of using DSSS, the 802.11 specification enables faster transmission rates — up to 11 Mbps data transmission rates.

The 802.11 network makes use of access point hardware. An *access point* is a receiver/transmitter that devices use in order to connect to a network. These access points can add significantly to the cost of a network. (They range in price from $250 to $1,200.) Because of the need for access points and LAN configuration, the 802.11 network technology can be expensive, as well as difficult to set up and use. However, the technology gains significantly in speed, reliability, and increased range, which can be up to 300 feet.

The 802.11 technology doesn't work as well as Bluetooth for ad hoc networking, because it requires somewhat complex setup. Ad hoc networking is one of the strengths of the Bluetooth environment. For this reason, the two technologies could coexist and augment each other, with users selecting Bluetooth for connecting peripherals to a PC and 802.11 for connecting the PC to the office LAN.

The 802.11 technology also is more susceptible to interference than Bluetooth. For example, microwaves are generated at the same 2.4-GHz frequency and have been shown to jam transmissions from Bluetooth devices operating in proximity (within a few feet) to the microwave oven. Of course, this problem can be remedied by moving away from the microwave oven when operating a Bluetooth device. The problem with the 802.11 networks, however, is more difficult to solve. Because the 802.11 technology doesn't use frequency hopping, it is much more vulnerable to interference than Bluetooth (or HomeRF). So, this technology is more likely to be affected by home appliances as well as Bluetooth devices operating in the 2.4-GHz band.

Compatibility is another problem for the 802.11 technology. Apparently, the 802.11 specification can be interpreted in different ways by different manufacturers. Consequently, a network card developed by one manufacturer might not work on an 802.11 network built by a different manufacturer. Steps have been taken to remedy this issue. The Wireless Ethernet Compatibility Alliance (WECA) now requires interoperability testing — just as the Bluetooth SIG does — in order for a product to display the 802.11 label.

Table 18-3 lists the advantages and disadvantages of the 802.11 technology.

Table 18-3 Advantages and Disadvantages of the 802.11 Technology

Advantages	Disadvantages
Speed	Limited range
Inexpensive	Integration with wired networks difficult
Fast (11 Mbps)	Too expensive and complex for home use
Reliable connections	Compatibility problems with products from different manufacturers
Long range	Requires physical access points
Easy integration with Ethernet networks	Difficult to configure and maintain
	No voice or telephony

Bluetooth limitations

Bluetooth's range limitation is evident when using the technology to connect to wireless LANs. Bluetooth was not initially envisioned as a LAN technology, but more and more that type of usage seems to be under consideration. However, 802.11/Wi-Fi and HomeRF both were designed as wireless LAN technologies, and these existing standards have much larger range than Bluetooth. The HomeRF range is 105 feet, and the 802.11 range is 300 feet — both significantly better than Bluetooth's 33-foot (10-meter) range.

Perhaps an even bigger disadvantage than range is the slow data transmission rate currently available in the Bluetooth environment. Theoretically, Bluetooth has a maximum transmission rate of 1 Mbps. In practical terms, however, asymmetric data transmission is closer to 721 Kbps, and symmetric data transmission is 432.6 Kbps.

IrDA rates are 4 Mbps, HomeRF rates are 10 Mbps, and 802.11 rates are 11 Mbps. Clearly, Bluetooth is at a serious disadvantage compared with these transmission rates.

The Bluetooth transmission rates are fast enough for many applications; voice transmissions, for example, work at these rates. Sending data to a printer doesn't need more than 400–700 Kbps, and this rate also is adequate for receiving data from a wireless mouse or keyboard. However, it's not fast enough for sending large files from one device to another.

Bluetooth wasn't designed to be a LAN technology; it was intended as a cable-replacement technology and for creating ad hoc point-to-point connections (which don't need to know the network address of a device). To enter the LAN arena, Bluetooth's rates must change. Currently, HomeRF and 802.11 are the technologies to choose for delivering large data transmissions at fast speeds.

Devices using Bluetooth technology do radiate ELF (extremely low frequency) and ULF (ultra-low frequency) magnetic waves, but these emissions are no greater than those generated by industry-standard cordless phones. So, the risk to human health is probably negligible.

ELF electromagnetic radiation is in the 3 to 3,000 Hz range and is commonly emitted from electrical power lines and many electrical appliances. ULF radiation is between 0 and 3 Hz and is the type of emissions common to telecommunications equipment and many industrial settings.

Comparison of wireless technologies

Table 18-4 lists the differences among the various wireless technologies that we discuss in the previous sections of this chapter.

Table 18-4 Wireless Technologies

Technology	Maximum Speed	Range	Tolerance to Interference	Mfg. Cost	Purpose
Bluetooth (RF)	1 Mbps	30 feet	Medium	$15 currently (goal = $5)	Cable replacement
IrDA	4 Mbps	3 feet	None	$2	Cable replacement
802.11	11 Mbps	300 feet	High	$100 – $300	Corporate or campus LANs
802.15	1 Mbps (greater speed projected)	30 feet	Medium	Low	Cable replacement

Best-Use Scenarios

Each wireless technology that we describe in previous sections of this chapter was developed with different objectives in mind, and as a result, their strengths are most evident in specific areas of use. For example:

- ✓ Bluetooth excels when used as a cable-replacement technology and in establishing private and public ad hoc communications. It currently doesn't have the range or bandwidth for wireless LAN applications.

- ✓ IrDA is a good cable-replacement technology if you have line-of-sight and proximity between two devices. It doesn't have the range or bandwidth for wireless LAN applications, nor does it have the capability for ad hoc public communications or voice capability for home applications.

- ✓ HomeRF is intended for home use, and that's what it does best. It carries voice and data transmissions with minimal interference, but it doesn't have the range for corporate LAN applications.

✓ The 802.11 technology excels in corporate and campus LAN environments. It has some difficulty with interference and lacks voice capability for home applications.

Bluetooth application scenario

As a cable-replacement technology, Bluetooth enables users to connect a wide range of computing and telecommunications devices without the inconvenience of plugging in cables. One application scenario involves a user who wants to synchronize data on one personal device with another — even if the other device is powered off or in sleep mode. For example, assume that the user receives a message on a cell phone. With Bluetooth, the user can configure the device to transmit the message to a laptop, even if the cell phone is still in the user's briefcase. Further, automatic synchronization can save a lot of time for mobile users. Any updates or changes to files on a desktop computer can be uploaded automatically to a laptop or handheld device when the devices are in range. Theoretically, the user wouldn't have to do anything to establish a link; the synchronization would happen automatically. Figure 18-1 illustrates how Bluetooth is used to connect wireless devices.

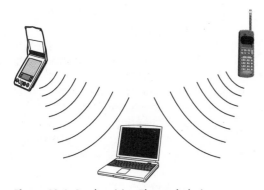

Figure 18-1: Synchronizing Bluetooth devices

IrDA application scenario

Similar to Bluetooth, IrDA can effectively establish ad hoc private connections. For example, in a retail store, a "smart" credit card could be used to send payment information to an IrDA-compatible card reader. The distance and line-of-sight requirements are easily met, because the customer is standing at the counter, next to the card reader. The user simply holds the smart card next to the reader, and the payment information is sent via infrared light. Although Bluetooth also could accomplish this ad hoc network, IrDA is a more secure technology, so payment information is not at risk.

HomeRF application scenario

With the HomeRF technology, users can set up a home network to share voice and data between PCs, peripherals, and PC-enhanced cordless phones. In this way, home users can share files, modems, and printers; forward incoming phone calls to multiple cordless handsets, fax machines, and voice mailboxes; review incoming voice, fax, and e-mail from a PC-enhanced cordless handset; and activate home electronic systems by spoken command. Figure 18-2 illustrates a HomeRF network.

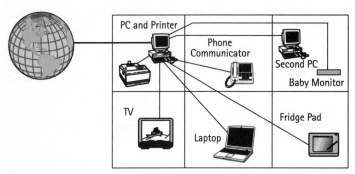

Figure 18-2: Creating a HomeRF network

IEEE 802.11 application scenario

One application scenario using 802.11 technology involves connecting multiple buildings in a metropolitan area using WLAN bridges. This type of network would be useful in a campus setting with buildings spread out over a significant area. The WLAN devices can make connections without requiring a T-1 line connection, and the bridges typically can extend LANs 1 to 5 miles (and possibly up to 20 or 30 miles) apart but within line-of-sight. These are conventional LANs that connect workstations by using wired connections (Ethernet, standard wiring, or fiber). A major benefit of the wireless LAN bridge scenario is that it spans multiple buildings without incurring the monthly costs of T-1 or higher-speed telecommunication lines. Figure 18-3 shows a network that implements the 802.11 technology.

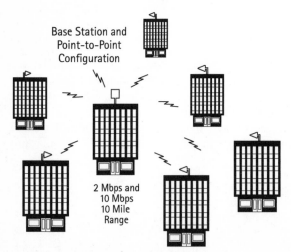

Figure 18-3: 802.11 WLAN bridges

Third-Generation (3G) Wireless

First-generation wireless systems are analog rather than digital. Examples of first-generation cellular systems include Advanced Mobile Phone System (AMPS), Nordic Mobile Telephone (NMT), and Total Access Communication System (TACS). These systems were popular in North America throughout the 1980s and 1990s and continue to operate in various parts of the world today. They provide voice transmission services but cannot carry any data signals. And no standards exist for interoperability among the various systems.

Second-generation (2G) systems are digital rather than analog. Digital cellular systems include Global System for Mobile (GSM) communications (the European standard), Digital AMPS (DAMPS), and Japanese Digital Cellular (JDC). Most 2G systems were designed primarily for voice transmission technologies that use digital encoding and provide some low-speed, circuit-switched data services for handheld applications (for example, mobile phone-based e-mail and Internet service). But as with first-generation systems, little or no compatibility exists among the different 2G systems. Bluetooth and the other wireless technologies discussed in this chapter are all examples of 2G cellular systems.

The third generation (3G) of wireless technology is a concept that intends to unify various wireless technologies at a high level in order to provide global roaming and voice-data convergence, and thus eliminate competing and incompatible systems. Developed by the International Telecommunication Union (ITU), the International Mobile Telecommunication 2000 (IMT-2000) standard is a modular platform that extends Europe's GSM communications standard.

GSM technology

GSM, formerly known as Groupe Spéciale Mobile, was designed as an international digital cellular service based on TDMA technology. The European version of GSM operates at 900 MHz and 1,800 MHz. In North America, GSM is available primarily in the Northeast, California, and Nevada and is used for PCS 1900 service. PCS 1900 uses the 1,900-MHz frequency and thus precludes interoperability with GSM phones that operate on 900- or 1,800-MHz networks.

The European Telecommunication Standards Institute (ETSI) was created in 1988 to establish telecommunications standards in Europe. In 1990, it published GSM Phase I specifications. By 1996, there were 36 GSM networks in 22 European countries. By January 2000, GSM networks existed in 132 countries worldwide.

A GSM network has the following elements:

- ✓ **Mobile station:** Handheld device used for voice and data.

- ✓ **Base station subsystem:** Subsystem that controls the radio link with the mobile station and monitors call status for handoff purposes.

- ✓ **Network subsystem:** Subsystem that sets up calls between a mobile unit and other fixed or mobile network users. Provides management services such as authentication. Main part of the subsystem is the Mobile Services Switching Center.

- ✓ **Air interface:** Radio link over which the mobile station and the base station subsystem communicate and over which the base station subsystem and the MSC communicate.

Each GSM network has an operations and maintenance center that oversees the operation and setup of the network.

GSM uses a combination of Time and Frequency Division Multiple Access (TDMA/FDMA) methods to divide the bandwidth. Two types of channels are available within this framework:

✓ Traffic channels carry voice and data.

✓ Control channels carry information used by the network for supervision and management.

TRANSMISSION METHODS

High-speed circuit-switched data (HSCSD), which was introduced in 1998, is a data transmission method with a rate of 57.6 Kbps and potentially higher speeds. The GSM standard was modified to support this method. This method enables GSM phones and mobile terminals to handle multimedia applications and download graphics-laden pages from the Web within seconds. In-house LANs also can be accessed via corporate intranets.

General packet radio services (GPRS) for GSM became available in 1999. It provides higher-speed data services for mobile users. Because it is a packet-switched technology, it's better for data applications than HSCSD. For example, it works well for e-mail and database access services. It also uses radio and network resources more efficiently and thus reduces the costs of providing connectivity. GPRS also provides mobile access to corporate intranets without a remote modem.

Enhanced Data for Global Evolution (EDGE) is to be the last GSM development before 3G takes off. This technology uses an alternative modulation scheme to provide data rates of 384 Kbps and higher using the standard GSM 200-KHz carrier. It supports both circuit- and packet-switched data. EDGE will enable GSM operations that don't obtain 3-G licenses to nevertheless offer competitive wideband services.

Although GSM is a 2G technology, the fact that the IMT-2000 standard is an extension of the GSM standard clearly marks GSM as a player in the 3G world.

GLOBAL STANDARDS

IMT-2000 intends to facilitate moving from the national and regional 2G systems of today toward 3G systems that will offer global service capabilities and interoperability. The ITU's role in this process is to provide direction and coordinate related technological developments. This is the largest telecommunications project ever attempted. It was conceived in the early 1990s, when mobile telecommunications provided only voice and circuit-switched low-speed data transmissions. With the rise of Internet, intranet, e-mail, e-commerce, and video services, expectations for sending and receiving transmissions across networks and terminals have increased.

Not a single standard or technology, 3G covers a variety of approaches to bringing high-speed Internet services to cellular networks. In most cases, 3G will be implemented in terms of upgrades to current systems that differ from country to country. New capabilities will be added as demand indicates the need. For example, Europe and Asia will convert from GSM to Wideband Code Division Multiple Access (W-CDMA). In North America, CDMA is likely to migrate to W-CDMA, but Time Division Multiple Access (TDMA) systems probably will move to EDGE. Although these systems are still mostly in the testing stage, each shows advantages and disadvantages. For example, although EDGE requires relatively minor infrastructure upgrades, its speed of 384 Kbps suffers in comparison with W-CDMA's 2 Mbps.

The 3G platform will provide digital voice transmission and broadband digital data transmission as well as videoconferencing and other data-related applications. It will have global roaming capabilities with a single low-cost terminal that will provide access to information and services to anyone at any time.

3G and Bluetooth

The Bluetooth specification will support 3G systems in delivering a wide range of services to users. For example, a 3G mobile phone with built-in Bluetooth capability would enable the local connection to be made via the Bluetooth radio, while the 3G network would handle the global part of the connection.

Current cellular systems don't transmit data fast enough to be practical as multimedia terminals, but 3G systems promise to change that by providing high-speed data transmissions. With rates of up to several hundred Kbps available to cellular phones, they will become multimedia terminals, offering full-featured Internet access. Clearly, the usage models outlined in the Bluetooth specification will realize their potential when Bluetooth technology interfaces with 3G systems.

Summary

As can be seen, there are points of convergence between Bluetooth and other wireless technologies as well as points of departure. In comparing the various wireless technologies, we make these key points:

✓ Currently, no clear winners or losers have emerged in terms of what each technology can provide.

✓ Bluetooth may nudge out IrDA in the end because of IrDA's limited range and line-of-sight requirement.

✓ HomeRF and Bluetooth are intended for different environments and are really more complementary than competitive technologies.

✓ 802.11/Wi-Fi could become the standard for all wireless networking — even home networks — should its costs come down and it becomes easier to use to the detriment of HomeRF.

✓ Many companies currently support 802.11 and Bluetooth standards, so these two technologies may be the survivors in the wireless marketplace.

✓ Looking ahead at the third generation of wireless technology, Bluetooth seems a viable technology for that arena. Bluetooth was designed to handle high-speed voice and data transmissions, and therefore was essentially ready for the 3G platform from the beginning.

✓ Bluetooth is designed with the idea of interoperability playing a major role in product development, which means that Bluetooth will work well with 3G technology.

Chapter 19 continues our look ahead to the future of the Bluetooth technology.

Chapter 19

Looking Ahead

In This Chapter

In the technology's current state of development, Bluetooth-enabled devices are primarily cable-replacement systems. To make connections without cables, the technology incorporates a tiny microchip in a radio transceiver that is built into digital devices. The Bluetooth unit makes connections instantly, facilitating both voice and data transmissions within a 10-meter range. The radio operates in a globally available frequency band, ensuring compatibility worldwide.

Although making connections without wires is a desirable feature for many end users, the technology's potential for doing much more as it matures keeps interest in Bluetooth high. Future Bluetooth devices will enable users to exchange information and synchronize files between devices without the use of cables. For example, a user will be able to transfer files easily from a laptop to a desktop computer without any setup requirements. Or, just by bringing devices in range of each other, a user will be able to synchronize personal information between a mobile phone and a laptop computer. Further, users will be able to perform these tasks without having to physically connect the devices, load files, or open applications. And with a range of 10 meters (about 33 feet), users will have more mobility than cables would provide. This is the promise of Bluetooth technology: cable-free connections, convenience, and mobility.

In this chapter, we examine Bluetooth's future, with the following objectives in mind:

✓ Reviewing Bluetooth's progress toward fulfilling its promise of cable replacement, convenience, and mobility

✓ Anticipating future Bluetooth products and usage scenarios

✓ Evaluating Bluetooth compatibility with 3G

✓ Assessing Bluetooth's potential for success

Functionality Without Cables

Bluetooth is intended to replace cables regardless of the type of application — voice or data. In a few years, as many as 80 percent of mobile phones may be Bluetooth enabled, carrying a chip that will provide wireless connection to similarly enabled notebooks, printers, and many other digital devices. And because Bluetooth can be used for various purposes (voice and data), it will eliminate the need for multiple types of cable connections.

Voice

Bluetooth supports both ACL and SCO links — thus enabling both voice and data transfers. The SCO links support real-time voice and multimedia traffic using reserved bandwidth. The Bluetooth specification is broad enough to support the use of telephones in several ways. First, home or office telephones will be able to access and use the wireless network to connect to the PSTN. This feature will enable users to make calls via a voice base station (incurring a usage charge), as well as provide access to services available on an external network.

Bluetooth technology also may enable telephones to act like walkie-talkies — the *intercom scenario* described in the Bluetooth specification. This type of connection does not incur a usage charge; instead, the two devices communicate directly with each other without the use of a base station or carrier service.

Finally, the Bluetooth specification enables the telephone to provide services that in the past have been available only on mobile radio networks and only through a connection with a cellular infrastructure.

The voice channels supported by the Bluetooth specification include a short-range, walkie-talkie type of connection and a radio link connection. The radio link connection would be used between a headset and a mobile phone to enable a user to talk on the phone while keeping hands free for other tasks (such as driving or using a keyboard). Ericsson already offers a headset with a built-in Bluetooth radio chip. And Plantronics has a headset in production that comes with a small radio add-on module that can be placed between the desktop phone and the wall socket, enabling use of the headset at a range of up to 10 meters. Meanwhile, Nokia has introduced the Mobil Connection Kit for use with the 6210 mobile phone. In this product, the Bluetooth radio and aerial are embedded in the battery, which connects to the phone in the form of a compact flash card with a PC adapter.

Video

The Bluetooth specification also supports the transmission of video signals between devices. Toshiba, one of the five founding members of the SIG, has developed an integrated circuit that enables video signal encoding and decoding in the MPEG-4 format. For example, video images captured by a digital camcorder are compressed in the MPEG-4 format, and then, using Bluetooth, they can be transferred to another device for editing. A key element of the MPEG-4 format is that video compression is suitable for unstable data transmission, which occurs when applications run over wireless connections and the Internet.

This type of communication between devices is handled by TCP/IP, which runs over the Bluetooth link-layer protocol. TCP/IP provides support for the Real-time Transfer Protocol, ensuring that video packets are correctly synchronized.

Although transmission speeds are not great at this point in the technology's development, Toshiba and others are working to boost the transmission rates and make Bluetooth an effective means for transmitting multimedia signals among various devices.

Data

The Bluetooth specification supports instant connectivity for data transfers. A user just needs a device equipped with a Bluetooth radio to begin ad hoc networking with other similarly equipped devices. For example, when a mobile device detects other Bluetooth-enabled devices, it can instantly connect and exchange business cards with these devices.

Currently, the data transmission rates are low, which makes transmitting large files inefficient. However, the SIG is working to change the specification to support greater transmission rates. After that has been accomplished, wireless connectivity will start to realize its potential.

Convenience

The Bluetooth technology promises to make wireless connections as simple as switching on the lights. One of the main advantages of Bluetooth is that it doesn't need to be set up by the user — all digital devices are intended to communicate spontaneously.

Bluetooth was originally envisioned as a cable-replacement technology that would provide instant connectivity in a personal area network (PAN) as well as enable ad hoc networking among a variety of users and devices.

Personal ad-hoc networks

Users will be able to set up all their Bluetooth-enabled devices so they automatically exchange information and synchronize with one another. For example, if a user accepts an appointment on a handheld device, the appointment is automatically accepted on the desktop PC as soon as the two devices are within range of each other. Or, if the user makes changes to files on a laptop PC, the updated files can be transferred automatically to the user's desktop. This capability will greatly simplify a mobile user's work life, providing a more efficient use of time, while the Bluetooth devices maintain the user's changing files and information behind the scenes.

Voice/data access point

The Bluetooth technology also will simplify access to other networks. Bluetooth connections will recognize and connect to different types of networks via voice/data access points. *Access points* are essentially bridges that enable devices to connect to a wired infrastructure, such as an Ethernet hub. The access points receive, buffer, and transmit data between the two types of networks, providing more flexibility in the Bluetooth ad hoc networking environment. For example, users could connect via an access point to a corporate intranet with their wireless devices.

Speed and security

The Bluetooth technology is designed to be fully functional even in very noisy radio environments, with voice transmissions audible under severe conditions. Bluetooth provides a high transmission rate (with efforts already under way to increase the rate), and data and voice transmissions are protected by error-correction methods as well as encryption and authentication routines for privacy.

Mobility

Enabling wireless communication among mobile devices on a global scale is an important component of the Bluetooth vision. The Bluetooth specification, which is intended to be a global standard for developing Bluetooth products, will ensure the compatibility of any devices or applications bearing the Bluetooth trademark. So, a mobile user traveling throughout the world will be able to connect to any other Bluetooth device, regardless of location or manufacturer.

In order to enable efficient mobile communications, the technology must offer low power consumption to avoid draining battery life. The Bluetooth technology will make low power consumption possible by implementing a single chip as part of the Bluetooth module, with radio frequency and logic components included on the same chip.

Current Bluetooth units have a 10-meter range and use only 1 milliwatt of power. Further, the radio chip will consume only about .3 milliamps in standby mode, which is less than 3 percent of the power used by traditional mobile phones. The specifications also define power-saving features that enable devices to move into power-saving modes when transmissions decrease or stop.

Bluetooth Promises

Since Bluetooth's beginnings in 1994, the promise of its technology has attracted wide support and been greeted with unparalleled enthusiasm throughout the computer and communications industry. SIG members hope that Bluetooth technology soon will be available in the marketplace, providing convenient, fast, and secure instant wireless connectivity, as well as establishing a global standard that will enable interoperability among devices, regardless of vendor, on a worldwide scale. During the next couple of years, member companies plan to build the Bluetooth technology into millions of electronic devices, including the following:

- ✓ Mobile phones
- ✓ Mobile computers
- ✓ Handheld devices
- ✓ Headsets
- ✓ Office equipment
- ✓ Cameras (still and video)
- ✓ Internet access and e-mail
- ✓ Office LANs

So, what will the end user be able to do with Bluetooth-enabled devices? The Bluetooth SIG and member companies envision numerous uses for the technology, including those outlined in the following sections.

Sketchpads

A special software is envisioned that will turn Bluetooth-enabled notebooks, palmtops, or Windows CE devices into sketchpads. Users can then use a stylus to annotate or draw on Word files, e-mail messages, graphics, or any Windows-based applications. The altered files can be transferred to other Bluetooth devices, so other users can review the files and save them to their devices. In this way, coworkers can obtain and review information quickly and efficiently and exchange the information with minimal effort.

Remote synchronization

Synchronization works not only among devices in a PAN, but also among devices of multiple users that are linked via a PSTN. This feature can be valuable if mobile users need to be notified immediately of time-critical changes. For example, if a meeting time has changed, the message can be sent from the workplace to the user's mobile phone. The mobile phone automatically connects to the user's organizer or laptop and updates the schedule. When the user next reviews his or her schedule, the changes will already be in place.

Printing

Using Bluetooth technology for wireless printing can provide users with versatility and flexibility in what and how they print. Imagine, for example, being able to send images from a digital camera directly to a printer — without the need for cable connections. Or, imagine taking a picture and sending the image to a Bluetooth-enabled cell phone, which in turn would relay the digital image as an e-mail attachment to one or multiple recipients, who can in turn send the images to the Bluetooth-enabled printer.

Car systems

Using Bluetooth-enabled devices in cars is an area the specification targets. Various devices, such as cell phones, pagers, and handheld computers, will be able to share information in a car. The Bluetooth technology creates the possibility of making every cell phone hands-free without the costly installations currently required to a car's interior. Because any Bluetooth-enabled device can communicate with any other similarly enabled device, products can be used interchangeably in the car without regard for manufacturer or operating system. For example, a device could get a phone number from a handheld phone and automatically dial it so the driver's hands never leave the wheel. Of course, Bluetooth-enabled headsets then would enable users to carry on conversations while keeping hands free for driving.

Home entertainment

Bluetooth technology is envisioned not just for the business world, but also in the home. For example, perhaps a Bluetooth-enabled digital television would notify users that a favorite program is beginning and ask if the program should be recorded for later viewing.

Another possible device that would be used in the home is a Bluetooth-enabled data pad. Used as a remote control, the data pad could be set up to control all entertainment devices in the home as well as any new ones that come into the home in the future — thus eliminating the need for multiple remote devices.

Yet another possible use for Bluetooth-enabled devices will be to keep track of products in the home, such as toothpaste or laundry detergent, and remind the user when to buy more.

Although these possible uses are still only in the speculative stages, Bluetooth clearly will open the doors of imagination and be limited only in how developers learn to implement the technology.

3G and the Future

The Bluetooth technology is the result of the joint achievements of five leading companies within the telecommunications and computer industries: Ericsson, Intel, IBM, Nokia, and Toshiba. More than 2,000 other manufacturers, from all parts of the world and various fields of business, have now also joined the Bluetooth family, making it by far the fastest growing industry standard ever.

Although Bluetooth is a second-generation (2G) technology, it is nevertheless being developed with an eye toward compatibility with the third-generation (3G) communications systems. The International Telecommunications Union (ITU) and regional standards bodies are developing the 3G technology, which is actually several wireless technologies unified at a high level to provide users with true global interoperability.

The 3G aim is to move from the 2G national and regional systems' incompatibility into a new generation of expanded coverage and new service capabilities by providing a set of universally accepted standards. The ITU will direct and coordinate technological developments in the communications and computing area so that manufacturers produce interoperable applications and hardware. Clearly, the Bluetooth specification fits into this framework very well. Bluetooth could easily dovetail into 3G systems by extending their reach to local devices such as handhelds and PDAs, while 3G technology would extend Bluetooth's range well beyond local device communications.

Other areas in which Bluetooth and 3G goals are compatible include the following:

✓ Both were designed from the outset to support wideband data as well as voice communications.

✓ Systems must deliver the same or better service than current systems and be inexpensive.

✓ Both must be flexible in terms of being able to support new products and applications.

✓ Both must be able to deliver high-speed data and voice transmissions.

Developing a truly global communications system — one that can access other devices, the Internet, and e-mail, to download information from the Web or from other devices — will require a hybrid solution. Bluetooth and 3G hold the promise of answering this need. A cellular phone that incorporates 3G and Bluetooth technology promises to become a powerful multimedia terminal. The 3G terminals would provide access to many different forms of information, such as Web browsing, e-mail, video, and voice, while Bluetooth devices would support multiple local connections. In other words, the 3G system would provide connections to a specific location, while Bluetooth is used to deliver transmissions to local devices. This combination means a considerable reduction in traffic on a 3G network, which in turn means lower cost to maintain and less possibility for RF interference.

Future Bluetooth

The next evolution of Bluetooth is already in the planning stages, with major revisions to the Bluetooth specification scheduled for release in the near future. Version 2.0 of the specification is intended to enhance the current version, adding new usage models and profiles as well as extending the capabilities of the basic performance specifications. New usage models that may be defined in the 2.0 version of the specification include wireless CD-quality headphones, wireless speakers and microphones, and wireless video displays. And these are just a few of the possibilities.

Bluetooth technology seems very promising. Offering wireless connectivity at low cost, providing convenient, easy-to-use products and applications, and maintaining global interoperability among products, Bluetooth has already captured the interest of computing and communications industry leaders. Whether Bluetooth becomes a part of our future, however, remains to be determined. Even though many companies have invested time and money in the technology, the ultimate success or failure of Bluetooth will be in the hands of consumers. Bluetooth's success will depend on how consumers respond to these questions:

✓ Does the product work as expected and promised?

✓ Does it provide cost-effective value to the consumer?

✓ Is it convenient and easy to use?

✓ Does it live up to the hype?

✓ Does it solve a real problem?

If consumers answer "Yes" to most of these questions, they will buy the products and want more, ensuring Bluetooth success. But in order for the answers to be positive, the products must live up to the Bluetooth promises.

Summary

The SIG expects that within the next few years, Bluetooth will be built-in to millions of mobile phones as well as other communications and computing devices:

✓ The first Bluetooth products on the market are likely to be basic cable replacements.

✓ After the Bluetooth chips attain critical market mass, new markets will open up for Bluetooth technology.

✓ Software development kits (SDKs) are available for Bluetooth developers. More competition in the SDK area and lower prices on Bluetooth chips will promote more development among manufacturers.

✓ The continuing development and refinement of the Bluetooth specifications will ensure product interoperability regardless of product design and manufacturer.

✓ 3G cellular telephony will offer national coverage and mobility, and coupled with the Bluetooth technology will be able to provide cost-effective interconnection for locally connected devices.

✓ New market opportunities will open up for Bluetooth as well as 3G products to extend the reach of cellular systems well beyond current boundaries.

If you need to refresh your knowledge of any Bluetooth concept or need a ready reference for Bluetooth terms, the appendix provides a glossary of Bluetooth terminology.

Appendix

Bluetooth Terminology

1G (First generation): Analog cellular phone technology.

2G (Second generation): Digital cellular phone technology, including CDMA, TDMA, and GSM.

2-in-1 handset: A phone handset that serves as both a remote handset and a network connection device.

3G (Third generation): The emerging technology generation of digital cellular phones that increases bandwidth to 384 Kbps for a stationary or slowly moving device (such as walking), 128 Kbps in a fast-moving device (such as a car), and 2 Mbps in fixed-based application.

Acceptor: A Bluetooth device that receives an action from another Bluetooth device (the initiator).

ACL (Asynchronous Connectionless): A packet-switched (asynchronous) connection created on the LMP layer of the Bluetooth protocol stack between two Bluetooth devices.

AM (amplitude modulation): A transmission mode that encodes its signal into a carrier wave by modulating the amplitude of the carrier.

AMPS (Advanced Mobile Phone Service): An analog cellular phone system that supports mobile devices in the 800-Mhz band. AMPS is used in North America and in more than 40 other countries.

AP (Access point): The designation for a wireless network connection point or interface device.

API (Application Programming Interface): A software library with routines that act as the go-between for an application and the operating system or interact directly to the hardware, such as a Bluetooth interface device, the Bluetooth protocol stack, or interface device.

Application layer: The group of protocols in the Bluetooth protocol stack that provide a user interface.

ARQ (Automatic Repeat Request): An error correction method in which the receiving station requests that a message be retransmitted when an error is detected.

ATM (Asynchronous Transfer Mode): A cell-switched transmission service that creates a logical circuit from end-to-end to ensure quality of service (QoS). ATM is available in a transmission speeds that range from 1.5 Mbps to 1 Gbps. ATM transmits voice, data, and video in fixed-length 53-byte cells.

Authentication: The process that verifies the stored link key or the PIN of a Bluetooth device attempting to establish a link. Authenticated devices are designated as trusted devices. Also used to verify the username and password of a user attempting to log into a network.

Authorization: The process used to determine the access level of a device that has been authenticated and indicated as trusted. Authorization includes the process of authentication.

Baseband: A form of digital data transmission that is carried over the physical communication medium — for Bluetooth, this would be RF.

Bluetooth: The open specification that defines wireless communication of data and voice signals.

Bonding: The creation of a link between two Bluetooth devices using the link key.

Browser: Application software used to download and display Internet Web pages.

Bus: The data lines used to transfer data between two devices.

CAN (Campus Area Network): A network type that interconnects buildings located on a single piece of ground or location, such as a college or business campus.

CDMA (Code Division Multiple Access): A spread-spectrum digital cellular technology in which each cell uses an individual code to identify a call, enabling multiple calls to be grouped on a single frequency.

CDPD (Cellular Digital Packet Data): An analog cellular technology that allows for more efficient data transmission on AMPS cellular radio systems.

Channel: A pathway for electrical or electronic transmissions between two or more points. .

Circuit-switched: A transmission mode on which a dedicated line is created to carry data for only one user at a time. *See also packet-switched.*

Client-server: A networking type in which a central device (server) provides requested services to other devices on the network (clients).

CODEC (Coder/Decoder): A device that converts incoming signals from analog to digital and outgoing signals from digital to analog for transmission over a digital communications service.

Connectable device: Any Bluetooth device within the range of a paging signal from an initiator device.

Connectionless: A transmission mode that does not provide management or administration of the transmitted data.

Connection-oriented: A transmission mode that creates and manages a communications session, including the retransmission of missed or erroneous message segments.

CPU (Central Processing Unit): The primary or central processing component of a hardware device that controls the interpretation and execution of instructions.

CRC (Cyclic Redundancy Check): A binary value created through a preset algorithm and used to determine whether any data is lost during transmission. The sending device calculates this value and attaches it to transmitted data packets. The receiving device recalculates this value and uses it to determine whether any data was lost in the transmission of the packet.

CVSD (Continuous Variable Slope Delta Modulation): A cellular telephone modulation method that attempts to match the size of the signal to the analog wave.

DCE (Data Circuit-Terminating Equipment, or Data Communications Equipment): In serial communications, the device placed between two communicating endpoints that facilitates the communications process, such as a modem.

Device layer: The protocols of the Bluetooth protocol stack that handle the interface to certain components of a Bluetooth device, such as the display, the keypad, and RF communications.

Discoverable device: A Bluetooth device that responds to an inquiry issued within its range. A device that is out-of-range to an inquiry is called a silent device or is said to be in nondiscoverable mode.

DLCI (Data Link Connection Identifier): The identifying code assigned to each endpoint of a frame relay circuit. The DLCI is used to represent the destination address for a packet.

DSP (Digital Signal Processor): A special type of coprocessor dedicated to processing the mathematics involved in supporting digital sound, images, and video signals.

DTE (Data Terminal Equipment): A serial communications endpoint device, such as a computer or terminal. *See also DCE.*

DTMF (Dual Tone Multiple Frequency): The system used on touch-tone telephones, in which each key is assigned a specific frequency or tone that can be identified by a microprocessor.

Dumb peripheral: A peripheral device that provides only a connection (cable detect) signal to a port on a Bluetooth device and does not generate signals of its own.

EIA (Electronics Industries Association): The trade association responsible for developing many telecommunications standards — including RS-232, RS-422, and others — used to connect serial devices.

ESMR (Enhanced Specialized Mobile Radio): A wireless communications system that links several portable transceivers in a network of repeaters, each of which has a range of 5 to 10 miles.

ETSI (European Telecommunications Standards Institute): A group that develops a range of telecommunications standards used throughout Europe and worldwide.

FEC (Forward Error Correction): A data-encoding technique that facilitates the repair of data received in error. Before transmission, error correction bits are interspersed in the data and can be used to correct the data should an error occur.

FCC (Federal Communications Commission): The governing administrative body that oversees telecommunications, radio, and television transmission in the United States.

FIFO (First-In, First-Out): A queueing method in which the first signal received is the first signal processed.

FM (frequency modulation): A transmission mode that varies the frequency of the carrier to blend the data signal into the carrier wave.

GSM (Global System for Mobile Communications): A digital cellular technology available in both the US and Europe that provides various services to cell phone subscribers, such as SMS.

HCI (Host Controller Interface): A command interface to the baseband controller of a Bluetooth device, which provides a uniform access method to Bluetooth baseband capabilities.

HDLC (High-level Data Link Control): A Data Link layer data communications protocol that embeds information in a data frame, enabling hardware devices to control data flow and perform error correction.

Headset: A combination microphone and earpiece that can be worn on a user's head and connected directly to a cell phone or via a Bluetooth wireless link.

HomeRF (home radio frequency): A wireless PAN technology that has a transmission range of 150 feet with transmission speeds of 1 or 2 Mbps.

Host: The hardware and software platform on which a Bluetooth application runs.

IEEE (Institute of Electrical and Electronics Engineers): Purportedly the largest technical professional society in the work. Among its initiatives is the development of networking and communications standards, such as the 802.3 and 802.11b standards.

IETF (Internet Engineering Task Force): The body that is responsible for maintaining Internet protocols, such as TCP/IP. The IETF operates under the supervision of the Internet Society Internet Architecture Board (IAB).

Initiator: A Bluetooth device that initiates an action with another Bluetooth device over an established link. *See also acceptor.*

IP (Internet Protocol): The TCP/IP Network layer protocol that defines logical network addressing — specifically, IP addressing.

IPX (Internetwork Packet Exchange): The native transmission control protocol on Novell NetWare systems prior to NetWare Version 5.

IR (infrared): A band of radiation with wavelengths longer than light but shorter than radio waves that lies outside the visible spectrum (at the red end). IR is used for wireless transmissions between computer devices and handheld devices, but requires a clear, unobstructed line-of-sight to connect.

IrDA (Infrared Data Association): The standards body that creates guidelines and standards for communications between electronic devices using infrared light signals.

IrOBEX (Infrared Object Exchange): A set of high-level protocols that facilitate the exchange of such objects as vCard and vCalendar over an infrared link.

ISDN (Integrated Services Digital Networks): A telephone company service that provides high-speed communications using standard POTS and PSTN lines. Two types of ISDN are available: BRI (Basic Rate Interface), which provides 144 Kbps of bandwidth, and PRI (Primary Rate Interface), which provides 1.54 Mbps of bandwidth.

ISM (Industrial, Scientific, and Medical): A public radio transmission band originally set aside for use in these three commercial areas. ISM operates at 2.4 GHz.

ITU (International Telecommunications Union): Also referred to as the ITU-T, this is the primary international telecommunications standardization body.

JATE (Japan Approvals Institute for Telecommunications Equipment): Organization responsible for granting compliance and reliability approval for terminal equipment that is to be connected to the public network in Japan.

L2CAP (Logical Link Controller and Adaptation Protocol): Bluetooth protocol that provides both connection-oriented and connectionless services to upper layer protocols of the Bluetooth protocol stack. L2CAP operates on the Data Link layer of the OSI model and the Baseband layer of the Bluetooth stack.

LAN (local area network): A network established to serve the needs of local network users that may or may not provide access to remote hosts outside the network.

LC (link control information): One of five baseband channel types used to carry Bluetooth data through the baseband layer of the Bluetooth protocol stack. The other four channel types are link management information (LM), user asynchronous data (UA), user synchronous data (US), and user isochronous data (UI).

Link key: The authentication key used to establish a connection between Bluetooth devices. *See also bonding.*

Link Manager: The software in the Bluetooth protocol stack that provides for link setup, authentication, link configuration, and other link-related services.

Link Manager Protocol (LMP): The protocol used to manage peer-to-peer communications between two Bluetooth devices.

LM (link management information): One of five baseband channel types used to carry Bluetooth data through the baseband layer of the Bluetooth protocol stack. The other four channel types are link control information (LC), user asynchronous data (UA), user synchronous data (US), and user isochronous data (UI).

MAC (Media Access Control) address: On a Bluetooth piconet, the three-bit address used to identify each of the participating devices.

MTU (Maximum Transmission Unit): The maximum size (in bytes) of a packet that can be transmitted across a link.

MUX (Multiplexer): A communications device that combines multiple data signals into a single composite signal for transmission over a single channel.

NTIA (National Telecommunications and Information Administration): The executive branch of the US government's representative on telecommunications and information technology issues.

NOS (Network Operating System): The system software running on a network's central server that manages the resources of the network and administers access and user permissions.

NVRAM (Non-volatile Random Access Memory): A type of memory circuit that holds its contents after the primary power source is removed. NVRAM can be implemented with SRAM (static RAM) connected to a battery power source or EPROM (erasable programmable read-only memory).

OBEX (Object Exchange Protocol): A set of high-level protocols that facilitates the exchange of such objects as vCard and vCalendar over either a Bluetooth or IrDA (IrOBEX) link.

OEM (Original Equipment Manufacturer): A company that remanufactures or repackages hardware and software from other manufacturers or suppliers.

OSI (Open Systems Interconnect) model: The widely accepted model for a layered approach to network communications that defines seven layers of function, each of which is defined independently of the other layers.

Packet-switched: A network communications mode that routes data using the addresses included in the message packet. *See also circuit-switched.*

PAN (Personal Area Network): A wireless network of devices located within the range of a wireless technology (Bluetooth, HomeRF, or IR) that serves a single person or a small group of people.

PC Card: A hardware expansion device that is installed in a personal computer (PC) via a PCMCIA slot to add features or services, such as a Bluetooth adapter. *See also PCMCIA.*

PCMCIA (Personal Computer Memory Card International Association): The standards association that develops and publishes standards for PC Card devices. *See also PC Card.*

PDA (Personal Digital Assistant): Handheld device used for a variety of applications, such as personal information management (PIM), address book, appointment calendars, and many online activities, such as e-mail and Internet access. Examples include the Palm Pilot and the Handspring Visor.

PDU (Protocol Data Unit): The generic name for a message or a portion of a message that is passed from layer to layer in a communications protocol model, such as the Bluetooth protocol stack or the OSI model.

Peer-to-peer: A networking type in which each connected device manages the access granted to other connected devices.

Piconet: An ad hoc network of Bluetooth devices that can support from two to eight connected devices in a peer-to-peer network arrangement.

Plug and play: A system hardware configuration method in which devices are discovered when they are attached to the host and automatically configured.

POTS (Plain Old Telephone System): The telephone service provided by the links between your home or office and the telephone company's central office facilities.

PPP (Point-to-Point Protocol): A transport protocol that encapsulates the PDUs from other protocols for transmission over communications lines.

Profile: A description of the intended use and application of a Bluetooth device, produced by one of the Bluetooth SIG's working groups.

PSTN (Public Switched Telephone Network): The interconnecting network used by telephone service providers to provide nation and worldwide signal transmission.

QoS (Quality of Service): The definition or parameters that define the level, quality, and speed of a communication service.

RF (radio frequency): The range of frequencies above the audio range and below visible light (between 30 KHz and 300 GHz) that is used for virtually all broadcast transmissions.

RFCOMM (Radio Frequency Communication): The ETSI protocol that provides serial cable emulation on a radio frequency transmission.

RS-232 (Recommended Standard 232): The definition, established by the EIA, of a certain serial communications interface, cabling, and connector.

Scatternet: The combination of many independent and nonsynchronized Bluetooth piconets.

SCO (Synchronous Connection-Oriented): A circuit-switched connection reserved for communications between two devices. SCO links are created on the LMP layer as reserved slots on a physical channel and used primarily for transmitting voice signals.

SDP (Service Discovery Protocol): The Bluetooth protocol that provides a means for applications to discover available services and their characteristics on a Bluetooth device.

Service layer: The group of protocols in the Bluetooth protocol stack that provide services to the application layer and device driver layer in a Bluetooth device. A *service* is software or hardware (or both) that provides information, performs a task, or controls a resource on behalf of another entity.

SIG (Special Interest Group): The founding members and other adopting companies form the Bluetooth SIG, which is the governing body for the Bluetooth technology.

SMS (Short Message Service): A system, similar to that used with pagers, that sends short text messages to cellular phones.

Spread-spectrum: A telecommunications technique that transmits a signal on a bandwidth that is larger than the frequency of the original signal. Frequency hopping is a form of spread-spectrum.

TACS (Total Access Communication Service): A 1-Gbps analog mobile telephone standard that is based on AMPS.

TCS (Telephony Control Protocol Specification): The Bluetooth specification module that defines the protocol requirements for the wireless-telephony and intercom profiles.

TCS-BIN (TCS Binary): The Bluetooth specification that defines a bit-oriented telephony protocol.

TCP (Transmission Control Protocol): A connection-oriented protocol that is the primary transmission protocol of the TCP/IP protocol suite.

TCP/IP (Transmission Control Protocol/Internet Protocol): The de facto protocol suite standard used on the Internet.

TDM (Time Division Multiplexing): A transmission technology that transmits multiple interleaved signals as a single transmission. The signals are interleaved by allocating each alternating time slice in the transmission.

TDMA (Time Division Multiple Access): A cellular phone technology that digitizes a voice signal to provide more signal traffic per transmission channel, with each call allocated a different time slot on a given frequency.

UA (user asynchronous data): One of five baseband channel types used to carry Bluetooth data through the baseband layer of the Bluetooth protocol stack. The other four channel types are link control information (LC), link management information (LM), user synchronous data (US), and user isochronous data (UI).

UART (Universal Asynchronous Receiver/Transmitter): A device that converts parallel data signals into serial data signals for transmission over serial communications services or coverts serial signals into parallel signals for use by computers and other devices.

UDP (User Datagram Protocol): A connectionless transmission protocol used to send control and status messages across a TCP/IP network.

UI (user isochronous data): One of five baseband channel types used to carry Bluetooth data through the baseband layer of the Bluetooth protocol stack. The other four channel types are link control information (LC), link management information (LM), user asynchronous data (UA), and user synchronous data (US).

UMTS (Universal Mobile Telecommunications System): The European version of the 3G wireless telephony system that provides service in the 2-GHz band, global roaming, and many personalized features.

US (user synchronous data): One of five baseband channel types used to carry Bluetooth data through the baseband layer of the Bluetooth protocol stack. The other four channel types are link control information (LC), link management information (LM), user asynchronous data (UA), and user isochronous data (UI).

USB (Universal Serial Bus): A hardware interface for low-speed peripherals, such as keyboards, mouse, printers, scanners, and telephony devices, with a maximum bandwidth of 12 Mbps and support for up to 127 devices on a single channel.

vCard: The electronic or virtual equivalent of a paper and print business card, typically in the form of a file exchanged between two Bluetooth devices.

WAN (Wide Area Network): A network that encompasses a wide geographical area, such as a state, county, or global. The Internet is a WAN.

WAP (Wireless Application Protocol): A set of communications protocol standards that enable users to access online services from a portable (mobile) phone or other device.

W-CDMA (Wideband CDMA): A 3G cellular technology that applies CDMA technology in place of TDMA to increase data transmission rates in GSM systems.

WPAN (Wireless Personal Area Network): *see PAN (Personal Area Network).*

Index

Symbols

mu symbol μ, 8

Numbers

A

G

H

I

continued

continued